# Japanese Politeness

Although the Japanese language is one of the most quoted examples in politeness research, extant publications focus on particular areas of politeness, and very few of them enquire into the varied aspects of Japanese politeness. In this book, Yasuko Obana provides an integrated account of what signifies Japanese politeness.

By examining how far previous assumptions can apply to Japanese, Obana exposes a variety of characteristics of Japanese politeness. By taking a diachronic approach, she probes into what constitutes politeness, extracts key elements of the term 'polite' in Japanese, and demonstrates how modern honorifics' apparent diverse, divergent uses and effects can be integrated into a systematic matrix. Furthermore, by quoting traditional Japanese language scholars' (*kokugo gakusha*) studies, Obana brings different views into the open. She also carves out politeness strategies in Japanese that have not been adequately explored to date, and which often conform to the way in which honorifics behave because they reflect social indexicality.

This book is a good reference for scholars in pragmatics, particularly for those who are working on politeness. It is useful for Japanese language teachers who want to know how to teach Japanese politeness to non-native learners. Postgraduate students of Japanese or pragmatics may also find this book useful for self-study.

**Yasuko Obana** is a Professor in the School of Science, Kwansei Gakuin University, Japan, teaching English to science students. She has published a number of articles in the field of pragmatics, including politeness and anaphora in text processing. When she was teaching Japanese to university students in Australia, she was analysing learners' errors in Japanese, which led her to publish *Understanding Japanese: A Handbook for Learners and Teachers* (Kurosio Publishers, Japan, 2000). She is now writing a co-authored book on Japanese pragmatics.

# Japanese Politeness
## An Enquiry

**Yasuko Obana**

Routledge
Taylor & Francis Group
LONDON AND NEW YORK

First published 2021
by Routledge
2 Park Square, Milton Park, Abingdon, Oxon OX14 4RN

and by Routledge
52 Vanderbilt Avenue, New York, NY 10017

*Routledge is an imprint of the Taylor & Francis Group, an informa business*



*British Library Cataloguing-in-Publication Data*
A catalogue record for this book is available from the British Library

*Library of Congress Cataloging-in-Publication Data*
A catalog record has been requested for this book

ISBN: 978-0-367-28060-4 (hbk)
ISBN: 978-0-429-29946-9 (ebk)

Typeset in Times New Roman
by Newgen Publishing UK

# Contents

# Preface

## Some characteristics of this book

This book is about Japanese politeness. It does not cover all of its aspects, but focuses on major issues that have been most frequently discussed in politeness research. The book utilises a number of original contributions based on my previous publications, therefore different approaches and arguments are often presented.

This book bears a number of noteworthy characteristics. First, when introducing previous theoretical assumptions and discussing current issues, I examine how far they can apply to Japanese language by providing examples from real conversations, dramas and films, as well as polite behaviour witnessed in actual social life. This gives me opportunities to elaborate on characteristics of Japanese politeness, what features of Japanese politeness differ from other languages, and why some extant assumptions do not suit Japanese politeness.

Second, this book often examines aspects of politeness diachronically. For example, in dealing with the definition of politeness, while previous studies synchronically observe phenomena and work out how politeness should be viewed or defined, I take a diachronic route, starting with fundamental psychological needs/wants, examining how they develop into social standards, to explain in what way features of politeness such as 'evaluations' and 'expectations' are borne out and intertwined with social norms of 'politeness'.

Diachronic examination also sheds light on the essential features of the translated terms for 'polite' in Japanese, *reigi tadashii* and *teineina*, which are contrastive with the term 'polite' in English. This contrast, in fact, accords with the survey/interview results of several scholars, and further clarifies why speakers of Japanese and English perceive the term 'polite' differently in their language.

Another diachronic investigation is pursued regarding the founding of honorifics and what elements of its origin, i.e. a language for gods and goddesses in prayers, persist in modern honorifics. It follows that many features that characterise modern honorifics such as 'distance', 'public performance' and 'upward-respect' originate in motivational factors for honorific use in ancient times. A diachronic enquiry into honorifics also presents the following finding. Honorifics today are manipulated in varied ways, not necessarily aiming at politeness, but expressing, as the speaker's choice, her psychological state on the spur of the moment (e.g. speech level shifts), yielding effects such as 'irony', 'conflict', 'self-defence' and 'profound gratitude'. These pragmatic effects appear to be beyond the nature of the so-called 'conventional' honorifics. However, a closer look at honorific phenomena reveals that conventional honorifics and honorific terms used in speech-level shifts bear close parallels, and constitute 'two ends of a continuum', both of which come down to the origin of honorifics.

Third, I do my best to use technical terms cautiously rather than accept them as axiomatic or simply borrow them from other disciplines without questioning. For example, I employ the term 'social norm' when discussing what constitutes politeness. To understand exactly what this term means, I examine how it is treated in sociology; it turns out that 'social norms' as defined in sociology are far more flexible and situationally changeable than have been believed in pragmatics, while basically functioning as a yardstick for evaluations and bringing forth expectations in social phenomena (politeness, in our case).

I also enquire into the question of the dichotomy, 'collectivism versus individualism', which was raised in the discussion on 'face' because Brown and Levinson's (1978, 1987) concept of 'face' was critically assessed as individualist, which does not fit the collectivist 'face' in other cultures. However, the more this dichotomy is investigated by going through many examples discussed in social psychology, the more questions and problems arise, which makes one wonder whether the dichotomy in fact exists or if it truly reflects the reality of different cultures. This naturally casts doubt on whether it is possible to draw a distinction between two types of 'face' by adopting such a controversial tenet in social psychology.

I employ the *uchi*/*soto* (inside/outside) distinction (the distinction between in-group and out-group) in determining who receives *kenjoo*-styles (humble styles) and is treated in the same way as the speaker, i.e. treated as a *uchi*-member. I use this term simply as the extension of the speaker's viewpoint to a referent person because Japanese language constantly places the speaker's viewpoint first on the speaker and then on someone who is socially closer to her (I call this viewpoint the 'Speaker's view' in this book). Therefore, I use the distinction as a tool to distinguish honorific styles. On the other hand, the distinction has traditionally been used to explain Japanese mentality, the nature of collectivism and even the uniqueness of Japanese psychology (e.g. *amae* – 'dependence'). I enquire into these claims, and conclude that those arguments for the *uchi* consciousness and its reflections in behaviour and social life are built on pure speculation without offering any objective methods (e.g. experiment) to verify their plausibility.

Finally, in this book, I enquire into Japanese politeness by introducing and reviewing previous studies published both inside and outside Japan. Especially by quoting traditional Japanese language scholars' (*kokugo gakusha*

国語学者) studies (normally written in Japanese), I bring different views into the open; some are biased, some others insightful and convincing, and others quite unacceptable due to the lack of logical backups or full explanations. Nonetheless, the works of these Japanese scholars enabled me to look at Japanese politeness in a broader way and to enrich arguments in this book.

## On a theory of politeness

In this book, I attempt to define politeness from a diachronic perspective, which makes it possible to extract features of politeness such as social norms, evaluations and expectations and to explain how they are borne out and intertwined with one another to constitute politeness. However, this is a macro sketch of politeness, and still far from the understanding of what politeness is and how it is involved in social actions because, in reality, it is much more complex and contextually subtle, and evaluations of politeness differ across cultures, even in different regions or groups of the same culture.

Establishing a theory of politeness is not my primary intention in this book, but I go a little deeper by introducing the concept of Role-Identity borrowed from Symbolic Interactionism (SI), a prevalent role theory in sociology. This is because I believe SI's Role-Identity entails processes to determine politeness, i.e. one's identity in a given situation and its implementation as a role performance are steps to determine appropriate behaviour. It should be noted, however, that identity and role are not isomorphic but different role performances are expected to occur even if the same identity (e.g. professor) is observed; e.g. professors may or may not use honorifics with their students (role performance) due to their different interpretations of what a 'professor' should be like (to this extent, identity contains subjective judgements). I also create sub-categories of Role-Identity because they help understand reasons for dynamic changes of politeness. For example, the interactants, who normally do not use honorifics with each other, may use honorifics when they are placed in a different situation (e.g. formal meeting). This can be explained as role shifts: from institutional to task-based role-identities. Another example is that the same speaker uses different strategies (e.g. direct versus indirect request strategies) in the same discourse because she changes her stance or psychological state as the interaction develops into a different phase. I explain this by using the term, 'Interactional Role-Identity'.

Politeness has been defined and its tool, Role-Identity, has been suggested, but this is not yet sufficient; we still have a long way to go before reaching a theory of politeness. However, it is beyond the scope of this book to go further. Therefore, a theory of politeness awaits another occasion, but here I would like to add something about which I am concerned.

It would be interesting to imagine how a theory could be built up. What if I established a theory of politeness with Japanese language in mind? Perhaps I would first classify politeness as 'indexical and module' types as defined by Brown (2011). This classification is necessary because indexical politeness (i.e. honorifics) is not a matter of mutual face work or rapport but a one-way signal indicating upward respect or a social distance whether it is vertical or horizontal. Furthermore, indexical politeness differs from module politeness (i.e. strategic politeness) in that the former is purely pragmatic and socially indexical with no semantic contributions, whereas the latter is semantic and semantic content becomes the target for the evaluation of politeness.

A second attempt at establishing a theory of politeness would involve differentiating role-based strategies from other types of strategy because many strategies in Japanese are constructed based upon one's recognition of role. Even in strategic planning (i.e. motivations for strategy construction), Japanese people first scrutinise those with whom they are interacting and then determine appropriate strategies according to their social relationships. Of course, this may also be true in other cultures, for example when a power difference between the two interactants needs to be emphasised. Nonetheless, in English, how one's behaviour affects the other is in many ways a primary concern (e.g. potential threat) in determining a strategy, whereas in Japanese, one's identity and accordingly its role performance are often considered prior to the nature of an utterance (e.g. request), which often entails linguistic terms. This means that, in Japanese, many strategies, like honorifics, are indexical in nature. When such role-identities (e.g. job responsibilities, task-roles at work or in group activities) are not evidently observed, individuals consider how their actions affect the other interactants, and choose appropriate strategies to mitigate potential threat.

These suggestions indicate that politeness starts taking on a different complexion once it is based on a different language or at least requires a different route from what has been explored in previous theoretical assumptions. Although I have studied a variety of politeness phenomena across cultures, and so make an effort to be fair and objective in research, I am in all honesty influenced by the ideological image of Japanese politeness and by the way in which Japanese politeness is organised. The purpose of politeness is, indeed, to achieve smooth communication, which may be universal; however, the perception of politeness, or its socio-pragmatic (or ideological) conception, seems to be different across cultures and influential in research enquiries without one noticing it. This, of course, is useful in completing this book, in which Japanese politeness is elaborately examined. However, it might become a hurdle when establishing a theory of politeness. I would be more cautious if an opportunity arose to write a book on a theory of politeness.

# Acknowledgements

To complete this book, many people helped me with advice and suggestions. In spite of living in Britain and Australia for 22 years, and now teaching English to Japanese students, I am still learning and struggling with English. Stuart Cunningham kindly proofread all the chapters. In addition, he advised me to elaborate on Japanese terms and expressions for readers who are not familiar with the language, and our discussions gave me opportunities to further improve the chapters. I would like to express my sincere thanks to Stuart.

I also thank Michael Haugh, my research associate since 2012. His excellent insights and innovative approaches enabled us to produce a number of research results whilst simultaneously inspiring me to deepen discussions in various places in this book. Michael also helped me a great deal when I was going through hard times and encouraged me to focus on my research.

I would like to express many thanks to my family, particularly my husband, Katsumi, who took over the household chores when he retired and has encouraged me to devote myself to my research. Many thanks to my mother, my mentor, who is always providing me with emotional support. I am grateful to my late father, who gave me an opportunity to study overseas and encouraged me to pursue my career.

I originally prepared a book for teachers and learners of Japanese. However, when I went through some difficulties with it, Andrea Hartill, senior publisher at Routledge, suggested that I amend it to a research monograph, and it transpired that I then really enjoyed writing this book. I would like to thank Andrea for her patient guidance.

This work was supported by Grant-in-Aid for Scientific Research (KAKENHI), the Ministry of Education (2015–2018 and 2018–2020).

# Note on transcriptions

The following abbreviations are used in the morphological gloss in the text:

Acc – accusative marker, *o*
Aux – auxiliary
Caus – causative auxiliary, *-seru/saseru*
Conj – conjunction
Cop – copula, *da* and its variations. When this appears as *desu*, 'Polite' is used in the morphological gloss
Formal – formal style converted from a dictionary form. For example, *gojistu* (later) is a formal style of *atode, nochini* and transcribed as 'later[Formal]'
Hon – honorific marking or conversion. If the meaning of a term appears at the same time, [Hon] is attached to the meaning. e.g. say[Hon]
Intj – interjection
MD – mood marker, usually utterance ending particle
Neg – negation, *-nai*
Nom – nominative marker, *ga*
Nomi – nominaliser, usually marked by the particle *no* (e.g. *~no da*)
Pass – passive auxiliary, *-reru/rareru*
Past – past tense, *-ta*
Polite – addressee honorifics, *desu/masu*
Prog – progressive or state auxiliary
Q – question marker, *ka*, *no*
Quote – quotation marker, *to*
TE – *te*-form, which bridges between a verb and an auxiliary, so-called *setsuzoku joshi* (conjunctional particle)
Top – topic marker, *wa*

Note. In the text, the reader will notice words and statements in bold or italic. Those in bold identify key concepts or statements that I highly value in my arguments or would like to draw the reader's attention to due to their controversial nature. Statements in italic indicate main points in each section or in given paragraphs. In the examples, specific phrases are underlined in the Japanese script and written form for ease of identification. Also note that, to avoid using he/she throughout, odd-numbered chapters refer to 'she' and even-numbered chapters to 'he'.

# Part I

# Politeness begins

# 1 Definition of politeness

This chapter examines how the concept of 'politeness' has been viewed in the last four decades from the perspective of pragmatics. It first looks at the etymology of the term 'politeness', and then briefly reviews previous studies on the definition of politeness. It is generally accepted that politeness research has gone through three stages. First, politeness was treated as a part of speech acts and it was customary to make a list of acts of politeness. Second, Brown and Levinson's (1978, 1987) 'face-saving' theory focused on face-threatening acts (FTAs), and designed strategies to mitigate or redress these acts. Though their theory has been criticised as well as praised, it is a seminal inspiration as it has invigorated politeness research since then. The third stage was informed by Eelen's (2001) criticism of normative ways of treating politeness that promoted discursive approaches to politeness.

## 1.0 Introduction

Politeness exists in every culture, and serves as "a key means by which humans work out and maintain interpersonal relationships" (Kádár and Haugh, 2013: 1). As members of society, we generally know (or think we know) how to behave politely and can judge whether or not the behaviour of another is also polite. Politeness is one of the disciplines we have been acquiring since childhood, and exists in our daily life as a matter of course; we live by and in it. This is why politeness is considered to be a folk concept, i.e. "a notion that has a general, popularly understood meaning particular to a sociocultural grouping, but which has not been formally defined or standardized" (Bernstein, 2010: 2). Because of this, it is extremely difficult to pin it down academically, especially when attempting to theorise it. Another difficulty with its theorisation is that, although politeness as a concept may be universal, its concrete examples are culture-laden, presenting diverse phenomena across cultures. Even within the same culture, regional and individual differences can constitute factors for different judgements on politeness. It is also true that politeness is contextually driven; the same behaviour is judged as polite in one context but as impolite in another. In this way, politeness is a complex and diverse phenomenon. In spite of these difficulties, 'politeness' has been one of the most discussed topics in pragmatics for the last four decades.

This chapter briefly looks at three major streams of politeness research by focusing on how politeness is viewed. Since this book focuses on Japanese politeness, I review previous studies from the viewpoint of how they can apply to Japanese.

## 1.1 The etymology of 'politeness'

The term 'politeness' is generally accepted as '**a social tool whereby we aim to achieve smooth and conflict-free communication**'. This idea is based on the etymology of the word 'politeness' It is derived from a Latin word *polit-us*, meaning 'polished, refined', and its related form is *polīre*, which, according to the *Oxford English Dictionary*, means 'to smooth or to polish'. Therefore, 'to be polite' signifies the management of smoothness by showing certain refined (polished) manners.

Smoothness, when applying it to social interactions, implies conflict-free communication. For example, agreeing with the other rather than disagreeing more likely achieves conflict-free communication. Empathy and sympathy may also serve as social lubricants in interaction. Praising is one means of creating a pleasant feeling in the other's mind. Honorifics also contribute to smooth communication as juniors (in status or age) are socially expected in many situations to use honorifics with their seniors,[1] and this kind of social conformity achieves trouble-free interaction.

Politeness also relates to its other origin, 'polished'. It implies that skill in politeness enables its users to maintain their dignity in social life. In extreme cases, it can be interpreted as a way of enhancing "*ego's* self-esteem and his/her public status in the eyes of *alter* with a supplementary aim of enhancing *alter's* self-esteem" (Watts, 1992: 45). Although this extreme interpretation, which Watts quoted from the definition prevalent in eighteenth-century British elite society, rarely arises in our modern society, its remnants still linger in certain polite situations today. For example, if someone says, 'I would like to have a cup of coffee', the listener may judge it as polite, but who is the speaker being polite to? As 'would like to' refers to the speaker's own wish, it is not addressed to the listener. It is not directly polite to a particular person, but meant to maintain the speaker's social dignity. Because this linguistic behaviour is accepted as appropriate by the society in which the speaker resides, it is labelled as 'polite'. In a similar way, the mastering of Japanese honorifics guarantees the user's good social image, and the skilful use of honorifics often makes the user appear educated. Perhaps this is one of the reasons why Watanabe (1974) describes modern honorifics as aiming at *hinkaku hoji* (品格保持), meaning, 'maintaining one's dignity'. Hundreds

1 There are, of course, exceptions. For example, some family-oriented companies apparently do not use honorifics between the employer and employees except for occasional uses of addressee honorifics, *desu/masu*, which are attached to the verb ending, and local casual restaurants seldom use honorifics with their customers in order to maintain a relaxed atmosphere.

of books on how to use correct honorifics[2] are published in Japan, claiming that 'competent adults should know how to use them', 'honorifics are a linguistic weapon in business', 'honorific use is a basic business manner', 'capable business people should be able to use honorifics' and even 'appropriate uses of honorifics create beautiful ladies'. Some of these may be quite subjective or biased, but all point to the etymology of politeness: 'polished'.

In sum, **politeness has two aims: to achieve smooth communication with others and to maintain our dignity as competent adult members of society**. Both originate from the same human desire to make other people have a better opinion of us and themselves. Therefore, from the viewpoint of its etymology, **politeness can be defined as 'a social tool whereby we aim to achieve smooth and conflict-free communication'**.

The concept of politeness, as defined above, exists in every human community, and its fundamental purpose applies in every language. However, this is valid only at the abstract and conceptual level because concrete examples of and practical approaches to politeness differ from language to language. The same behaviour may be interpreted differently from one community to another. In other words, politeness is a culture-laden term, and its practice reveals particular socio-psychological details of the standards or norms that have historically evolved in each language community (see Chapter 2 on how politeness begins and evolves).

Let us consider a simple example. If a guest arrives at Brisbane airport, we might ask her, 'How was your flight?' or 'Did you enjoy your flight?' This is a common polite enquiry. On the other hand, a Japanese person in the same situation will ask, *otsukareni natta deshoo*, meaning 'You must be tired.' This is also polite. What, then, is the reason for this difference? One patriotic answer is that the Japanese expression is more considerate to the guest than the English greeting. In fact, when I asked several Japanese people living in Australia what gives rises to the above difference, most of them gave this patriotic answer. On the other hand, 'How was your flight?' allows the guest to freely talk about her journey and does not impose upon her the evaluation of a third party. The guest is, therefore, the judge and the question maker is merely accommodating. From this viewpoint, *otsukareni natta deshoo* may sound imposing because the guest may not be tired but is now obliged to feel tired. However, from another viewpoint, this expression implies that the

2 A major explanation for the considerable sales of how-to books on honorifics is that honorifics are not acquired but learnt in adulthood. They are consciously learnt, memorised, practised and finally (or hopefully) used smoothly. According to one of the surveys conducted by *Bunka-choo* (文化庁, the Agency for Cultural Affairs, an extra-ministerial bureau) in 1995 reveals that only 15.1% of Japanese speakers regard themselves as fluent in honorifics, 52.2% as just good at using honorifics and 29.2% as not being able to use honorifics sufficiently while wanting to use them more skilfully. While feeling that they are not able to use honorifics, 95.7% of the respondents to the NHK survey in 1987 answered that they consider honorifics necessary and indeed essential in working situations.

speaker will consider the guest's condition when planning the rest of the day for her. In this way, different viewpoints yield different social actions and yet have the same intention: politeness.

## 1.2 Politeness as part of speech acts: A set of rules

This section and onwards briefly looks at the history of how 'politeness' has been viewed or defined. As it is beyond the scope of this chapter to review the entire history of politeness research, I focus on the following three main areas: (1) speech act theory, (2) face theory and (3) discursive approach. The most recent developments will be examined in Chapter 2, since commonly used terms associated with the concept of politeness, such as 'evaluation', 'social practice' and 'expectation', in recent studies are closely related to the discussion in that chapter of how politeness begins and evolves.

Politeness was once treated as part of speech acts. Speech acts mean communication in which the speaker through the use of language intends to perform in relation to the other (usually listener) and to evoke the other's response. They include requests, invitations, greetings, questions and many other purpose-oriented interactions in which speaker and listener are both involved to achieve their own aims.

As a notable scholar in Speech Act Theory, Grice (1975) originally established four maxims underlying the cooperative conversational principle in transactional discourse. Grice's cooperative principles and maxims are directed toward 'effectiveness' in conversation. The four maxims are:

1. The maxim of quantity – Give the most helpful amount of information.
2. The maxim of quality – Information should be truthful.
3. The maxim of relation – Be relevant.
4. The maxim of manner – Behave in a clear, brief and orderly manner.

At first glance, these maxims may work well, especially when busy business people need to deal efficiently with work matters; in this particular case, effectiveness is indeed treated preferentially. However, in many other social interactions, politeness is not aimed only at effectiveness. On the contrary, real interactions often contradict those maxims and yet would not be considered 'impolite' at times. This is because, in our social interactions, we often stray from the topic upon which we originally focused but by letting the discourse wander can nonetheless enjoy a smooth conversation.Politeness, after all, is a matter of conflict-free communication. We are not in court or talking with a lawyer who is paid by the hour.

Social interaction does not necessarily strive to gain only relevant and brief information, but often aims at social **grooming** (Dunbar 1988). 'Grooming' in human society refers to social interactions by means of which we stay in touch with our friends and family and ensure strong social relationships.

This implies that grooming does not necessarily aim at achieving the maxims above because the interactants do not dormally plunge into the targeted topic without preamble, but enjoy digression in the course of information delivery and accept idle talk, through all of which they strengthen their solidarity. What is more, we are not always truthful in social interactions. For example, creating an excuse when turning down an invitation to a party, though it is not 'truthful' in a strict sense, is perhaps more polite than telling the truth, which is that we prefer not to be invited because we do not want to hear the host's lengthy bragging. Nonetheless, Grice's maxims surely laid the foundation for pragmatic approaches to language phenomena, and became a trigger for promoting politeness research thereafter.

Grice's idea led Edmondson (1981), Lakoff (1973, 1975, 1977), Leech (1980, 1983) and Searle (1975) to go further and suggest rules of politeness. They are concerned with how to act in cooperative conversation, and interpret 'politeness' as a set of rules for Speech Acts. For example, Lakoff (1975) presents three rules: (1) Formality – keep aloof, (2) Deference – give options and (3) Camaraderie – show sympathy. On the other hand, Leech (1983) suggests six maxims of the politeness principle: tact, generosity, approbation, modesty, agreement and sympathy.

The problem with these approaches in Speech Act Theory is that their rules remain at the abstract level, eliminating particular contexts of human interaction. For example, Lakoff (1975) provides the first rule, 'Formality – keep aloof'. Indeed, formality is required in certain contexts; however, even in an overtly 'formal' context, keeping aloof is not constantly required throughout the interaction. Actual interactions involve showing both involvement and distance between interactants, depending on how communication develops. Another example is Leech's (1983) suggestion that 'agreement' is a principle of politeness. Indeed, agreement may avoid conflict between the interactants and achieve smooth communication. However, it is not realistic to assume that we always agree with each other for the sake of smooth communication (there may be yes-people, of course, but such people are often not respected; do you agree?). What if a different opinion is inevitably aired? How can we negotiate to reach a consensus? Do we not bring a different polite approach to start negotiating? Speech Act Theory, then, does not accurately reflect reality because *politeness is not just a set of fixed rules, but is more transitional and contextual.*

Japanese politeness is equally flexible and negotiable. Honorifics as a part of Japanese politeness are also contextual and changeable. As is shown in the following chapters, the use of honorifics can be judged as polite or impolite, depending on the relationship between the interactants, i.e. how appropriately one measures a social or psychological distance between oneself and another, and in what context the interactants are placed (and probably what they are talking about; a serious request may require a higher level of honorifics while a casual invitation maintains a lower level). For example:

(1–1) 田中君、ちょっと千円貸してくんない？財布忘れてきたんだ。
Tanaka-kun, chotto sen-en kashi-te-ku-n-nai?
a little 1000 yen lend-TE-give-Nomi-not
Saifu wasure-te-ki-ta-n-da.
wallet forget-TE-come-Past-Nomi-Cop
'Tanaka, can I borrow 1000 yen? I forgot to bring my wallet.'

*chotto* → literally 'a little', to indicate that the speaker is not asking too much
*kashi-te-ku-n-nai?* ← a shortened form of *kashi-te-kure-nai?*

(1–2) 田中さんのほうから今回の企画についてプレゼンしていただきます。
Tanaka-san no hoo kara konkai no kikaku nitsuite
from this time of plan about
purezenshi-te-itadaki- masu.
present-TE- receive[Hon]-Polite
'Mr Tanaka is going to give a presentation about the forthcoming plan.'

*~no hoo kara* → lit. from the direction of (someone), indirectly referring to Tanaka as a courtesy to Tanaka

Suppose the speaker (who is probably male as deduced from his speaking style in example [1–1]) and Tanaka are close colleagues. In example (1–1), the speaker casually asks Tanaka if he can borrow money by using the plain forms *kashite kun nai* (can [you] not lend) and *wasurete kitanda* (I forgot), as well as an informal term of address, *-kun*. This is a private communication between the speaker and Tanaka whether they are at work or somewhere else (and yet the speaker is strategically polite to Tanaka by phrasing his request in a negative and interrogative way and by explaining why he is making such a request). On the other hand, example (1–2) shows that the same interactants are situated in a formal meeting, and the speaker as chair announces Tanaka's presentation. Because they are both exposed to the public, they are expected to be formal, and so the speaker uses honorifics about Tanaka's action (*purezenshite itadaki masu*) and addresses Tanaka with *-san* (Mr/Ms). These examples show that the same people use different speech styles in different situations. This is because people have different roles[3] in different situations (e.g. friends in one situation, meeting attendees in another), according to which their linguistic choices differ to suit their role (and the given situation).

3 Obana (2009) and Haugh and Obana (2011) call such roles '*tachiba*-roles' (*tachiba* = standing place). The same concept is termed 'Role-Identity' by Turner (2011), and throughout this book I employ the latter as it encompasses more varieties of role, ranging from institutional to interactional and improvised roles. See footnote 5 in this chapter, and Section 2.3 for further details.

The above counter-examples indicate that, although Speech Act Theory was a pioneer in the development of subsequent politeness research, it remains at a theoretical level and does not reflect reality. This is because *politeness phenomena cannot be recapitulated as a set of rules due to their diverse and context-dependent characteristics.*

## 1.3 Face-saving view: Brown and Levinson's politeness theory

Based on Goffman's (1967, 1971) notion of 'face', Brown and Levinson (1978, 1987) introduced a 'face-saving' view. They claim that *the notion of 'face' is universal, and that politeness arises through face-saving strategies.* Their work has prompted numerous discussions on the concept of face as well as on the applicability of their strategies to other cultures. However, Brown and Levinson's attempt is worth considering because they were the first to try to develop a comprehensive theory of politeness, and a great deal of research has been devoted to politeness since then.

According to Brown and Levinson, all competent adult members of a society are concerned with their *face, the self-image they present to others.* 'Face' consists of two kinds of desire (face-wants): the desire to be unimpeded in one's actions (*negative face*) and the desire to be approved of (*positive face*). These two types of face are the basic wants of any individual in social interaction, and politeness is motivated by the desire to maintain face. However, communication may involve acts that threaten the other's face. Brown and Levinson (1987) assert that *many actions are intrinsically face-threatening acts* (*FTAs*); "by their very nature, they run contrary to the face wants of the addressee and/or the speaker" (70). Therefore, *politeness is manifested as face-saving strategies in order to minimise FTAs.* They list 15 positive and 10 negative politeness strategies (listed in Endnote 1 of this chapter).

Brown and Levinson's theory has also prompted numerous reviews, controversies and criticisms, which largely point in the following directions:

1. Their concept of 'face' comes from individualist societies and does not apply to collectivist societies.
2. Their FTAs are not universally applicable. The same behaviour may or may not be face-threatening across cultures. Thus, their strategies may not apply to other cultures.
3. Politeness is not always manifested in the form of strategies.

Concerning the first point, strong objections were made by scholars studying Asian languages (e.g. Chang and Holt, 1994; Gu, 1990; Hill et al., 1986; Ide, 1989; Ide et al., 1992; Kummer, 1992; Mao, 1994; Matsumoto, 1988, 1989; Morisaki and Gudykunst, 1994). They all argue that Brown and Levinson's 'face' raises territorial concerns for interactants regarding autonomy and privacy, the values of which are based on individualism in Western cultures. For example, Matsumoto (1988) and Gu (1990), addressing

Japanese and Chinese cultures, respectively, argue that Brown and Levinson's concept is untenable in these Asian cultures because their notion of 'face' is not applicable to socio-centric societies, where 'face' predominantly refers to one's placement in social relations with others. Matsumoto (1988) points out that what is most significant to Japanese people is not their right to act freely but, rather, their position in a group in relation to others, acceptance by the group and the duties assigned by the group. In a similar way, Ide (1989) uses the term '*wakimae*' (discernment), arguing that Japanese politeness is evidence of showing one's *wakimae* in relation to others, or where one stands in relation to others. Therefore, Brown and Levinson's concept of 'face' is alien to Japanese society.

The above argument is closely related to the dichotomy that exists between **collectivism** and **individualism**,[4] which is one of the most explored areas in social psychology. However, while this study has identified many interesting socio-behavioural differences, it has also encountered numerous questions and controversies. These issues are discussed in detail in Endnote 2 of this chapter, but here we look at a few examples. Takano (2008) presents 19 experimental results (deduced from research conducted by himself as well as others) that contradict the traditional view of Japan as a collectivist society and the US as an individualist society. One of these results is that American and Japanese subjects, who responded to questions concerning 'conformity' and 'cooperation', showed little difference in their psychological attributes. As one of the reasons why the results contradicted the prevalent belief, Takano (2008: 55–56) assumes that many previous survey questions are not appropriate because they imply that the researchers associate developed countries with individualism and developing countries with collectivism. For example, the question of whether or not good environmental conditions for workers are strongly desired, which was expected to be agreed upon by collectivist cultures (or developing countries), is not appropriate for distinguishing between the US and Japan since both countries, as developed nations, have already facilitated such conditions.

Takano (2008: 59) also contends that, while 'conformity' is strongly associated with collectivism, American subjects in the experiment conducted by Asch (1956) were influenced by the researcher's associates, who outnumbered the genuine subjects and deliberately selected a wrong answer. The 'conformity' rate was 37%, which, according to Takano, Americans found shocking because their society was believed to be independent and self-reliant.

As shown above (and in Endnote 2), *a closer look at studies on the dichotomy between individualism and collectivism makes us wonder if it is ever possible to divide the world into two types of culture*. Despite this, the arguments against

4 Collectivism is defined as "any of several types of social organization that ascribe central importance to the groups to which individuals belong", whereas individualism emphasises "individual freedom", placing "great value on self-reliance, on privacy, and on mutual respect" (*Digital Britannica Concise Encyclopaedia*). See Endnote 2 of this chapter for further details.

Brown and Levinson's 'face' above resort to the belief that Asian cultures are collectivist and Anglo-Saxon cultures are individualist; thus, 'face' allegedly functions differently in those two types of culture. This means that those scholars who criticise Brown and Levinson's 'face' unconditionally accept the idea of the dichotomy between collectivism and individualism.

The second point questions the universality of FTAs across cultures. For example, Brown and Levinson's classification of 'indirectness' as a negative politeness strategy may not be applicable to all cultures. It has been reported that, in south Western and Slavic cultures, directness connotes sincerity and straightforwardness signifies cordiality (e.g. Sifianou, 1992; Wierzbicka, 1995). Pan (2000) argues that, in Chinese culture, a direct suggestion is considered a display of goodwill and Katriel (1986) identifies the Jewish preference for 'straight-talk'.

It seems, then, that utilising the same strategy (e.g. indirectness) in *different cultures evokes different FTAs*. Furthermore, even in the same culture, the same strategy (e.g. indirectness) is not always judged as 'polite'. For example, the Japanese language commonly exhibits indirect approaches in requests (by using a question to give options), assertion (by using *omowareru* [it seems], *~ja nai desu ka?* [is it not?] to avoid a confrontation) and invitation (by using a negative form, e.g. *issho ni ikonai?* – Wouldn't you like to come with me?). However, *requests as the fulfilment of one's entitled duties are quite directly made due to the implementation of one's Role-Identity*,[5] such as occupation (e.g. doctor, teacher), social status (e.g. student, parent), responsibilities (e.g. project management) and assigned tasks (e.g. meeting chair). If one's role is clearly recognised among the interactants, it entitles one to request directly. For example, the meeting chair is entitled to make direct requests such as:

(1–3) この件については、今週中にメールでお返事ください。
Kono ken nitsuite wa, konshuu-chuuni meeru de o-henji-kudasai.
this matter about Top this week during mail by Hon-reply-please
'Please send me your reply on this matter by the end of this week.'

The chairperson expects the meeting attendees to give their opinions on the item they have discussed. Although she uses honorifics, the request (the underlined part) is quite direct and imperative. This is because the speaker plays a role as chair, which entitles her to make a direct request as long as the request content remains within the domain of tasks the chair is expected to fulfil. On the other hand, indirect requests when performing

5 I employ the terms 'identity' and 'role' as conceptualised by Symbolic Interactionism, a role theory in sociology, to explain what processes are involved with the presentation of politeness. Throughout this book, I use 'Role-Identity' (Turner, 2011), which emphasises that identity (e.g. job categories) emerges in interaction and role performances are based on the identity. See Section 2.3 for details.

one's professional duties indicate that one is not confident and so is judged as indecisive (see Chapter 9, in which strategies in the honorific world are examined). Therefore, while requests (and other actions that involve the other person) in general take indirect approaches in Japanese society, those which implement one's Role-Identity do not follow suit, and in this case one's role entitlement acquires priority over the consideration of FTAs (concerning the comparison between direct and indirect requests in Japanese; see further examples in Section 8.2.1).

Brown and Levinson's strategy examples seem to be problematic, too. Obana (1996) discusses Japanese strategies in the world of honorifics (I call them 'honorific strategies'; see Chapter 9) to show that many of Brown and Levinson's positive politeness strategies are not consistent with the way in which the Japanese show deference. For example, in relation to Strategy 2 (approval, sympathy) of positive politeness, juniors in age or status in Japanese society cannot freely praise their seniors, particularly concerning the *professional performance* of the latter. Therefore, students, for example, would sound rude if they said to their lecturer 'Your lecture is very good,' or 'Your book, professor, was very interesting' because *judgemental statements are not acceptable* no matter how much the students intend to praise the lecturer (see further examples in Section 9.3). Another example is Strategy 9 of positive politeness, "Assert or presuppose S's knowledge of and concern for H's wants", does not conform to the world of honorifics. This is because juniors are expected to directly offer what they assume their seniors want (even if their guess might miss the mark!). Therefore, juniors would not ask, for example, 'Aren't you hungry? Would you like to have lunch?'; instead, they can suggest, 'It's almost lunch time. How about lunch?' Juniors also would not ask, 'Would you like me to help you?'; rather, they would directly offer help: 'I'll help you!' (this will be discussed in detail in Section 9.4).

The third issue, 'politeness is not always manifested by strategies', has been raised particularly by scholars of Japanese politeness. Japanese honorifics are classified as part of Strategy 5 of negative politeness in Brown and Levinson's framework (cf. Endnote 1 of this chapter). They define honorifics as "direct grammatical encodings of relative status between participants, or between participants and persons or things referred to in the communicative event, deriving from frozen outputs of politeness strategies" (Brown and Levinson, 1987: 179). However, Ide (1989) contests that the use of Japanese honorifics is not a strategy but the socio-pragmatic equivalent of grammatical concord. Thus, honorifics are ascribed to socially prescribed norms, manifested by *wakimae* (discernment), while strategies resort to the speaker's own intention ('volition'); in other words, the former are conventionally fixed while the latter are volatile.

I agree with Ide's view that Japanese honorifics are not a strategy, but it does not mean that they exist in contrast to strategies. First, honorifics are not 'ritualistic' or 'prescribed', as Ide claims. As will be discussed in Section

3.2 and Chapter 7, honorific phenomena are quite diverse, negotiable and flexible, and even contingent in some cases. Second, the concept of *wakimae* is not accurately interpreted. It is because *wakimae* means 'one's knowledge of how to behave in social interaction or how to distinguish one thing from another (e.g. good and bad, private and public)'. As social interaction is diverse and dynamic, improvised and changeable, so is the behaviour of *wakimae* to suit different interactions. For example, in Japan women are traditionally prohibited from stepping into a *sumo* ring. However, the tradition was broken in April 2018, when the Kyoto city mayor suddenly collapsed while making a pre-tournament speech to the audience. A woman, a nurse, climbed into the ring and gave the mayor emergency treatment. Thanks to her prompt treatment, the mayor later recovered from his stroke. However, the woman's action created much controversy. In fact, when the woman was treating the mayor, the sumo wrestling referee (行司: *gyooji*) was so upset that he tried to push her out of the ring. In the end, the media and viewers praised her action as appropriate at that particular moment. The woman's action in dealing with an emergency was the implementation of a *wakimae* (i.e. what to do appropriately) in spite of her violation of the traditional *wakimae* (i.e. women should not go into the ring). This means that though *wakimae* may be associated with a habitual social-action (e.g. bowing when greeting) in some contexts, it can be momentary behaviour in other contexts. *Wakimae* is, therefore, contextually-driven.

*Wakimae* behaviour may also differ from group to group in so far as it meets the requirement of the group to which one belongs. For example, in one company, younger workers can freely express their own opinions, and so their frankness is granted as a *wakimae*. Another company, however, does not allow young workers to freely express themselves; instead, they are expected to talk with their section manager first, and then their opinions will be discussed in a company meeting. Following this company policy may indicate a different *wakimae*. However, this policy may change when a new president arrives. Or younger workers may file a petition for more freedom and eventually win and then a different *wakimae* will be established.

*Wakimae* is not a technical term to define a particular linguistic phenomenon. It is a social action that reflects one's sense and sensibilities in a given situation. Therefore, it applies to varied social interactions as long as one's verbal or non-verbal act suits the given situation and is accepted as appropriate. It also does not belong to Japanese culture only, as Ide (2006) claims. It applies to differing cultures where social interaction is expected to go smoothly; as Pizziconi (2003) appropriately points out, *wakimae* is essential in communication, regardless of the language. As such, the scope of *wakimae* behaviour is so broad that all kinds of appropriate behaviour, not to mention Brown and Levinson's (1987) strategies, can be categorised as *wakimae* once they are felicitously selected. The idea of *wakimae* will be further discussed in Chapter 6, in which I clarify how honorifics should be grasped in pragmatic principles.

## 1.4 Discursive politeness

Although Eelen (2001) did not offer an alternative theory, he raised a number of questions that had been neglected in previous studies till then, which established the next stage of politeness research: the discursive approach to politeness. This section discusses the points focused on by Eelen:

1. Previous theories as normative accounts of politeness
2. *Habitus* as an alternative view of politeness
3. Politeness to be examined discursively
4. Evaluations of politeness to be conducted by the hearers not the linguist

### *1.4.1 Previous theories as normative accounts of politeness*

Eelen critically reviewed previous major studies on politeness to label their examples (of politeness) as 'social norms' (in fact, he devotes a great deal of space in his book to pointing out normative accounts of those examples). For example, Brown and Levinson's (1987) face and rationality are regarded as "standards people are expected to live up to – in simple terms, social norms" (Eelen 2001: 126), Ide's (1989) *wakimae* as "to conform to the prescribed norms" (124), and Watts' (1992) politic behaviour as "norms of behaviour" (127). Janney and Arndt's (1992) 'tact' is equally considered to be part of norms because "tact relies on cultural assumptions.... And such cultural assumptions are normative ways of interpreting behaviour" (125). For Eelen, 'social norms' are "prescribed" (124), and "translated into social/cultural principles that guide language behaviour" (187). Therefore, norms are not "relative to the individual, but become absolute, objective entities operating on the level of society/culture" (187). Therefore, normative accounts of politeness, in his opinion, illustrate that "politeness can be seen as a system, mechanism or force involved in the establishment and maintenance of the Parsonian functional integration of society" (203).

I agree with Eelen that politeness is not a set of prescribed rules but, rather, is dynamically transformative and contextually-driven. Therefore, politeness should be examined in accordance with the surroundings in which an utterance is made, i.e. outside factors (e.g. interactional contexts, topics, places and the interactants' relationships), or through inner factors (e.g. emotions, motivations, expectations and beliefs that form the basis for the judgement of politeness). However, I cannot agree with Eelen's interpretation of 'social norms' because social norms neither exhibit a set of rigid rules nor exist as objective entities beyond individuals' social actions. As will be discussed in Chapter 3, social norms used as an indispensable term in sociology are not defined as Eelen describes, but, rather, as "highly dynamic in that social norms arise, hold sway to differing extents and in different ways for a whilst and fall into disuse" because social norms "lie at the intersection of our individual and societal purposes and adaptions" (Edmonds, 2014: 189–190). In fact, social norms have "no reality other than our beliefs that others behave according to them and expect us to behave according to them" (Bicchieri, 2006: 22), and so, "implement *informal social order* that is not imposed externally" (italics in original) but internalised in one's mind. Because of this, "what is acceptable or not seems very changeable according to the time, place and social context of any action" as it "critically [relies] on the perceptions of individuals" (Xenitidou and Edmonds, 2014: 1). Individuals differently perceive what is acceptable or not in different contexts, and act accordingly, assuming that their choice of a particular act will be accepted in a particular context. This also implies that, while social norms may be contingent in a given circumstance, they certainly serve as a social cornerstone for individuals to conform to and rely on when judging others' behaviour. In other words, social norms "touch upon our individual and collective identities, both in playing a part in their formation as well as resulting from these" (Edmonds, 2014: 190).

### *1.4.2 Habitus as an alternative view of politeness*

As an alternative principle (perhaps alternative to 'social norms'), Eelen suggests *habitus*, which was originally introduced by Bourdieu (1977) as a sociological term, and defined as "the durably installed generative principle of regulated improvisations" (78). Eelen interprets this as follows:

> *Habitus* outlines a social mechanism that caters for regulated behaviour without the need for positing some external objective regulating force. It captures a process of structured creativity or collective individuality. (2001: 222)

In other words, *habitus* potentially encompasses not only "the behavior of persons sharing a common set of experiences" because it exists within, not outside of, the historical process, but also changes "in response to changed external circumstances" (Littleton, 1979: 181).

Although *habitus* emphasises the nature of changeable and contextually transferrable aspects of behaviour, its base lies in dispositions shaped by past experiences and systems, which consequently contribute to shaping current practices (Bourdieu 1984: 170), and so *habitus* is a social practice that guides behaviour and way of thinking.

Indeed, with *habitus* Eelen intends to direct politeness from a set of rigid rules to more flexible and negotiable social actions. However, if the term 'social norms' is accurately grasped, it is evident that there is little difference between *habitus* and social norms. They are both established as the backbone of social practices (e.g. politeness behaviour) developed through past experiences and configurations (see the discussion in Chapter 2 on how politeness evolves and a further explanation of 'social norms' in Chapter 3). *Habitus*, just like social norms, is developed as socially ubiquitous "schemes engendered by history"

(Bourdieu, 1984: 82), although it allows changes over time as well as transferability in specific contexts just as do social norms.

Now it is clear that *habitus* as a concept of politeness creates not only contingent behaviour but also a regulated custom or social practice that guides us on how to behave in various social settings. *Social practice refers to daily routines that are habitually performed in our society*, and is "seen as determining the conceptual content of our belief" (Esfeld, 2003: 19). Eelen himself claims that politeness is a social practice (2001: 220–227), which is understandable since the term 'social practice' was introduced by Bourdieu (1977) as recursive performances of *habitus*. In this regard, Eelen admits certain regulated or normative characteristics of politeness, although his criticism of the rigid conceptualisation of de-contextualised utterances by previous studies is worth consideration and has been influential in subsequent studies on politeness.

### *1.4.3 Evaluations of politeness to be examined discursively*

Perhaps this view is Eelen's most significant contribution to politeness research. Until then, politeness was defined as a list of rules or strategies without consideration of the contexts in which it is expressed. In arguing against Brown and Levinson (1987), Van der Bom and Mills (2015: 183) point out that their theory "entails a … sentence-focussed model of communication, which forces them to assume that elements in conversation have single functions". On the other hand, "discursive approaches are a more localized, interactive and context-focussed form of analysis which takes into account the interaction between participants [and] chooses longer stretches of discourse for analysis" (187). Ever since 'discursiveness' was suggested by Eelen, it has been customary in politeness research to provide a naturally-occurring interactional discourse for analysis and to judge politeness through varied cues and clues extracted from that discourse. Let us examine this concept using an example.

The following example is an excerpt from the drama series, *Hanzawa Naoki*, in which Hanzawa, as the protagonist, is being bullied by senior members in the bank. He challenges them and eventually exposes their illicit activities:

(1–4) 小木曽：東京では、ずいぶん世話になったね、半沢融資課長。
Ogiso: *Tookyoo dewa, zuibun sewaninat-ta ne, Hanzawa yuushi kachoo.*
Tokyo in a lot get help-Past MD loan section manager
'You helped me a lot in Tokyo, Loan-Section Manager Hanzawa.'

半沢：融資部が行う裁量臨店に、わざわざ人事部の小木曽次長までお越しいただけるとは。
Hanzawa: *Yuushi-bu ga okonau sairyoorinten ni, wazawaza*
loan-division Nom conduct internal audit to all the way

*jinji-bu* *no Ogiso-jichoo* *made okoshi-itadakeru*
personnel-section of Ogiso-deputy chief even come[Hon]-receive[Hon]
*towa.*
MD

'This is an internal audit in our Loan Division, and yet even Deputy Chief Ogiso from the Personnel took the trouble to come here. I'm honoured indeed.'

(*Hanzawa Naoki*, Part 3)

Example (1–4) appears to be an appreciative interaction between Ogiso (senior) and Hanzawa (junior) with Ogiso's *negirai* (労い: the expression of a senior's appreciation for his junior's work) for Hanzawa's work when they had a meeting in Tokyo, and Hanzawa's *kyooshuku* (恐縮: feeling a sense of obligation to Ogiso because he had taken the trouble to come to Hanzawa's Osaka branch from Tokyo to join the audit). However, given that Ogiso intends to drive Hanzawa into a corner while Hanzawa struggles to retaliate against Ogiso and his group, which is the main story line of the first three parts of the series (each part lasts 90 minutes), the interaction in example (1–4) is far from a polite or amicable exchange.

The context of their previous encounter means that Ogiso's utterance, *zuibun sewa ni natta* (you helped me a lot), does not convey its literal meaning; rather, it is a sarcastic reminder of Hanzawa's counterattack to Ogiso's accusation in Tokyo, which occurs in Part 1 of the serial. His facial expression is not amicable but spiteful, which conforms with his negative remark. On Hanzawa's part, Ogiso's attendance at the audit breaks tradition because an audit is normally conducted within the branch but Ogiso belongs to the main branch in Tokyo. Hanzawa is fully aware of Ogiso's intention, which was clearly stated in the previous scene when Hanzawa was talking with his friend colleague: Ogiso's persistent desire to attack Hanzawa. Therefore, Hanzawa in example (1–4) is sarcastic when he uses *wazawaza* (taking the trouble) and *itadakeru* (could receive + honorific marking). That is, *wazawaza* in a negative context means an accusation aimed at the other's unnecessary action, and *e*- in *itadakeru* means 'possible', which displays the speaker's gratitude if the other person's action is in the speaker's favour ('I fortunately can receive [that from you]), but in a hostile context implies that he is annoyed by Ogiso's action. Although Hanzawa maintains appropriate honorifics as he is junior, i.e. follows a social norm, such honorifics in turn enhance the sarcasm he intends to deliver to his senior because in reality he means that Ogiso should not attend the audit, and so Ogiso's presence is annoying. Since Hanzawa is junior to Ogiso, he does not show his negative emotion on his face, but rather looks cool and composed.

Having watched the drama unfold, the audience can perceive what Ogiso and Hanzawa's utterances in example (1–4) imply in reality, and understand that they are both being sarcastic (and, as proof, the story following the interaction in example [1–4] develops into a more severe battle during the audit). In this way, accurate analysis of example (1–4) is derived from an examination of the entire context of the serial, from Parts 1 and 2 to the beginning of Part 3, during which the relationship between these characters as enemies is created, played and maintained. Discursive analysis, therefore, identifies that the polite linguistic exchanges on the surface (*negirai* and *kyooshuku*) are actually a sarcastic reminder and a sarcastic expression of annoyance, respectively.

The discursive approach has been criticised for its attention to minute, fragmentary and individual utterances (Terkourafi, 2005), for its non-theorised nature (Haugh, 2007) and for its focus on judgements by individual participants (Haugh, 2007; Locher, 2012). Nonetheless, the examination of contexts surrounding the utterances in question, which is now a customary practice in linguistic research, is important in order to extract cues and clues from relevant contexts for precise and convincing judgements, though of course this approach loads researchers with extra burdens in their analysis.

### *1.4.4 Evaluations of politeness to be conducted by the hearers not the linguist*

Eelen (2001: 128), by defining politeness as "to act appropriately", describes how politeness should be evaluated in the following way:

> [B]ecause a polite communicative act is always aimed at some addressee on which it intends to have some effect, the hearer's expectations about politeness need to be met in order to be successful. Social appropriateness is thus closely related to hearer expectation…. Acting politely thus equals acting appropriately equals acting according to the hearer's expectations.

Eelen further claims that politeness research should focus on politeness that, first, is "about commonsense notions of politeness" or a folk concept in which lay people perceive an utterance as polite or not (240). In other words, the discursive approach aims to assign hearers or participants to evaluate politeness rather than analysts or researchers, as the latter have traditionally spotlighted politeness. Second, research should focus on a theoretical conceptualisation of politeness.

While some of Eelen's ideas are quite influential, the tenet here has been criticised mainly for predicting bleak prospects for future politeness research. First of all, the absence of an analyst means that there is no prior assumption of, for example, where the data will be subsumed, what contextual features contribute to judgements of politeness and how those features can then be categorised. As Haugh (2007: 303) appropriately points out, "if the analyst is not able to identify with some degree of certainty evaluations of (im)politeness that arise through a close analysis of the interaction, what indeed has been accomplished?" This is because we cannot keep looking at interactions one by one and asking lay people whether they are polite or not. A mere collection of fragments of interaction without involving the analyst's certain assumptions would never lead us to understand what politeness is, what constitutes politeness and why and how politeness differs in different contexts as well as across cultures. A theoretical conception is necessary because it shows the analyst's view of how politeness is analysed and judged, predicts other phenomena yet to be analysed, and facilitates efficient applications to other languages. It must be the case that a theoretical conception is testable; new evidence may rebut it, but theory-building in any scientific research inevitably goes through such trial and error.[6] A good theory passes tests, and can encompass more phenomena and explain them extensively.

Another question about Eelen's (2001) "evaluations by hearers" is where 'evaluations' come from. Evaluation is a broad term in psychology used to cover a variety of judgements individuals perform. Their own attitude, likes and dislikes, and stance or viewpoint in each specific discourse are all considered 'evaluation'; such judgements may differ individually and are loaded with personal tastes. On the other hand, there is another type of evaluation which adheres to collective or social patterns of behaviour and which categorises these patterns as pro-social or anti-social, though some patterns may be judged differently by individuals on the basis ofthe particular benefits/losses those patterns bring about. Let us call this type of evaluation '**social evaluation**', as used by Li (2014) and Abdai and Miklósi (2016). Li (2014: 189–207) elaborates on the nature of social evaluation, which "reflects the fundamental interests and needs" (194) of the society to which people belong and that "has an actual effect on the integrity, the social consciousness and social practice"[7] (189).

In a similar way, politeness is closely associated with social evaluation. Eelen's term 'common sense', when preferring to utilise the first form of politeness rather than the second for analysis, is also related to social evaluation. Though different definitions have been observed in sociology, common sense is largely understood as "organized and typified stocks of taken-for-granted knowledge upon which activities are based and that, in the 'natural attitude', are not questioned", or "tacit knowledge ... in which people draw on implicit rules or 'how to carry on' and which produce a sense of organization and coherence" (Scott, 2014 [1994]: 100).

Evaluation of politeness may be derived from hearers' common sense; however, before it becomes tacit knowledge, those hearers (as well as other people, including the analyst) have heuristically learnt and acquired the skills necessary to behave in social interaction. Abdai and Miklósi (2016: 3) describe "the

6 This is called 'falsifiability' of a theory, which is Karl Popper's (2002 [1934]) basic principle about science; any scientific hypothesis is testable through certain methods (e.g. experiments, surveys) and, if it is not possible, Popper does not admit such a hypothesis as scientific.

7 However, Li admits that social and individual evaluations are not clearly distinctive because individual evaluation often reflects the standard of social evaluation as a social performer, but at the same time carries an individual's own subjective measurements.

development of fully fledged social evaluation in humans" that begins at the infant stage and continues into adulthood, whereby *eventually people build up a certain (regulated) guideline in their mind in order to optimise evaluations.* Whether this guideline is called social norms (in this book) or *habitus* (Eelen's choice) or even 'common sense', evaluation of politeness is neither ad hoc or random nor belongs only to hearers. Social norms and evaluations are largely shared by people in the same community; the community may be as large as a nation or as small as the group to which one belongs.

It is indeed true that politeness evaluation may differ at times, and the analyst should articulate and explain what features signify such differences. However, as examined above, (social) evaluation, no matter who it belongs to, is a collective ability and socially practised based on certain standards. To make this clearer, let us look at an example from Japanese.

The formulaic expressions, *arigatoo* and *sumimasen*, are often interchangeably used, both meaning 'thanks' while the latter can also be used for apology in other situations. As Coulmas (1981) and Kumatoridani (1988, 1999) point out, thanking and apology often take on similar attributes in many interactions, and "are not as distinctly different as widely believed" (Kumatoridani, 1999: 624). Coulmas (1981) pays attention to 'indebtedness' that is shared between expressions of thanks and apology. In a similar way, Jautz (2013: 7) argues that thanking formulae not only acknowledge and evaluate positively what one has done for the other, but also "are associated with negative feelings, as the speaker acknowledges a debt of gratitude and thus humbles their face".

Obana (2015) differentiates between *arigatoo* and *sumimasen*, assuming that the domain of one's Role-Identity (cf. footnote 5 of this chapter) in a given context is key to distinguishing them. For example, a university student asking her professor a question about her dissertation would express *arigatoo gozaimashita* (*arigatoo* honorific-marked, addressee honorific marked with the past tense), but never *sumimasen deshita* (*sumimasen*, addressee honorific marked with the past tense) when leaving the professor's room. This is because giving dissertation advice is categorised as one of the professor's professional jobs or the fulfillment of her role-identity (institutional role, in this case). On the other hand, if the same professor offers coffee to the student after the discussion, the student may say *sumimasen*. This is because offering coffee is not one of the roles the professor is expected to play; it exists outside the domain of her role responsibilities. Therefore, the same student differentiates between using thanking formulae in dialogue with the professor by perceiving what kind of social action is taking place and how the action should be categorised by assessing the stances she and the professor are currently assuming.

The assumption above is the analyst's evaluation of the occurrence of the thanking formulae, and to prove this, Obana (2015) asked 215 native speakers of Japanese which formula, *arigatoo* or *sumimasen*, they would use in each context. In relation to the dissertation, all 215 subjects answered *arigatoo gozaimashita*, but with regards to the offer of coffee, 153 subjects chose *sumimasen* and 62 chose *arigatoo gozaimasu* (and 47 people responded that use of both is possible). The latter case is noteworthy because, although a majority of the subjects chose *sumimasen* just as the analyst claims, some subjects chose *arigatoo gozaimasu*, thus we have some individual differences here.[8] This is not hearers' evaluation but a questionnaire survey; nonetheless, the analyst's assumption conforms with a majority of people's judgements while admitting a different choice by some individuals. It should follow that the analyst examines why, in one context, *arigatoo* was unanimously selected while, in the other, individual differences were observed.

When controversial or grey areas of evaluation are predicted, hearers' opinions, statistics or surveys may be of help to back up the analyst's assumptions, but the most important point here is that **evaluation of social actions is largely a collective assessment**, and not entirely free from the social standards we social beings conform to.

Eelen attempted to break away from what he calls 'social norms, which he associated with a rigid and static set of theorised rules, and to move to a discursive, non-analytic and hearer-based method. However, the terms he used, such as 'evaluation', '*habitus*' and 'common sense', which were supposed to support his postulation of politeness, are in fact not far away from normative accounts of politeness.

## Endnote 1: Brown and Levinson's positive and negative strategies

Brown and Levinson listed a number of face-saving strategies, but essentially they consist of four orientations under the two face types (modified version of Fraser 1990: 229–230), as follows:

Negative face

1. Acts threatening to the hearer's negative face – e.g. advising, ordering, suggesting.
2. Acts threatening to the speaker's negative face – e.g. accepting a request or an offer.

Positive face

3. Acts threatening to the hearer's positive face – e.g. disagreeing, raising taboo topics, complaining and criticising.
4. Acts threatening to the speaker's positive face – e.g. apologising, accepting compliments and confessing.

8 Obana's (2015) analysis contends that the difference is based on where individuals primarily place their value, i.e. whether they are 'pleased' with the offer of coffee (in the case of *arigatoo*) or 'obliged' to the professor (*sumimasen*).

To avoid potential FTAs, Brown and Levinson suggest 15 strategies for positive politeness and 10 for negative politeness:

Positive politeness

1. Notice, attend to H (his interests, wants, needs, goods)
2. Exaggerate (interest, approval, sympathy for H)
3. Intensify interest in H
4. Use in-group identity markers
5. Seek agreement
6. Avoid disagreement
7. Presuppose/raise/assert common ground
8. Joke
9. Assert or presuppose S's knowledge of and concern for H's wants
10. Offer, promise
11. Be optimistic
12. Include both S and H in the activity
13. Give (or ask for) reasons
14. Assume or assert reciprocity
15. Give gifts to H (goods, sympathy, understanding, cooperation)

Negative politeness

1. Be conventionally indirect
2. Question, hedge
3. Be pessimistic
4. Minimise the imposition
5. Be deferent
6. Apologise
7. Impersonalise S and H
8. State FTA as a general rule
9. Nominalise
10. Go on record incurring a debt or as not indebting H

## Endnote 2: Collectivism and individualism – are they real?

One of the major criticisms of Brown and Levinson's (1987) face theory is that their 'face' belongs to individualist societies but does not apply to collectivist societies. In this Endnote, I examine whether the dichotomy between collectivism and individualism can be materialised in politeness research. This is because the criticism of Brown and Levinson's face is based entirely on this dichotomy, and yet no question has been raised regarding whether or not the dichotomy is validated in order to establish a sound base for distinguishing between the two types of face.

Collectivism and individualism are terms employed by anthropologists, sociologists and social psychologists, and used as a yardstick whereby universal features are sought through the observation of social behavioural patterns across cultures (e.g. Barnlund and Yoshioka, 1990; Brislin and Yoshida, 1994; Cousins, 1989; Kim et al., 1994; Luce and Smith, 1987; Shweder and Bourne, 1982; Triandis and Brislin, 1980; Triandis et al., 1990). Perhaps, one of the most comprehensive collections of cross-cultural studies can be found in Smith and Bond (1998), who review numerous previous works, comparing different cultures according to communication styles (e.g. in friendship, a small/large group), organisational behaviours (e.g. cooperation, negotiation) and many other social interactional situations. Triandis (1995) also provides a number of experimental results that are used to distinguish between individualism and collectivism.

Hofstede (1991: 51) views collectivism and individualism as follows:

> [I]ndividualism pertains to societies in which the ties between individuals are loose ... Collectivism as its opposite pertains to societies in which people from birth onwards are integrated in strong, cohesive ingroups.

In general, individualism is most characteristic of Northern and Western Europe, the United States, Australia and New Zealand. Collectivism, on the other hand, is most prevalent in Southern and Eastern Europe, Latin America, Asia and Africa. Kim et al. (1994: 2) highlight distinctive differences between individualism and collectivism, as follows:

> [I]individualist societies emphasize "I" consciousness, autonomy, emotional independence, individual initiative, right to privacy, pleasure seeking, financial security, need for specific friendship, and universalism. Collectivist societies, on the other hand, stress "we" consciousness, collective identity, emotional dependence, group solidarity, sharing, duties and obligations, need for stable predetermined friendship, group decision, and particularism.

In a similar way, Yoshida (1994: 243) adds features such as "harmony and good interpersonal relationships" to collectivist values and "behaviour bringing merit to specific people" to individualist values. A more extreme opinion is found in Brislin and Yoshida (1994: 78–80), who claim that "individualists carry a sense of separation from their extended family and from their community ... Collectivists are more willing to downplay their own goals in favour of group preferences". Smith and Bond (1988: 171) ascertain that communication styles differ between the two types of society: "Communication in collectivist cultures is more indirect, less succinct and less interpretable without knowledge of its context than that typically found in individualist cultures." They quote the value configuration of Sagiv and Schwartz (1995), which indicates that value types such as "security, tradition, benevolence and conformity" direct societies toward collectivism, while "hedonism, stimulation, and self-direction" are more characteristic in individualist societies (Smith and Bond, 1988: 53).

Overall, collectivism and individualism have been treated as bi-polar, and a great number of researchers have endeavoured to seek contrastive behavioural patterns. Of course, some scholars (e.g. Schwartz, 1990; Tyerman and Spencer, 1983; Triandis, 1994; Trompenaars, 1993; Wierzbicka, 1994) warn that this dichotomy may mistakenly lead to diametrically opposed binarism. Triandis (1994: 42) and Trompenaars (1993: 49) carefully assert that both types exist in every culture, however one or the other is manifest more conspicuously in different situations, and each society may tend to be more susceptible to a particular type. Therefore, just because one society is categorised as individualist, it does not necessarily mean that it behaves individualistically in every social situation.[9] For example, Tyerman and Spencer (1983) argue that British society, though it is alleged to be typically individualist, may allow collectivist situations to be formed, such as long-term groups led by their leaders' orientation, where members increase intergroup cooperation, and their behaviour within their group is regulated by a long-established set of social norms. They use the example of boy scouts. We could also easily associate this example with other team activities such as sports organisations (e.g. football, basketball, baseball), where conformity, a strong sense of solidarity and team trust must be constructed in their players' minds. In a similar way, Hofstede (1980) found an interdependent pattern in an individualist society when the subjects in his experiments knew they were relating to a cooperative partner. Wierzbicka (1994:19) does not oppose the use of the bi-polar method to investigate a typology of communication patterns, but hesitates to use it for categorising societies as one or the other type.

Smith and Bond (1998: 49) admit that social psychologists rarely attempt to predict the behaviour of specific individuals, but provide interpretations of average results from persons in those countries examined. This implies that, while they support the bi-polar classification of societies, they also acknowledge fuzzy, non-conforming and exceptional areas in each type of society.

Those careful approaches, however, have in fact been distorted and even ignored when two apparently opposite societies are compared in experimental studies (mainly by questionnaires or by asking subjects directly). This is because the aim of these studies is to extract and emphasise differences, and so they cannot offer a compromise solution between the two value types.

9 If we accept this cautious approach, then, our central issue on face is more problematic because the discussion on face entirely relies on the existence of the dichotomy between individualism and collectivism. If Brown and Levinson's face is criticised as belonging to individualism, then which part of British society, for instance, does this refer to? Does this mean that in the military and boy scouts, British people have a collectivist's face and when they go home, they have an individualist's face? Which face, then, is brought forth in accounting for politeness?

I do not intend to argue whether or not the world consists of these two types of culture. However, a closer examination of how those experimental results were extracted raises a number of questions and may take issue with the validity of the dichotomy between individualism and collectivism. First, many variables listed as typical features in contrastive studies have never been clearly defined, and have been used without questioning their applicability. For example, Yoshida (1994) claims that a collectivist society places a high value on harmony and good interpersonal relationships. However, variables such as 'harmony' and 'good interpersonal relationships' have never been questioned. I believe that every society aims at these features in communication, and politeness is a means of achieving them (and politeness exists in every culture). Yoshida also states that an individualist society is likely to encourage behaviour that brings merits for specific people. However, business organisations surely seek merits for their own group members, even in Japanese society while Japan is assumed to be a typical collectivist society. If these members are not 'specific people', who are they? Kim (1994) also proposes that collectivist cultures are guided by the requirement not to impose on the hearer and not to hurt the hearer's feelings. However, this conclusion is too generalised to be accepted because the requirement quoted here is fundamental human psychology because no one wants to be imposed on or hurt whether they belong to an individualist or a collectivist[10] society (provided such societies exist). In this way, variables used to characterise the two types of society are often accepted as axiomatic, and have never been defined. Therefore, the meaning of terms such as 'harmony', 'autonomy', 'self-direction' and so on remains obscure and could be misleading when applied to describing other societies yet to be categorised.

A second question about those experimental results is whether or not their methodological processes are appropriate. For example, Smith and Bond (1998: 106–109) refer to the result of different patterns in 'describing oneself'; e.g. Americans use many more generalised trait descriptions than the Japanese. It was then concluded that Americans describe themselves in a more abstract manner and Japanese characterise themselves situationally or via interpersonal relationships.[11] However, it is quite difficult to accept this conclusion because such results may depend on types of question in experiments. If the question is familiar to a particular group of people, they will describe themselves successfully, meeting the researcher's expectations. On that account, we should consider whether or not questionnaires were prepared fairly for both groups;

10 For example, Brown and Levinson's (1987) strategies to avoid FTAs specifically refer to Kim's 'requirement'. Does this mean, then, that Brown and Levinson's strategies should be categorised as collectivist features while their 'face' is considered individualist?

11 I am under the impression that the American way is more subjective than the Japanese way because, even if describing oneself in an abstract manner, it may be from the image of oneself while describing oneself in a given situation, i.e. describing how one behaves in a given situation is more objective without resorting to one's own image of oneself.

otherwise, they might have prevented one group of people from 'describing themselves' successfully, resulting in belying the researcher's expectations. Then the question is not a matter of the dichotomy of sociological types, but is to do with the appropriateness of methodologies. Smith and Bond, in fact, admit that social psychology has largely been developed in Western countries, and so the Western view is inevitably involved in preparing experiments.

Furthermore, it is questionable whether the way of describing oneself in different cultures should signify the dichotomy between collectivism and individualism. Because of the over-emphasis on the bi-polar theory in social psychology, research topics have been extended to include more detailed phenomena, such as romantic relationships, communication with foreigners, self-disclosure and so on. Just because two societies show different attitudes toward these topics, it does not necessarily mean that they are derived from differences between collectivism and individualism. Some other social, historical or political reasons may be involved. For example, regional differences often exhibit diverse attitudes (e.g. foreigners in rural areas in Japan are treated differently from those in urban areas; communication styles naturally differ in these areas within the same culture). Upbringing or class differences in the same culture may present varied degrees of self-disclosure than similar classes in different cultures.

Takano (2008) contends that prior to those experiments exist the researchers' preconceived idea or even ideological belief that Japan is collectivist and the US individualist (he collected experimental results in which Japan and the US are compared). He also states that such a preconceived idea is prevalent in each society and formed as a common view (*tsuusetsu*: 通説 – lit. prevalent theory). Takano (2008: 128f) offers as an example of common views Japanese people's loyalty to their company, which is one of the most accepted features constituting collectivism. However, contrary to this common belief, a number of questionnaire results showed that American workers demonstrated more loyalty than did Japanese workers. For example, the All-Japan Federation of Electric Machine Workers' Union (電機労連: *denki rooren*) conducted a survey in Japan and the US in 1988, and found that, in response to the question of whether those workers want to do the best to contribute to their company, only 29% of the Japanese workers answered 'yes' in contrast to 64% of the American workers. Takano quotes a few more similar results presented by different research institutes. He by no means intends to conclude that Japan is an individualist society; rather, he uses these examples to warn us not to be misled by prevalent beliefs.

It is not my intention to solve dilemmas and controversies concerning the dichotomy between individualism and collectivism in social psychology. However, it is evident that controversies and problems surrounding the concept of the dichotomy exist, and yet those linguists who argue against Brown and Levinson's (1987) 'face' base their ideas upon this disputable and unstable concept without questioning its validity, and even take it as axiomatic in their arguments.

# 2 The underlying meaning of politeness

## How it begins and evolves

This chapter first introduces recent developments in politeness research since Eelen's (2001) suggestion of the discursive approach. A number of definitions of politeness have been offered such as 'communities of practice' (Mills, 2003), 'rapport management' (Spencer-Oatey, 2008[2000]) and 'relational work' (Locher and Watts, 2005). While they incorporate the discursive approach in their analysis, they also give access to 'norms' of politeness for evaluation. Kádár and Haugh (2013) incorporate 'evaluations', 'social practice' and 'expectations' into the concept of politeness, and these terms are essential features that constitute 'social norms'. This makes one wonder where these terms come from and how they constitute politeness. To address this issue, this chapter then moves on to examine those terms from a different perspective. While many previous studies on politeness synchronically observe politeness phenomena and work on how politeness should be viewed or defined, I take a diachronic route to clarify what features constitute politeness (I call this the 'underlying meaning of politeness') by explaining how politeness is borne out of our fundamental human needs/wants in social life, how such needs/wants are developed into social standards (social norms), and how social standards and another human behaviour, 'evaluation', are intertwined with politeness.

### 2.1 The recent development of politeness studies: What 'politeness' constitutes

Since the work of Eelen (2001), researchers on politeness are more cautious in evaluating utterances by presenting a long sequence of interactional exchanges surrounding those utterances in question. They often incorporate the method provided by Conversation Analysis in order to be more objective, authentic and indicative of cues and clues for appropriate evaluations. This means that, although Eelen did not develop the notion of *habitus* into a systematic theoretical framework, which I assume was an alternative to normative accounts of the previous studies, his contribution to the re-thinking of evaluations and the way in which data is to be presented is significant in the history of politeness research. On the other hand, since the work of Brown and Levinson (1978, 1987), no rigorous, systematic framework has been observed in politeness research except that of Spencer-Oatey (2008[2000]), though in line with Brown and Levinson. Rather, suggestions on how politeness should be viewed or what politeness constitutes seem to be the most recent developments in politeness research, while more diverse politeness phenomena are analysed in a particular language as well as across cultures.

In this section, I take a look at recent studies on the definition of politeness, and discuss noteworthy terms used in those studies in processing what politeness constitutes. This will be helpful when discussing (and understanding) the 'underlying meaning of politeness' in Section 2.2, where many of those terms are employed in defining politeness from a diachronic perspective.

### *2.1.1 Communities of practice*

Mills (2003, 2011) adopts the term 'communities of practice', which was initiated by Lave and Wenger (1991), to discuss how politeness is co-constructed by members of a community. Valuing the discursive approach suggested by Eelen (2001), Mills stresses the importance of the 'community-based' and 'discourse level' model in politeness analysis.

Lave and Wenger's (1991) 'communities of practice' derives from their view of how 'learning' is achieved socio-culturally. According to them, learning is not accumulated by isolated individuals, but is a social process situated in the practice of communities, which contributes to the development of individuals' membership in their community as well as their identity. At the same time, a community of practice has the potential to change by experiencing the ebb and flow of newcomers during the process of obtaining membership, which may contribute to the further development of their community. Or a community may radically change when old members are replaced by newcomers.

Given the concept of communities of practice as above, politeness as a social practice is learnt and co-constructed (and shared) by the community of practitioners. However, while this is a reasonable explanation of how politeness is learnt and practised, the question of where 'such politeness is to be learnt' remains unsolved. For this, Mills (2011: 75) implies that "individuals assume that certain norms are accepted within a CoP (Community of Practice)" or "there are certain socially-derived norms at work within the group". This means that *Mills admits the existence of 'social norms',*[1] *based on which politeness is evaluated*, although she also (2011: 79) stresses the greater

1 Although Lave and Wenger themselves do not use the term 'social norms', they define a community of practice as "a set of relations among persons, activity, and world, over time and in relation with other tangential and overlapping communities of practice" (1991: 98), and a community of practice is built up by people who participate in the process of collective learning and share the domain of interest. They also admit that such a process can be generalised and applied to other communities. This indicates that a CoP itself establishes social norms within that community over time.

leeway a CoP affords individuals to "make choices about how they will speak from within a set of options approved of by the CoP".

### *2.1.2 Discursive face*

Geyer (2008) reinstates Brown and Levinson's (or more precisely Goffmanian) 'face' in her argument by revising it as one's "interactional self-image, which is determined in relation to others, discursively constructed during a particular contact, and closely aligned with the participant's discursive identity" (50). She calls such face "discursive face', 'interactional face' or 'interactional self-image' (ibid). Although she warns that face is not identical to politeness since "facework, ... encompasses a wider range of practices than polite behaviour", she does assert that "evaluations of facework and appropriateness constitute the basis for evaluations of politeness" (7).

Not only does Geyer emphasise the discursive nature of her 'face', she also uses face more extensively; it is not limited to individuals' identity but extended to a more collective one such as 'institutional face'. In this sense, Geyer's 'face' is equivalent to 'identity', which is a prevailing concept in discourse analysis, and Geyer (2008: 48–52) herself introduces studies on discursive identity to "link these diverging views to our understanding of face" (48).

In discourse analysis and sociolinguistics, "identity is not fixed", but rather "is constructed within established contexts and may vary from one context to another" (Omoniyi and White, 2006: 2), resulting from "processes of negotiation and entextualization that are eminently social" and therefore, identity "entails 'discursive work'" (De Fina et al., 2006: 2). In this way, identity can be defined as "a situatedness of the person in terms of standing in the context of a particular social relationship or group" (Gecas and Burke, 1995: 45).

What is normally conducted when dealing with identity in sociolinguistics and discourse analysis is that an interactional context is scrutinised to find certain linguistic terms, expressions and styles that point to a particular identity. For example, Drew and Sorjonen (1997) find personal pronouns used in interactions that index the participants' institutional identity such as 'we' referring to their own company. Kinuhata and Yang (2007) discuss military terms developed during the world wars, such as *jibun* (self) when referring to oneself, *-de arimasu* (it is that...), a report style used at the end of the sentence. Particular use of language also reveals which social identity the speaker brings to the fore. For example, Deckert and Vickers (2011) give an example of a black American woman's use of 'O-kay' in a particular way when strongly agreeing with the other interactant. In discourse analysis, the whole discourse is often examined, which involves the emerging of certain identities. For example, Johnson (2006) examines an interview with a teacher, which eventually reveals that the interviewee is 'a good teacher' although there is no mention of this quality in the interview.

There are, however, two points to be noted concerning 'identity' or Geyer's 'face'. First, albeit the prevalent idea that identity, just as Geyer's "face", emerges as an interactional product, the above examples imply that *identity encompasses socially enacted features* no matter how much its interactional 'discursiveness' is emphasised. This is because 'face' or 'identity' is not manufactured by the discourse-context, but its most suitable facet of 'face' or 'identity' is selected out of the multi-layered identities of one's self to suit the given context, and the self's multi-faceted identities are socially developed (see the Endnote to this chapter). For example, institutional identity that is disclosed in the linguistic term 'we' is culturally learnt and recursively occurs in many other contexts. In a similar way, newcomers to the military camp learn particular terms from existing soldiers, which in a sense plays a part in building new members' identity as 'soldiers'. This is well explained by Symbolic Interactionism (SI), which is a prevalent role theory in sociology; the self's identity emerges in ongoing interaction[2] but, at the same time, a role performance substantiated by an identity[3] (e.g. role-identity as a teacher performing his job [role] at school) "depends on a shared set of expectations.... *[W]e observe and enact these shared expectations*" (Sandstrom et al., 2010: 145, italics added) (see Section 2.3 for further details).

Another point to be noted is that, while particular linguistic terms used in a context may single out a certain identity, the reverse does not necessarily work out. This is because one's identity to some extent includes one's subjective enactment (belief or custom) of how to implement one's identity in one's behaviour. Or, more precisely, one's identity (e.g. a public servant) is not always in a one-to-one relationship with its behavioural implementation in reality (or one's role performance). For example, workers at the Driver and Vehicle Licensing Centre (運転免許更新センター: *unten-menkyo kooshin sentaa*) surely identify themselves as public servants, and work for visitors who need their driving licence to be issued or renewed. They are expected to use at least addressee honorifics with visitors. However, I recently noticed that there is one person at the centre in my area who uses abrupt forms or *tameguchi* (ため口: peer language) with visitors. I was initially annoyed (not as a linguist, but as a visitor). However, I heard some young visitors praising that officer's behaviour (when we were waiting for a renewed licence) because the paperwork required before attending the counter is quite tedious and yet (according to those young people) the officer gave elaborate advice in a friendly manner. I am not sure whether the officer's language is deliberate or he simply does not know honorifics. However, those young visitors' comment

2 However, Core-Identity is the most trans-situational because it is defined as "one's personal identity to oneself" (Hewitt, 1989: 334), including "personal history, biological information and aspects of personality" (Vryan et al., 2003: 371). Core-Identity is placed at the top of the hierarchy of transactional needs (identity categories) by Turner (2011).

3 As the self is not composed of a unity but "made up of modules, and the modules are made up of modules themselves" (Erdelyi, 1994: 7), multi-layered identities can be displayed in the same situation (e.g. a black American woman may speak in away that is a mixture of black, American and female identities).

was quite convincing as the centre as a whole is beaurocratic and aloof rather than amicable; thus, the officer's *tameguchi* may have enhanced his aura of kindness (elaborate instructions) and softened the uptight atmosphere. Thus, in this case, his non-honorific use, even if it deviates from the norm at the centre, has a positive effect. This shows that, while all of the workers identify themselves as public servants, their role performances (e.g. honorific use or not) may differ. That particular officer sees his role as to serve visitors in a kind manner, which in his mind comes before honorific use as a public servant. Therefore, identity is not completely aligned with its implementation as a role performance.

### *2.1.3 Rapport management*

The concept of 'rapport management' was suggested by Spencer-Oatey (2005, 2008[2000]) and, although it seems to remain in line with the framework developed by Brown and Levinson (1987), its modifications, changes and additions attempt to overcome the inadequacies for which Brown and Levinson have been criticised. For example, Brown and Levinson's "negative face issues are not necessarily face concerns at all", and instead Spencer-Oatey's 'face management' is "the management of face sensitivities" and "positive social *value*" (2008[2000]: 13), while placing Brown and Levinson's 'negative face' in 'sociality rights and obligations', one of the three key factors that influence 'rapport'; these factors are called 'the bases of rapport' (14). Furthermore, she introduces 'rapport management domains', in which "politeness is managed through multiple aspects of language use" (20). I interpret her bases of rapport as motivations for politeness behaviour, and domains as tools for actual implementation of those bases. This can be illustrated as shown in Figure 2.1, based on Spencer-Oatey's (2008[2000]: 14) figure, with my additional interpretations.

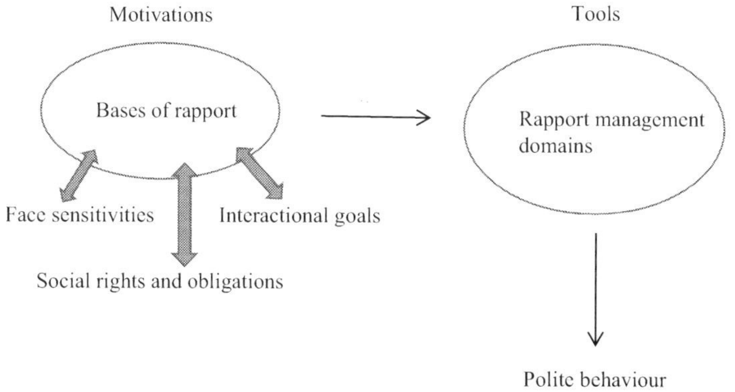


*Figure 2.1* Bases of rapport and rapport management

Honorifics are categorised as the 'Stylistic Domain' (21), which includes tone, lexical and syntactic choices. On the other hand, Brown and Levinson's face-saving strategies belong to the 'Illocutionary Domain', which "concerns the rapport-threatening or rapport-enhancing implications of performing speech acts". This seems to solve the controversy over 'collective face' entailed in honorifics in contrast with Brown and Levinson's (1987) 'individual face', for which they received criticism (cf. Section 1.3), without referring to face issues. Spencer-Oatey made many more suggestions (e.g. emotions, directness–indirectness), but here I discuss how far her Rapport Management Model (RMM) can apply to Japanese honorifics.

Indeed, honorifics are not a strategy but markings on the utterance that has strategically been constructed (see Section 6.2), and so honorification itself may be a matter of stylistic concern (or, more precisely, grammatical conversion). However, *actual choices of honorific terms often reveal how the speaker intends to achieve his goal in interaction*. In other words, honorific levels and terms can be manipulated to indicate the speaker's psychological state or his stance in relation to the other interactant. Speech-level shifts are a typical example, which occur because speakers are "active agents who strategically choose to use honorific or non-honorific forms to achieve their interactional goals"[4] (Cook, 2011: 3658). For example, between close friends who normally do not use honorifics with each other, their profound gratitude or sincere apology may prompt honorific use (Obana, 2017); by exalting the other at that moment, the speaker indicates her deep emotion.

Even in the use of conventional honorifics, variations in level (supreme to lower levels) imply the speaker's strategic manoeuvres to achieve his goal. For example:

(2–1) 波野：やめてくださいよ、粉飾だなんて。
Namino: Yame-te-kudasai yo, funshoku da-nante.
stop-TE-please MD window-dressing Cop-MD
'Window-dressing (settlement of our accounts), don't say that, please.'
半沢：では、この赤字決算、どう説明していただけるんですか。
Hanzawa: Dewa, kono akaji-kessan doo
then this deficit-settle how
setsumeishi-te-itadak-eru-n-desu ka?
explain-TE-receive[Hon]-possible Nomi-Polite Q
'Then, how could you please explain about this deficit balance?'
波野：あ、まあ、それはよく調べてみないと。
Namino: A, maa, sore wa yoku shirabe-te-minai to.
er well that Top well investigate-TE-try Conj
'Er, well, (we don't know unless we) investigate that in detail.'

4 Some effects of speech-level shifts are polite, some impolite and some neutral: see Section 7.2 for a detailed discussion.

半沢：私が調べましょう。総勘定元帳見せてください、…
Hanzawa: Watashi ga shirabe-mash-oo. Soo-kanjoo motochoo mise-te-kudasai.
I Nom check-Polite-MD general-ledger show-TE-please
'I'll check (it for you). Please show (me) your general ledger.

波野：今、税理士事務所にありまして。
Namino: Ima, zeirishi jimusho ni ari-mashi-te.
now accountant office at exist-Polite-TE
'Right now, it's in our accountant's office, so…'

半沢：そうですか。では法人税の領収書を見せてください。…
それも税理士事務所ですか？社長に会わせてください。
Hanzawa: Soo-desu ka. Dewa hoojin-zei no ryooshuusho wo mise-te
so-Polite MD then corporate-tax of receipt Acc show-TE
kudasai. … Sore-mo zeirishi-jimusho desu ka. Shachoo ni awase-te-
please that-too accountant-office Polite Q boss to meet-TE
kudasai.
please
'Is that so? Then show (me) the receipts of your corporate tax… .
Is that also in the accountant's office? Let me see your boss.'
(*Hanzawa Naoki*, Part 1)

This is an excerpt from the drama series *Hanzawa Naoki*, in which Hanzawa, as the manager of the loan section in his bank, is talking with Namino, a member of staff from the company who appears to have committed a window-dressing settlement of accounts (loan-fraud) and hidden the loan (borrowed from Hanzawa's bank) somewhere else. At the beginning, Hanzawa uses quite a high level of honorifics (*doo setsumeishite itadakerun desu ka.*[5] How could you kindly explain?) with Namino because Namino's company is Hanzawa's customer (and in reality, too, the norm at banks is that customers are treated with high levels of honorifics). However, as Namino starts replying indistinctly, Hanzawa changes his honorifics to the lowest level, which is shown in his subsequent lines (the underlined parts) because Hanzawa is determined to find out whether their loan was genuine or meant to be stolen under the name of deficit-accounts. The expression *~te kudasai* is a direct request in the polite but imperative form despite the presence of an addressee honorific, and quite demanding for a bank staff member talking to his customer. However, the use of such an expression indicates that Hanzawa is beginning to be suspicious, and determined to find out the truth. While his customer is in a dither, Hanzawa is clearly demanding, and yet his maintenance of honorifics, though at the lowest level, narrowly protects the social stances of himself and others (bank and customer).

5 The expression *itadak-eru-n-desu ka* contains honorific-marked humble stance *morau* (beg to receive), tentative possibility *-e*, and addressee honorific *desu*, and question *ka*.

Honorific use, therefore, cannot be categorised only as a matter of stylistic choices. By manipulating honorific levels and selecting particular honorific terms, speakers intend to deliver diverse illocutionary forces, yielding a variety of pragmatic effects. Such manipulations are often goal-oriented and intentionally controlled by the speaker. The so-called 'conventional' honorifics (or norms of honorifics: see Chapter 3) are themselves not a strategy, but indexical (indexing distance by recognising the social relationship between the interactants; see Section 6.2.4). However, when honorifics, while maintaining their indexical nature, are manipulated by differentiating their levels within the same discourse, as shown in example (2–1), they give rise to other pragmatic effects.

### *2.1.4 Relational work*

'Relation work' was initiated by Locher (2004), and further developed by Locher and Watts (2005), and places value on interpersonal relationships rather than individuals' performances; in this respect, relational work takes a similar approach to 'rapport management' (Spencer-Oatey, 2005, 2008[2000]). This concept covers impoliteness as well as politeness, examining a variety of interpersonal relationships that develop, change and persist.

Locher (2004: 85), in arguing against Eelen's (2001) criticism of the normative accounts of previous studies, concedes *the existence of norms in politeness*, and calls norms "a kind of competence that interactants acquire over time". She then adds that politeness evaluation comes from "the *expectations* the interactants have about the speech event at hand" (italics added). At the same time, "norms are not to be understood as static rules, but as in a flux, shaped, altered and maintained by [the] same members of society". I agree with Locher's view, but then the question is where those terms, 'social norms', 'evaluations' and 'expectations', come from and how they are developed and interrelated in yielding 'politeness'.

As has been shown, politeness research today inevitably incorporates the terms 'social norms', 'evaluations' and 'expectations'. In the next section, I examine the nature of politeness from a diachronic perspective to explain how those terms are brought forth to constitute the concept of politeness, and how they are inter-connected.

## 2.2 A diachronic approach

This section discusses what politeness constitutes from a diachronic perspective, which I call the 'underlying meaning of politeness'. It starts with the basic human needs/wants of involvement and independence: politeness is the means of maintaining the balance between involvement and independence. The balance is achieved by consulting social norms (of the society or community the interactants belong to), which are historically and socially accumulated evaluations. Such social norms yield expectations that other members of the society or community follow, and politeness is a part of social norms.

### *2.2.1 Involvement and independence as basic human needs/wants*

In sociology, 'society' is defined as "a large complex of human relationships, ... referring to a system of interaction" (Berger, 1966: 38). "Each person is dependent on others; their survival cannot be separated from their relationships with others, and in turn, relationships depend on the mutual coordination of actions among social actors" (Foley, 1997: 261–262). 'Socialisation' is "the process by which a child learns to be a participant member of society" (Berger, 1966: 116). As a result of socialisation, "each of us carries within us in the *habitus* a great number of relational patterns developed through our history of structural couplings with others" (Foley, 1997: 262).

This sociological view of the relationship between man and society can give the impression that society manufactures people for the purpose of integrating them into its pre-existing system to allow it to continue. However, at the same time, we individuals are willing to conform to the rules, movements and changes of our society. Let us call this '**involvement**' (the term borrowed from Scollon and Scollon [1995] and Scollon et al. [2012], but see the discussion below); it is our willingness to become part of the society to which we belong.

The term 'involvement' as used in this book is a fundamental aspect of human psychology that drives one to be a member of groups one has chosen or belongs to. In reality, it becomes a motivation to incorporate numerous and varied social actions from international and social affairs to joining one's local community and family solidarity. It should be noted, however, that unlike Scollon et al.'s (2012) 'involvement', which, as one of the two aspects of 'face', is directly coupled with politeness strategies and explained in a similar way to Brown and Levinson's (1987) 'positive politeness strategies', *'involvement' in this book remains a more simple and natural psychological need humans possess.* This is because 'involvement' (my interpretation) itself does not yield or constitute 'politeness'. Rather, politeness emerges out of the conflict or negotiation between involvement and independence (my interpretation; see below) in our psychology. In other words, politeness is borne out of the balance between these opposite needs/wants. Furthermore, 'politeness' is a collective and culturally-established social action, but 'involvement' is a more crude psychological need individuals possess. Therefore, these two notions, politeness and involvement, cannot be dealt with on the same plane; in order to reach politeness, involvement needs to go through a few more steps to be collectively configured (this is further discussed in the Endnote to this chapter).

'**Independence**' is another quality contrasting with 'involvement'. We need and want to be free and independent from involvement with our society (at this point, degrees of involvement and freedom are not questioned as they vary according to different individuals and circumstances). This means that we are social creatures but, at the same time, are trying to maintain our own independence. This does not necessarily mean that we wish to live alone without socialising with other people. Rather, it emphasises our right not to be completely controlled by our surroundings. It is our wish to be free from obligation to or imposition from others. This is because we know that once we are involved in the process of socialisation, not only will we enjoy sharing and solidarity, we will also assume duties and responsibilities, be in debt to others and sometimes feel as if we have no choice. We wish to have a certain amount of autonomy, or independence, from such social burdens, and prefer to have the right to choose what we want ourselves.

The term 'independence' is borrowed from Scollon and Scollon (1995) and Scollon et al. (2012), but unlike their concept of independence, which is another aspect of face and equated with Brown and Levinson's (1987) negative politeness strategies, *'independence' in this book, just as 'involvement', is a fundamental of human psychology because it itself does not yield or constitute politeness*. 'Involvement' and 'independence' as used in this book should be understood as our basic human needs (see the Endnote to this chapter). Tannen (1986: 30) claims that these features are "universal human needs", but "trying to honour these conflicting needs puts us in a double bind".

Man and society are not separable, and every social being experiences those two needs/wants. The balance between such needs/wants is difficult to maintain. First, everybody has those needs/wants. Second, they are opposing and contradictory emotions. One solution is to say that everybody has every right to pursue independence and involvement. However, do they freely pursue them? In reality, they do not. We do not like certain responsibilities, but we still fulfil them. We may want the freedom to visit our friends anytime we want, but in reality we do not do so at three o'clock in the morning. We may feel like turning up at the party at a time that suits us, but in fact we do our best to be on time. Why?

Here is another part of human nature that makes the pursuit of our basic needs/wants more difficult: **our constant consciousness of others**. We wish to pursue our needs/wants, involvement and independence, but our consciousness of others controls us in pursuing them freely, because we hope to look good to and be accepted and appreciated by others. Therefore, in actual socialisation, we negotiate, compromise and have second thoughts when striving for involvement and independence. In other words, our awareness of the outer world directs us to think carefully about how to pursue our involvement and independence, which results in conducting negotiations and adjustments to satisfy our own needs/wants and those of others. This is where politeness comes in as a tool for negotiation. **Politeness, therefore, is a negotiation tool for striking a balance between involvement and independence by considering our consciousness of others.**

### *2.2.2 Evaluations as the basis of politeness*

Tannen (1986: 31) explains that the reason why the choice between involvement and independence is not entirely free is that "it is informed by the individual's cultural knowledge". The cultural knowledge shared among people in their society moulds their behaviour in a certain direction. It is social criteria or standards that help to maintain a good balance between our consciousness of others and basic needs/wants in society. Where, then, do such standards come from?

Let us think about the word, 'good'. 'Good' is opposite to 'bad', but whether something is considered good or bad is actually the result of our judgement. As Shakespeare's Hamlet says, 'there is nothing either good or bad, but thinking makes it so' (*Hamlet*, Act II, Scene 2); here, 'thinking' is a judgement. *There is nothing intrinsically good or bad*[6] in this world, but *our* **evaluation** *is brought in to measure something as good or bad.* 'Catching fish' may be good from the viewpoint of lovers of fishing, but may be bad from the perspective of animal lovers. There is no absolute 'good' or 'bad' when considering phenomena around us. Even 'morality' is the result of our judgement at the social level.

Our daily life involves numerous evaluations of almost everything surrounding us. By comparison, by weighing and by measuring, almost all phenomena in our daily life are evaluated. Many linguistic terms already imply the results of such measurements; for example, the contrasted terms warm–cold, tall–short, high–low, big–small, clean–dirty, beautiful–ugly may already carry the results of human judgement. Some are still neutral but others quite judgemental. The term 'clean' gives a certain image, and in general we take it as 'good' and 'dirty' as 'bad' (cf. Lakoff and Johnson, 2003).

While the word level connotes a certain evaluation, this is even more notable at the sentence level because words which themselves have a relatively neutral meaning may be coloured by our judgement when they are placed in a certain linguistic context. Peng (2000: 197) gives the following example:

(2–2) 子供を食い物にするあんな奴は人間とは言えない。

Kodomo o kuimono ni suru annna yatsu wa ningen to
child Acc take advantage of such bloke Top human being Quote
wa i-e-nai.
Top say-can-not

'That guy who takes advantage of children cannot be regarded as a human being.'

Peng explains that the word *ningen* (human beings) used in example (2–2) is not an objective description of a sentient being, but connotes certain evaluations of 'human beings'. The basic level of morality (e.g. thou shalt

6 Some fundamental acts against humanity, of course, may be universally 'bad', although they are still conditional; e.g. killing another human being is considered to be a crime, but killing in war is justified; stealing seems to be universally wrong, but stealing from another country through military force has been justified throughout history. However, this argument should be left to other academic battles.

not kill) is posited upon the framework of 'human beings', and anyone who would violate such morality is not worthy of being called a 'human being', although they biologically remain one (*kuimono ni suru* [lit. to use as food], and *yatsu* [scornful term to refer to a third person] are also judgemental terms, but here Peng intends to show different connotations of the same word in different contexts). Therefore, the word *ningen* contains both biological description and evaluative bearing that satisfies our basic morals. Peng (2000: 197) states that, "the world of meaning presents not only the recognition of facts, but also the evaluated world coloured by our judgemental filters" (translation my own).

In this way, evaluation involves subjective judgements, and may differ individually. However, certain evaluations may be shared by members of a society adhering to collective or social patterns of behaviour; they are called 'social evaluations' (cf. Section 1.4). Social evaluations are often historically handed down, and accepted by and prevalent in society; they then function as social standards, a yardstick by which to judge social behaviours as acceptable or not. Social standards may be quite rigorous like laws, called 'codified norms', or may be unspoken as social indices that are commonly categorised as '**social norms**' (see Chapter 3 for more details). A social norm in sociology is understood as "a shared expectation of behaviour that is considered culturally desirable and/or appropriate" (Scott, 2014[1994]: 519). However, social norms are not a set of prescribed rules like law or traffic rules, but "lack the formal status of rules" (ibid). *They are a guideline to help us interpret the phenomena of social actions, determine how to behave in a given situation and evaluate others' behaviour. They are a point of departure, from which we negotiate, adjust and revise our behaviour to fit the on-going situation* (e.g. queuing is a social habit or norm well established in British society, but may be broken when someone is in a hurry).

Our society is loaded with numerous varieties of social norm. In Australia (and many other Western societies), strangers say hello or nod to each other in a lift while, in Japanese society, very few people perform this kind of gesture. In Japanese cities, even neighbours may not greet each other, but in many rural areas greetings to neighbours as well as to strangers are a common practice. In Australia, if someone sneezes, another person nearby says 'bless you' whereas sneezing in Japan does not invite such a greeting. There may be gender norms. It is still a general custom that women cook and men do repairs and car washing (however, in my home, my husband cooks as he retired a few years ago and I work at a university, which is our home-norm). In the library, people are quiet and whisper if they need to talk. These are just fragments of social norms, and listing them is an endless task. We live in and with social norms in our daily life and, as some of the examples above have already indicated, **politeness is part of social norms**. Just as social norms are socially co-constructed evaluations, so is politeness. As social norms allow contingent and contextually-driven actions while maintaining their nature as a social cornerstone, so does politeness.

The reason why politeness varies across cultures is that evaluations have been developed and standardised differently as individual societies experience different histories, environments and political situations. For example, we may think that 'thank you' is a universal expression of gratitude to someone who gives us a gift or offers kindness. However, in Swahili and some other African languages, the giver of a present says 'thank you' to the receiver. Giving away something in such cultures means having a divine opportunity to gain cooperation of the other under God's blessing (Asada, 2001: 29).

Let us look at another example. Formulaic routines such as greetings are part of politeness. 'Hello' in English can be used with everybody we meet, including strangers. On the other hand, *konnichiwa*, which is customarily translated as 'hello', is not used between company workers who meet in the same section every day. They may utter *ohayoo* (good morning) to their workmates in the morning, but there is no greeting in the afternoon except bowing or just smiling (or *yaa* [hi] to close colleagues). Family members and close friends never greet with *konnichiwa* except when meeting after 20 years' separation. School children do not utter *konnichiwa* to their class teacher at school; they just bow when meeting the teacher in the corridor. However, if they meet their teacher at a shopping centre on a Sunday, they may utter *ah, sensei, konnichiwa* (Oh, Ms, hello!). It seems that *konnnichiwa* is used with new people, or those with whom we are not close and do not see regularly, or when bumping into someone outside the workplace or school, with whom *konnnichiwa* is not usually used at work or school. It is evident that *konnnichiwa* and 'hello' exhibit pragmatic differences; while 'hello' is a friendly gesture with anyone the speaker meets, *konnichiwa* indicates creating some distance or taking a new turn. They are both polite (when used appropriately), but their pragmatic conditions and effects are different.

It should be noted that social norms of politeness are not always constant within the same society. There are regional, institutional, gender and even individual differences in the implementing of politeness as well as the evaluating of others' behaviour. They are called "**local norms**" (Fine, 2005[2001]: 143). For example, we generally learn that honorifics should be used with seniors in the workplace, however in a company where their relatives are also working, younger staff use very few honorifics with their seniors.[7] We also know empirically that individuals have their own codes of norms. For example, in Japan some professors use plain forms when interacting with their students on the basis of egalitarianism while others may use polite forms (addressee honorifics) as they believe that a little aloofness makes them appear professional.

**Social norms in a society are established through socially accumulated evaluations (or social evaluations) of activities.** Once social norms are prevalent as tacit knowledge in a society, people expect others to conform to them. Bicchieri and Chavez (2010) claim that one of the conditions necessary for

7 Relational behaviour confirmed by the author through informal interviews at a few companies in Osaka.

a social norm to exist and be followed is “the presence of empirical and normative expectations” (Bicchieri and Chavez, 2010: 151). “A social norm explanation presupposes consistency between beliefs and behavior. In particular, it requires consistency between participants’ beliefs about normative expectations and their subsequent choices” (159), although Bicchieri and Chavez, through their experiment on game-plays, note that inconsistencies do occur when individuals “revert to selfish behavior on others”. Therefore, *social norms carry* **expectations**, *and expectations, whether they are fulfilled or upset, warrant and feed evaluations*.

In this section, I have demonstrated the underlying meaning of politeness from a diachronic perspective. It starts with our basic psychological needs/wants, involvement and independence, which are negotiated and/or balanced by taking our consciousness of others into consideration. Politeness is an element of social norms that are collective cultural standards; social norms have historically been established based on our experiences of evaluations of all sorts of activities. These evaluations, in turn, create expectations as they are customarily practised. This will be further discussed in Chapter 3 to show how social norms (politeness), evaluations and expectations are inter-related.

I have addressed what constitutes politeness. However, this macro view is still far from the understanding of what politeness is because politeness in reality is much more complex and contextually subtle; how politeness emerges in interaction is still intangible. It is not my primary intention to establish a theoretical framework of politeness in this book, but in the next section, by introducing the way in which Symbolic Interactionism deals with identity and role, I attempt to go a little deeper to examine what processes are involved in achieving politeness.

## 2.3 Identity and role in Symbolic Interactionism[8]

### *2.3.1 Symbolic Interactionism*

Role Theory is a sociological discipline that explains how individuals form their social identities, how they act accordingly (role performance) and the consequences resulting from performing their roles in social life. Goffman (1959) explains the relationship between social identities and roles in terms of theatrical actors who play a role on stage.

Role Theory has been variously adapted[9] in accordance with the focus of specific sociological research. Symbolic Interactionism (SI), identified by Mead (1934) and further developed by Blumer (1969), for example, is quite distinctive from other role theories. First, SI asserts that *identity and role, while carrying a socially shared set of expectations, emerge in interaction* since they

8 This section is an excerpt from Obana (2016), and changed to suit the flow of the section.

9 There are five perspectives: cognitive, functional, organisational, structural and symbolic interactionism.

are "perceived and interpreted during interaction with others" (Vryan et al., 2003: 368). However, identity and role are not automatically prompted in a given interaction. Before they emerge, *the situation in which the interactants are placed needs to be defined.* We have a habit of interpreting all sorts of things in our interactional situation. Where we are, how we experience the atmosphere, the topic of conversation and how it is going, who the other participants are – whatever we encounter in the given situation is an object for our subjective interpretation. Such objects do not possess intrinsic meanings, but we attach meanings to them and use them as '*symbols*', according to which we define the situation. Once the situation is defined, we formulate our behaviour (role performance based on our identity in the defined situation), but during the interaction, *our identities and role performances may be negotiated, adjusted or even altered to fit the on-going interaction and to fit with the other participants.* This is because interaction is fluid and changeable – and so is identity. Roles, which are specified by identities and embodied in social behaviour, are also negotiable to fit the on-going interaction. In other words, "interaction is ... centrally a matter of negotiating identities and roles" (McCall, 2003: 328).

Second, *SI differentiates 'identity' from 'role'*. This is because one's identity (e.g. a teacher in relation to students) is role-performed differently according to specific situations (e.g. school policies, class dynamics and even one's subjective beliefs regarding how to behave in relation to one's students). In other words, a role is specific to a given context, and "a perspective from which the person acts in a defined situation" (Hewitt and Shulman, 2011: 218), i.e. "roles are a property of the situation (51f).

SI is basically a sociological device to explain in what way people determine how to behave in social interaction. I employ SI's principles to explain what processes are involved in determining appropriate behaviour because *politeness, like 'identity' and 'role', is a social action reflecting how one has perceived and interpreted the situation in which one is placed.* In other words, polite behaviour, just like 'role', is the implementation of one's perspective in a given context. Furthermore, politeness, like 'identity' and 'role', emerges in interaction, and is negotiable and adjusted to fit the ongoing interaction. Therefore, **politeness is the result of the evaluation of a role performance that has been implemented by identity**. For example, when a junior faces her senior at work, and identifies herself as a 'junior' in status to the other (Institutional Role-Identity; see below), i.e. when the situation has been defined, then she uses honorifics with her senior (a role performance). Furthermore, the distinction between identity and role in SI is a useful tool in politeness research because it serves to explain why the same identity (e.g. young company boss) may be implemented as different role performances (e.g. using or not using honorifics with older employees).

*SI's concept of 'role/identity' is also convenient to analyse the indexical nature of Japanese politeness* because one's identity is directly entailed in indexical politeness. Honorifics index a social or psychological distance, and linguistically implement the social relationship between the interactants (see

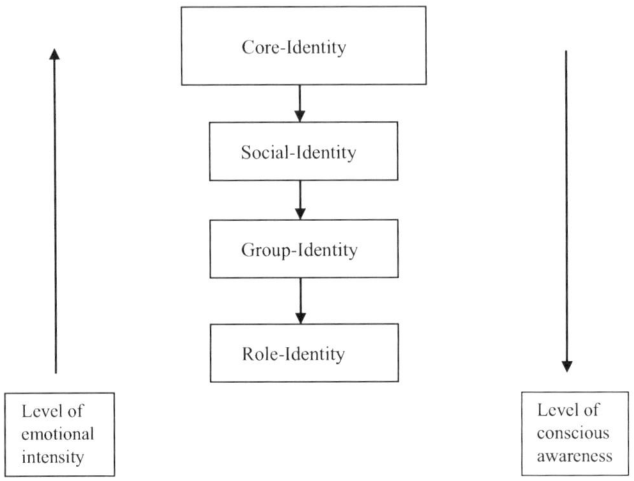


*Figure 2.2* Turner's (2011) model of the Hierarchy of Transactional Needs

Section 6.2.4). Similarly, strategies employed in the world of honorifics ('honorific strategies'; see Chapter 9) reflect the interactants' social relationship. Therefore, indexical politeness inevitably informs one's identity in a defined situation (e.g. university student at a seminar) in relation to the other (e.g. professor in charge of the seminar), and the use of honorifics and honorific strategies as a part of one's role performances are the linguistic evidence of the identity.

Since traditional role theories focus more on the effect of roles on sociological phenomena (e.g. the effect of a doctor's role on patients in hospital), the concept of roles/identities has been regarded as axiomatic, and thus the term, 'role/identity' is often used as a generic term that applies to all levels of social phenomena.[10] However, Turner (2011, a revised version of 2002) sub-categorises identities as four 'transactional needs' according to levels of emotional intensity and conscious awareness in identity construction. Figure 2.2 presents Turner's (2011: 335) model, though it is simplified to suit the discussion here.

According to Turner, the four transactional needs are "the universal needs that are *always present*, and indeed are *always activated* when people interact in encounters" (2011: 333, italics in original). First, Core-Identity is "the conceptions and emotions that individuals have about themselves as persons that they carry to most encounters" (334), which is equivalent to "one's

10 The types of identity introduced by Turner in Figure 2.2 are prevalent in many other studies, and Turner adopted the most pervasive terms. However, to my knowledge, Turner is the first to organise those types of identity as a concept.

personal identity to oneself" (Hewitt, 1989) or to 'personal identity' (Goffman, 1963), including "personal history, biological information and aspects of personality" (Vryan et al., 2003: 371). Vryan et al. (372) state that Core-Identity, or personal identity, is particularly trans-situational,[11] compared with the other identity types that are more contextually (socially or interactionally) constructed. Therefore, the level of emotional intensity in the case of Core-Identity is the highest of all the identity categories shown in Figure 2.2, as Core-Identity is the most personal and is almost unconscious in one's mind (on the other hand, Role-Identity is the most consciously recognised as it is publically determined, and often one is assigned a certain role in a given situation; therefore, the 'level of conscious awareness' is the highest as shown in Figure 2.2).

Second, Social-Identity is one's categorical identity in relation to others. It includes racial, ethnic, gender and national identities. Third, Group-Identity is individuals' "incumbency in corporate units such as groups, organizations and communities" (Turner, 2011: 334). This identity is "the perspective or culture (norms, values, beliefs, goals) of a given corporate unit individuals have internalised as part of the structure of self" (ibid). Fourth, Role-Identity is "the least encompassing level of self" because role identities "are attached to specific roles, typically played out in the divisions of labour of corporate units – for example, schools, workplaces, families" (ibid). Role-Identities are closely related to Group-Identities because specific roles are often derived from the values and norms attached to a given corporate unit. That is, Group-Identity is a more abstract concept and Role-Identity provides its substantiation with specific examples of roles in social interaction.

Role-Identity is somewhat different from the other identities. Through roles such as 'mother', 'teacher' and 'friend', one determines one's identity in a given situation. Therefore, it is called "situational identity" (Vryan et al., 2003: 368), which leads to "role enactments specific to a given context" (372). "A role is a perspective from which the person acts in a defined situation" (Hewitt and Shulman, 2011: 218), and situational identity is established on the basis of an individual's role. A role is "a resource that participants in a situation use in order to carry out their activities", and this situation "provides a container for roles"; thus, "roles are a property of the situation" (51f).

The identities in Figure 2.2 are not separate categories but intertwined in actual interaction, though one identity can be more strongly presented than others at a particular moment in interaction. Furthermore, as the interaction proceeds, one role can shift to another or a different role can be added to the

11 However, it does not mean that Core-Identity is fixed and unchanged. By experiencing social activities in one's life (e.g. education, work, socialising, family-making), one's Core-Identity may be reshaped or altered, i.e. the other social and situational identities and roles influence and contribute to the formation of one's Core-Identity (personal conversation with Professor Turner at the SI conference, 2016).

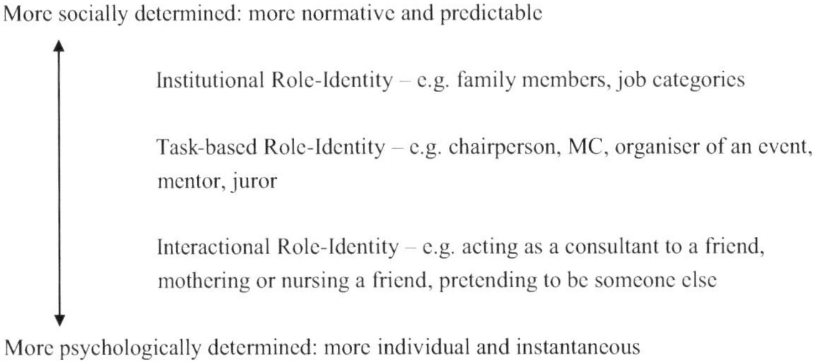


*Figure 2.3* Sub-categories of Role-Identity

*Note*. Sub-categories of Role-Identity are determined by recognition of 'role' in a given situation, which establishes one's identity. Therefore, strictly speaking, those sub-categories are all 'roles', but to differentiate them from the general term 'role', I apply 'Role-Identity' to the sub-categories throughout this book.

initial role. As the nature of ongoing interaction changes, roles also make adjustments to fit the situation.[12]

### *2.3.2 Sub-categories of Role-Identity and politeness*

Individuals' linguistic choices are often determined by identifying themselves as a certain role in interaction. This applies to all of the identities in Figure 2.2.[13] However, further sub-categories of Role-Identity can be established because more individually and psychologically oriented actions in daily life may also determine linguistic choices (Obana, 2012a, 2016). Individuals' daily tasks and short-term jobs that fall outside the identities in Figure 2.2, such as chairing a meeting and playing the role of MC at a friend's wedding, may also influence linguistic choices at the time of those role-plays, and individuals' psychological states can contribute to their opting for particular linguistic forms. Figure 2.3 illustrates the expansion of Turner's Role-Identity shown in Figure 2.2.

Figure 2.3 shows sub-categories of Role-Identity ranging from more socially determined roles to more temporary task-based roles, and to improvised or interactional roles that are more psychologically or individually determined at a certain point of time in an interaction.

12 This also applies to politeness behaviour since politeness is a linguistic implementation of identity in role performance, though politeness is most concerned with Role-Identity in Figure 2.2.

13 As discussed in Section 2.1, a particular use of language identifies the speaker as a certain social category such as black American woman (= Social-Identity), and as a representative of a company (= Role-Identity).

**Institutional Role-Identities** such as job categories (teacher, employer, doctor) are social roles that bear certain expectations or responsibilities individuals are obliged (or willing) to fulfil. These roles carry more or less a normative force despite individuals' somewhat different role performances, and "the performance of a job depends on a shared set of expectations ... we observe and enact these shared expectations" (Sandstrom et al., 2010: 145). When the situation in which we are placed is defined, we determine how we organise our social behaviour. Thus, Institutional Role-Identity is predictable just as Mead's (1934) term, the '*generalised other*', illustrates that we conform to certain patterns of behaviour during social interaction.

Institutional Role-Identity is implemented in linguistic terms, such as jargon in particular professions (e.g. *gaisha* meaning 'a murdered victim' as used by police), job titles (professor, prime minister), academic writing styles (Hyland, 2012) and addressing terms (nicknames to co-equal friends [Perinbanayagam, 2012: 39], Mum and Dad, Sir). The so-called 'conventional' honorifics and honorific strategies are also the linguistic implementation of Institutional Role-Identity.

As interaction is fluid and variable, roles that fit each situation can change or be negotiated. **Task-based Role-Identity** is created upon request or consensus in interaction, and lasts until the required jobs are completed. For example, colleagues in the same company, who normally may not use honorifics with one another, more likely use honorifics at a meeting as they are exposed to the public. On ceremonial occasions, the president of a company, who normally may not use honorifics with his employees, often uses honorifics with them in his speech. These honorific shifts are due to an awareness of Task-based Role-Identity as public speakers.

Let us take another example of Task-based Role-Identity. A student's task is to organise a seminar tour of his group and it commences upon request and ends when the tour is completed. During this period, the student acts as an organiser, and his group members, including the professor in charge of the seminar group, follow the organiser's requests and respond to his enquiries. This task-role is also recognised by all other members of the group, who identify themselves as recipients (another Task-based Role-Identity) of the organiser's task-role, and thus deliver an acceptable performance of their role. In the case of Japanese, the organiser's task-role is linguistically implemented, for example, in polite imperative forms in request as long as the content of the request is within the domain of his tasks as the organiser (see example [9–21] in Chapter 9). Other examples of Task-based Role-Identity are observed in duties assigned to a chairperson (cf. example [1–3] in Chapter 1), a mentor and a group leader to fulfil their responsibilities in situations that foreground their task-roles.

More psychologically-determined and improvised roles are called '**Interactional Role-Identity**', whereby the interactants momentarily create roles in accordance with how they feel about themselves in relation to the other interactants. These roles are the most changeable, dynamic and psychologically driven. For example, friends are an institutional role-identity; however, when one of them starts consoling another like a sister, this is a psychological identity and is determined voluntarily. Since Interactional Role-Identity is the least socially enacted, its role performances may more often fail to be accepted by the other interactant. The tone of language like a kind sister, for example, may be interpreted as soothing or condescending, depending on the situation, timing, the interactants' closeness and/or the recipient's psychological state. On the other hand, it is the Interactional Role-Identity that creates dynamic and vibrant exchanges in interaction, and reveals the interactants' psychological states.

Politeness mainly deals with the types of Role-Identity shown in Figure 2.3, ranging from its more socially enacted to more psychologically determined or improvised behaviours. The so-called 'conventional' honorifics and formulaic expressions such as greetings are the more socially practised Role-Identity, and speech level shifts (see Section 7.2) are a typical example of psychologically-driven Role-Identity, i.e. an Interactional Role-Identity, revealing what psychological stance the speaker is taking toward the other on the spur of the moment during the interaction.

The concept of Role-Identity seems to be a useful tool when explaining many examples of Japanese polite phenomena because roles are often implemented in linguistic terms in Japanese. The following chapters, examining examples of Japanese politeness, illustrate the types of Role-Identity involved with them.

## Endnote: 'Face' ≠ 'involvement and independence'

I have addressed the issue of the underlying meaning of politeness lying in our basic needs/wants, involvement and independence. I use these terms to avoid confusion with Brown and Levinson's 'positive and negative faces'. They sound similar to 'involvement and independence' because both are closely related to basic human needs/wants. Brown and Levinson are right in saying that these basic human needs/wants are universal, and contribute to the concept of politeness. However, it is doubtful that their notion of face is directly equated with human needs/wants. This is because *basic human needs/wants, or what I call 'involvement and independence', are the self's default desires*; they are natural, intuitive and fundamental human emotions. On the other hand, *'face' is something that has been culturally or socially (even group-orientedly – see below) moulded and has become part of one's belief system to be endorsed by the public*; in other words, 'face' is a social persona or a public presentation of the self. Therefore, it differs across cultures because it has culturally (and historically) been configured to conform to the way in which a society is operated. It also may differ from group to group as well as between individuals since group as well as individual faces are equally public selves that have been shaped through their own experiences.

Maintaining certain social standards as well as following their evaluation criteria is the manifestation of politeness. To violate such standards may cause loss of face, whether it is the loss of one's individual face or one's group face, depending on where one is situated. In either case, 'face' is a public arena or value experientially shaped by one's cultural knowledge, while admitting individual differences in its components because 'face' as one's belief system or value involves one's subjective or personal validation.

Politeness is a collective and social phenomenon, and one's face is learnt according to the way in which social standards are constituted in one's society; thus, the value of face differs across cultures, just as does the value of 'politeness'. Therefore, our basic human needs/wants cannot be equated with face; the former are pure human emotions prevalent universally, and the latter is based on specific cultural values acquired in order to conform to the standards in the society to which individuals belongs.

So far I have focused on the culturally-cast aspect of face in order to distinguish it from the basic (thus unprocessed) psychological nature of involvement and independence. However, it should be noted that face involves multi-layered identities of the self, and one (or more) of them emerges in a given interaction; in other words, the given context summons a particular type of face to suit that context. In this respect, face is contextual. However, it is not manufactured by the context; rather, a part of the self's face is selected out of one's face-modules.

# 3 Politeness as a social norm, its contingency and discursiveness

In Chapter 2, while discussing the underlying meaning of politeness from a diachronic perspective, I claimed that social norms serve as a cornerstone in determining and judging politeness, and argued that historically developed evaluations in a given community constitute social norms of politeness. However, social norms as used in sociology, just as politeness, are not a set of prescribed rules, but a point of departure, from which we negotiate, adjust and revise our behaviour to fit the on-going situation. This chapter elaborates on the nature of social norms, through which 'evaluations' and 'expectations' are extracted and form a triangular mechanism with social norms. It also discusses how norms of politeness are correlated with tranformative polite phenomena by employing Bicchieri's (2006) term, 'grammar of society' in describing social norms.

## 3.1 The term 'social norm' as used in sociology[1]

Ide (1989) defined Japanese honorifics as *wakimae*, and described them as "a set of social norms" and "the socio-pragmatic equivalent of grammatical concord" (227), i.e. linguistic norms that speakers are obliged to adhere to. This created an impression that social norms as used by Ide are "conventional and ritualistic" (Kádár and Mills, 2013: 143) and 'static' (e.g. Cook, 2011; Saito, 2010). However, the term social norm is not appropriately grasped in arguing for and against the *wakimae* view. In spite of the central importance of the term 'social norm' in sociology and social psychology, associated with numerous discussions and a variety of theorisations, in our linguistic enquiries it has never been thoroughly or adequately examined.

When Eelen (2001) suggested that the 'hearer's evaluation' should be administered in a discursive way, he critically reviewed previous major studies on politeness to label their examples (of politeness) as social norms (cf. Section 1.4). For Eelen, social norms are a set of prescribed rules or codes because they are "absolute, objective entities" and "cultural assumptions"

1 This section is an excerpt from Obana (2017) and changed to suit the flow of the section.

(187). Perhaps because of this, discursive approaches thereafter have avoided the term 'social norm' as if its use might oppose or deny discursiveness of politeness. However, the term 'social norm' as used by Eelen is not adequately interpreted.

In sociology, the term 'norm' plays a key role in explaining our social behaviour and conformity to or deviation from our community's regulatory systems and common beliefs. Norms prescribed as rules are called 'codified norms' or 'injunctive norms' (e.g. legal rules, public regulations, traffic rules), which are dealt with separately from social norms. Social norms implicitly govern our lives as *guidance* for how to interpret the situation in which we interact, how to behave in that situation as well as how to judge others' behaviour.

Although the concept of social norms means different things to different scholars (e.g. social norms as 'instruments of value realisation' by Baurmann et al. [2010], as 'a Nash equilibrium' by Bicchieri [2006] and 'expectations via social identities' by Symbolic Interactionism [SI][2]), there are common features those scholars generally agree on. First, social norms are not a static, fixed set of rules. *They emerge rather than are given, and are constructed and re-constructed as societal climate changes.* For example, Hechter and Opp (2005[2001]) use the no-smoking norm, which did not exist or was safely ignored two decades ago. The anti-smoking norm emerged as the number of health-conscious people increased and gradually dominated the ideological debate regarding whether smoking is an acceptable social practice.

Unlike codified norms, social norms are interpreted as "what is acceptable or not seems very changeable according to the time, place and social context of any action" because they "critically rely on the perceptions of individuals" (Xenitidou and Edmonds, 2014: 1). Individuals perceive differently what is or is not acceptable in different contexts, and act accordingly, assuming that their choice of act will be accepted by those around them. Because of this, social norms are not always executed when people judge a norm to be neither preferable nor desirable in a certain context. A good example for this was given in Section 1.3, where a woman's violation of the *sumo* tradition (i.e. a norm that women are not allowed to get into a *sumo* ring) was eventually accepted due to her prompt action in giving the mayor in the ring emergent treatment.

Second, *social norms are strongly "supported by shared expectations"* (Bicchieri, 2006: 10); "people are socialized in a way that leads them to acquire a disposition to comply with social expectations" (Heath, 2011: 67). While social norms are considered contextual and changeable, they are not totally

2 Symbolic Interactionism (SI), a role theory, which was initiated by Mead (1934) and developed by Blumer (1969), emphasises that identities emerge in interaction, and are negotiable in accordance with changing interactions. At the same time, identities (particularly social identities) carry shared expectations so that "we can readily adjust our behaviour to actions of others around us" (Sandstorm et al., 2010: 145). "Norms are an outcome of socialization that, in turn, is based on expectations held by most members of a community" (Fine 2005[2001]: 149). See more details of SI in Section 2.3.

uncontrolled because "people may choose what they prefer, but what they prefer in turn conforms to social expectations" (Parsons, 1951: 9). Bicchieri (2009[1997]: 25) goes further by stating that "a social norm depends for its existence on a cluster of expectations. Expectations ... play a crucial role in sustaining a norm."

Third, it is generally accepted that social norms have no reality, but present only *our beliefs*, which are based on expectations that "others behave according to them (= social norms) and expect us to behave according to them" (Bicchieri, 2006: 22). By conceptualising a social norm as "an equilibrium", Bicchieri and Chavez (2010: 151) use the term, "conditional preference", meaning that people conform to a social norm because they believe it exists, and because they believe others conform to it. This is a socially-constructed mutual expectation that serves as a pivot to evoke the implementation of social norms.

Lastly, *social norms are closely related to 'evaluations'* because "approval and disapproval are sanctions that *presuppose* the existence of norms that everyone expects to be followed" (Bicchieri, 2009[1997]: 25, italics in original). Sociologists tend to use the term, 'sanction' (e.g. excluding someone who has violated his group norm, giving a reward to someone who has done something desirable for their community) when referring to responses as the result of evaluations of a certain behaviour in a given situation. This may be because the term 'evaluation' is too broad to be used as a technical term since it refers to all kinds of value in money, amount, number as well as moral judgement. However, as discussed in Sections 1.4 and 2.2.2, 'evaluation' in relation to politeness in this book refers to 'social evaluation': a collective, socially-prevalent tool for the judgement of social actions, reflecting the values, needs and interests of the society to which people belong.

To sum up, social norms are a guideline for people to determine how to behave and to interpret, judge and evaluate others' behaviour. People tend to conform to a social norm because they believe it is valued and desirable in their community or society. However, social norms are not a list of prescribed rules; they emerge in social interactions and are negotiable in accordance with the way in which the community to which one belongs changes. On the other hand, social norms are sustainable as long as they are activated by the expectation (or shared belief) that individuals conform to social norms assuming that other individuals conform to them also. This means that *social norms, for their existence, strike a balance between stability and flexibility*. Therefore, **social norms, expectations and evaluations form a triangular mechanism in which they evoke, rely on and control one another**, as illustrated in Figure 3.1.

Figure 3.1 shows that:

1. Social norms are socially and historically constructed evaluations, and evaluations presuppose the existence of social norms. In other words, social norms are derived from evaluations, and evaluations serve as a tool for judging conformity to or deviation from social norms.

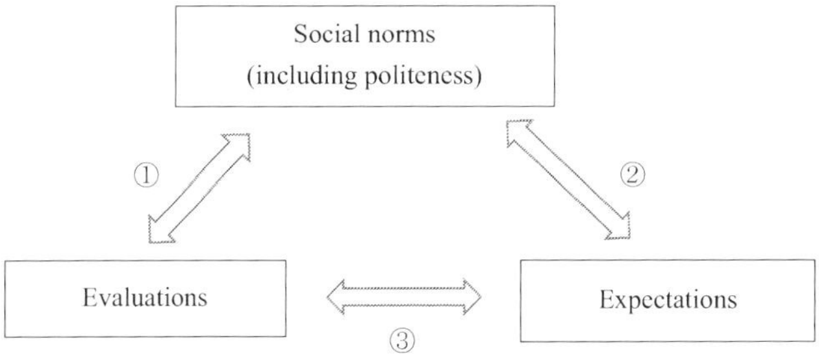


*Figure 3.1* the mechanism of social norms, expectations and evaluations

2. Social norms, for their existence, rely on shared expectations, and expectations stabilise social norms as a more reliable resource for determining social behaviour.
3. Evaluations, once socially constructed, yield shared beliefs or expectations, and expectations assist or affect evaluations.

As politeness is a part of social norms, it comprises the mechanism of Figure 3.1. Politeness is a cluster of evaluations, and evaluations serve as a tool for judging our behaviour as polite or not polite. Politeness presupposes the expectation that others behave according to norms of politeness. Evaluations, which reflect social norms of politeness, feed and control expectations and vice versa. Therefore, politeness, evaluations and expectations are intertwined.

*Social norms are implicit in our social practice.* What we learn from our parents and at school and what we experience in social gatherings are eventually internalised to inform our understanding of social norms. The same is true of politeness. Politeness is implicit in our social practice. Politeness is learnt and internalised in our mind. Although politeness, just as social norms, is negotiable and changeable, depending on a given context, *norms of politeness serve as a cornerstone and, therefore, are implicit in a variety of social practices.*

Eelen (2001) suggested that the 'hearer's evaluation' may be valuable since the evaluation of the speaker or the linguist may differ from theirs. However, the process of evaluation calls for a certain yardstick regardless of who evaluates. Furthermore, *habitus* Eelen suggested, if closely examined (cf. Section 1.4), can be equated with social norms because it is socially acquired as "a set of acquired dispositions of thought, behaviour, and taste to constitute the link between social structures and social practice" (Scott, 2014[2004]: 296).

Kádár and Haugh (2013) do not refer to social norms in their discussion; however, their statements that "politeness constitutes *a social practice*" and "politeness [is] ultimately located in *evaluations* of social actions" (Kádár and Haugh, 2013: 6, italics added) undoubtedly involve the nature of social norms.

First, a 'social practice' is something that is regularly repeated in social activities; it is defined as "the customary, habitual or expected procedure or way of doing something" (*Digital Oxford English Dictionary*). Social practices are "enduring entities reproduced through recurrent performance" (Shove et al., 2012: 8), though they have potential to change dynamically. Second, 'evaluation' means 'judging how good or bad something is', which surely requires a point of departure from which to process the judgement. Therefore, the concept of politeness described by Kádár and Haugh (2013) points to that of social norms, as I have discussed above.

It should be noted that social norms are not the same all the time in the same language community. We must recognise regional, institutional and group differences, called '**local norms**' (Fine, 2005 [2001]: 143). For example, in Tokyo, customers at a *kushiage* restaurant serving deep-fried meat and vegetables on bamboo skewers are provided with an individual dipping-sauce plate. In Osaka, however, a large pot of sauce is provided at each table and people share it, dipping each skewer once only. While people in Tokyo regard sharing a pot as unhygienic, those in Osaka believe that the sauce will become rich with oil and thus tastier, and the practice is not unhygienic because they dip skewers only once. This is a regional difference, and each region has established its own (local) norm.

Politeness phenomena also encompass local norms. For example, people in Osaka address the Japanese emperor's family in a different manner to those in Tokyo and the media, who refer to them with *sama* (様: an honorary term of address attached to the person's name). People in Osaka, on the other hand, address the emperor's family members with *san* (the informal form of *sama*), for example *tennoo-san* (天皇さん: emperor) and *koogoo-san* (皇后さん: empress) not because they downgrade the emperor and his family (indeed, they even call gods *kami-san* [神さん] and divine justice *o-tento-san* ([お天道さん]). It is because those in Osaka have traditionally treated gods and spirits in nature as their ancestors and felt close to them. The same sentiment seems to apply when they refer to other people even if they occupy a higher social rank (quoted from the newspaper, *Nihon Keizai Shinbun*, 16 January 2013).

Individuals also establish their own norms. As shown in Section 2.1, where a staff member at the local Driver and Vehicle Licensing Centre uses *tameguchi* (peer language) as his normal style of interaction with visitors while his colleagues use at least addressing honorifics as public servants (a social norm), an individual's belief may be reflected in his language use, and when it is recursively implemented, it becomes that particular individual's norm.

Observing the nature of norms as such, one may wonder how social norms create local and individuals' norms, and even their contingencies, and how they are related to one another. To explain this, I borrow the term the 'grammar of society' used by Bicchieri (2006), who tries to explain how social norms as the central axis are configured as a social practice.

## 3.2 Politeness as a social norm and its contingencies

Bicchieri (2006: ix) compares norms to the '**grammar of society**' for the following reason:

> [Like] a collection of linguistic rules that are implicit in a language and define it, social norms are implicit in the operations of a society and make it what it is. Like a grammar, a system of norms specifies what is acceptable and what is not in a social group. And analogously to a grammar, a system of norms is not the product of human design and planning.

However, I use the 'grammar of society' more extensively by observing the reality of how the grammar of a language serves in various contexts where the language is utilised, manipulated, controlled, twisted and even taken advantage of for individuals' idiosyncratic use. Figure 3.2, although by no means a complete list of manifestations of a grammar, indicates that based on the use of grammar as a point of departure, we can manipulate our language to create unique linguistic products: complex structures, written and spoken styles as well as personal styles, deviated word orders and gendered differences in language. And yet, the grammar of the language we use is implicit however uniquely we create a phrase, sentence, paragraph and text; the grammar serves as a cornerstone in our language use.

As politeness is a social norm, it performs just as the grammar of a language presents varied manipulations; it creates conventional manners and customs, geographically different behaviours and contextually-driven actions. However, social norms of politeness are implicit in all these apparent diversities. For example, although the officer's *tameguchi* (peer language) at the Driver and Vehicle Licensing Centre (see Section 2.1) was positively accepted, it does not mean that *tameguchi* itself is polite, but rather his kind and friendly manner was more distinctive, which allowed his *tameguchi* to be more readily accepted. Or, alternatively, his use of peer language enhanced his image of

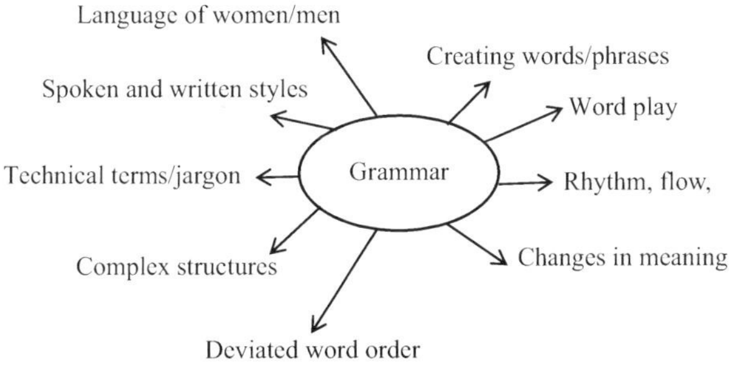


*Figure 3.2* Grammar and language use (Obana, 2017: 305)

kindness and friendliness; after all, honorific use creates distance and distance signals aloofness. Therefore, no use of honorifics, which seemingly violates the norm as a public servant at the counter, turns out to be in line with a different norm of politeness (friendliness, kindness). In this way, *social norms of politeness are multi-layered and different categories of such norms are convolutedly intertwined so that an apparently deviated behaviour in one context (as it is not socially expected in this particular case) can be judged as polite when looking at it from the perspective of another norm of politeness.*

There is no doubt that individual differences are significant in dealing with politeness. For example, in Section 1.4, I referred to individuals choosing between *arigatoo* and *sumimasen* when responding to a professor's offer of coffee to a student; some used the former and others the latter. The difference emerges from the values of those individuals; i.e. how *obliged* the student feels toward the professor (in the case of *sumimasen*) or how pleased she is with the offer of coffee (in the case of *arigatoo*). And yet, both formulae come down to an element of the politeness norm: 'thanking' for what the speaker receives as a benefit from the other person.

It was indicated in Chapters 1 and 2 that Japanese honorifics also dynamically change and yield a variety of pragmatic effects. However, a closer look at such diverse uses and effects reveals that norms of honorifics are implicit in those varieties, persisting as the basis for diverse uses of honorific terms; *those diversities are derived from norms of honorifics*. Obana (2017) explains this in a way analogous to Bicchieri's social norms as the 'grammar of society'.

Honorifics are, strictly speaking, 'markings' on an utterance that has strategically been constructed, and despite their complex and numerous forms, they function merely as the indexing of 'distance' (see Section 6.2 for details). The concept of distance typically applies to the following social situations (or motivations):

1. Social status and age differences
2. Formal situations (ceremony, public speech, meeting)
3. Familiarity (strangers, people less familiar to the speaker)

**These three motivations lay the groundwork for norms of honorifics that are so-called 'conventional honorifics'**, and evaluations are borne out of these norms, which constitute beliefs shared as expectations in Japanese society. However, at the same time we are creative creatures; we learn to manipulate, take advantage of and expand the use of honorific terms, whereby we negotiate and re-define our interactional relationships, express our emotional states and deliver subtle changes in dealing with others. And yet, norms of honorifics are implicit in these applications and derivations; they are a point of departure, from which honorific terms are extensively applied to a variety of situations, giving rise to differing effects and socio-pragmatic interpretations, as illustrated in Figure 3.3.

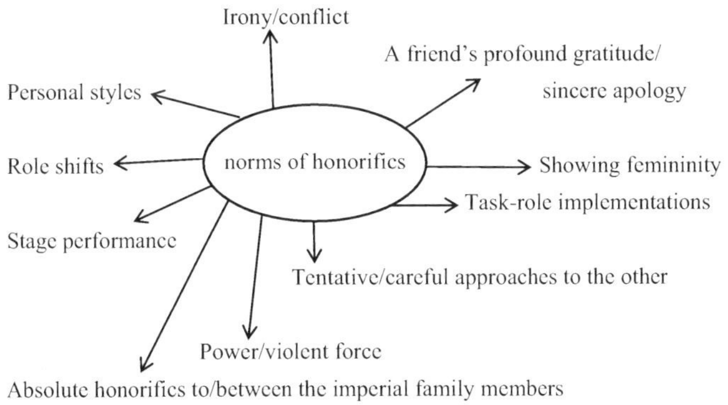


*Figure 3.3* Norms of honorifics and applications/deviations of honorific use (Obana, 2017: 306)

*Note.* I do not include dialectal polite forms in this figure as they constitute different forms and meanings, which should be categorised separately as another type of norm.

Figure 3.3 shows how dynamically honorific terms can be used in various situations. Detailed discussions with examples will be provided in Chapter 7, but here I briefly refer to some of the examples in Figure 3.3.

Women's language contains honorific terms to show their femininity; they are called *bikago* (美化語: self-beautification terms). By creating a certain distance between the (female) speaker and others, the speaker achieves some gracefulness (i.e. a little aloofness creates an air of high class elegance), which enhances her femininity together with her lady-like attitude. Absolute honorifics are still preserved in modern Japanese for use in relation to and between Imperial family members; for instance, in May 1919, the new emperor, when talking about his parents (the ex-emperor and empress) at a press conference, used honorifics about their behaviour.

There are also personal styles in honorific use. As discussed earlier, some professors use plain forms when talking with their students on the basis of egalitarianism while others use addressee honorifics as their basic style to maintain a little aloofness with their students.[3] This is a matter of personal choice, but choice is informed by the nature of norms of honorifics: distance. Distance, here, is manipulated as the speaker's choice and determines the manner in which each professor wants to interact with her students.

There is another example of personal style in honorific use (see the detailed discussion in Section 7.3.3). In a drama series called *Aiboo* (*Partners*), the protagonist always uses polite forms (mainly addressee honorifics) with his

3 For example, ten informal interviews with professors were collected by a student assistant, each lasting 20 minutes. Two professors used plain forms as their manner of address and the rest used polite forms. An element of this data was used and analysed in Obana (2012a, 2019).

subordinates, children and even criminal suspects, an approach in direct contrast to that of his fellow detectives, who differentiate their speech levels in accordance with power, social status and age difference. The protagonist's personal style of honorific usage conveys to the audience that he is cool, self-controlled, graceful and intellectual (and he acts accordingly throughout the drama).

'Role shifts' refer to different speech levels used between the same interactants as a result of their differing task-based roles (cf. Section 2.3.2; also see examples in Section 7.3.1) in different situations. For example, in the drama series *Tsuri-baka nisshi* (*Diary of Fishing Fools*), the protagonist, Hamazaki, is an inefficient and incompetent employee in a company owned by President Suzuki. In company situations, Hamazaki, as a subordinate, uses polite forms with Suzuki. However, Hamazaki is an excellent angler while Suzuki is an earnest but poor angler and is trying to learn the skill from Hamazaki. In fishing situations, therefore, Hamazaki is superior to Suzuki and so uses plain forms, speaking almost rudely to Suzuki. In this way, the same characters change their task-based roles and their language changes accordingly. However, no matter how diversely honorific terms appear to be utilised to yield varied pragmatic effects, norms of honorifics (motivated by social differences, formal situations and familiarity) are implicit in these diversities.

Norms of honorifics also serve as the basis for evaluations that appear to be individually different. For example, when very few honorifics are observed in a casual local restaurant, this is evaluated as 'appropriate' by customers because they agree with the restaurant's attempt to create a friendly and intimate rather than refined yet aloof atmosphere. The restaurant's measure of distance from its customers is warmly received and so this becomes a norm in this restaurant. However, when service is delayed the restaurant owner is apologetic and may become more polite, depending on how slowly meals are delivered, how close she is to particular customers (e.g. how regularly they visit the restaurant) and how pressed for time the customers are (e.g. they may have to go back to work straight after lunch). The restaurant owner has good reason for using high-level polite forms, but how they are evaluated may depend on individual customers. For example, the owner's apologetic approach using honorific terms may be judged as 'polite' because:

a. Customer A may feel that she is being treated as an important customer.
b. Customer B may think that the owner is humble and formal and is thus genuinely apologetic.

On the other hand, the same behaviour may be evaluated negatively because:

c. Customer C may not like the owner being suddenly humble.
d. Customer D may feel that his intimate conversation with the owner thus far has been ruined.

Examples a–d above are in no way intended as an exhaustive list of the myriad of possible reasons explaining customers' subtle positive or negative reactions. However, the point here is that, in spite of various motivations for positive and negative evaluations, norms of honorifics can be traced as the basis for those motivations:

a. A social relationship that exists between the customer and owner in a service industry
b. Formality
c. Social distance
d. Familiarity

In sum, although social norms of politeness may be socially enacted, they can be negotiated, adjusted and changed in accordance with the nature of a given situation. In other words, **social norms of politeness permeate in our society as a cornerstone while balancing their stability and flexibility**.

## Summary of Part I

In Chapters 1–3, while reviewing previous studies on the concept of politeness, I have addressed what constitutes politeness and its origins. While many previous studies synchronically observe politeness to reach conclusions, I take a diachronic route to explain what features constitute politeness. First, the basic human need for involvement and independence (according to my interpretation) is experienced by everyone; involvement and independence are opposites and contradictory; and our constant awareness of other people directs us to attempt to strike a balance between involvement and independence. For this, negotiations and adjustments are essential to satisfy our own as well as others' independence and involvement. This is where politeness comes into play as a tool for negotiation.

Second, negotiations for involvement and independence are not based on individuals' free choices but on certain standards that have been established (but not prescribed) in society. Such standards originate in our nature as human beings whereby we evaluate almost everything in our daily life. When evaluations are historically handed down and accepted throughout a society, they become social standards, or social norms, functioning as a yardstick to judge social behaviour. Furthermore, social norms carry expectations that members of a society act based on their shared social norms; this is called the 'generalised other' (Mead, 1934), a perspective that we imaginatively adopt when forming our own behaviour. Therefore, social norms, evaluations and expectations form a triangular mechanism; social norms, for their existence, rely on expectations, and expectations, whether they are fulfilled or upset, warrant and feed evaluations, and socially developed evaluations are added to or take the place of existing norms. Social norms are not a rigid set of rules. Social norms are a point of departure, from which we negotiate, adjust and revise our behaviour to fit the on-going situation.

# Part II

# Honorifics

# 4 The term 'polite' in English and Japanese

## Conceptual differences

Although the concept of politeness and features that constitute politeness have been discussed, which may apply to politeness universally, actual politeness phenomena are diverse, contextually-driven and even contingent at times; they differ across cultures, regionally in the same culture, from group to group within the same region and contextually and environmentally (e.g. social relationships, situations in which the interactants are placed). This makes us wonder if we are in fact communicating on the basis of a common understanding, i.e. through the shared perception of 'politeness'. Therefore, this chapter examines whether or not the term 'polite' and its equivalent translations in different languages are perceived in the same way. A number of research results commonly agree that 'polite' in Japanese and Chinese is predominantly associated with reservedness and formality whereas 'polite' in English incorporates features such as friendliness and kindness.

### 4.1 Etymology of the term 'polite' in Japanese: *Reigi tadashii* and *teineina*

This section examines the dictionary meanings of polite in English and its translations in Japanese. In Section 1.1, 'politeness' was defined from the viewpoint of its etymology as 'a social tool whereby we aim to achieve smooth and conflict-free communication'. It is derived from the Latin word *politus*, meaning 'polished, refined', and its related form is *polīre*, which means 'to smooth or to polish' (*Oxford English Dictionary*). Therefore, 'to be polite' signifies the management of smoothness and/or certain refined (polished) manners. This etymology conforms to the dictionary definition of 'polite': "having or showing behaviour that is respectful and considerate of other people" (*Digital Oxford English Dictionary*).

'Polite' is translated as *reigi tadashii* (礼儀正しい) and *teineina* (丁寧な) in Japanese. The former means 'to be correct in *reigi*' and *rei-gi* is the combination of two *kanji*, 礼 and 儀. The *kanji* 礼 is a simplified character, which symbolises 'kneeling reverently (the right part of the *kanji*) when worshiping gods and goddesses (the left part[1])'. Its original character is 禮, symbolising the pedestal (the left part of the character) on which offerings for gods were placed (the right part means 'abundance', thus 'abundant offerings'). This character was later used to refer to human behaviour. However, during the Zhou (周) dynasty (1046–256 BCE) in China, 禮 was strictly limited to the duties and behaviour of higher ranked persons in court. Confucianists expanded its use to individuals' behaviour, referring to morals and disciplines people are expected to follow, and worshipping gods was replaced with revering the other person (*Digital Britannica Encyclopaedia*, Japan). This meaning persists in modern Chinese and Japanese. *Rei* in modern Japanese also means 'bowing' and 'gratitude or a gift as a token of gratitude', which are concrete actions, conforming to the definition above.

The other *kanji* 儀 is another hieroglyphic character, consisting of 'a person' (the left part of the *kanji*) and 'a sheep' (the top segment of the right part of the *kanji*) with 'slashing with a knife' (the bottom segment of the right part of the *kanji*), i.e. this *kanji* originates in a ritualistic ceremony by sacrificing a sheep to be offered to gods:

儀 ← 亻(= person) + 羊 (= sheep) + 我 (= slashing with a halberd)

The ritualistic and solemn implications of this character were later expanded to human behaviour, referring to ceremonial manners and rules of etiquette. The character combines with others to highlight the ritualistic aspect of actions and events, e.g. *soogi* (葬儀 funeral), *gyoogi* (行儀 manners), *gishiki* (儀式 rife).

Following the etymology of 礼 and 儀, *reigi tadashii* (礼儀正しい) means that our "manners and behaviour are correct in the light of social order and institution and/or social norms" (my translation) (*Sekai dai-hyakka jiten* 世界大百科事典).

Now let us examine the other translated term, *teineina* (丁寧な). The *kanji* 丁寧 comes from the name of an ancient Chinese war-drum, which circulated a warning or call to attention to soldiers. Because the drum did not effectively echo across the military units, it was beaten many times to make sure that everybody heard it. The manner of beating the drum later applied to ways of dealing with people, goods and important matters (e.g. request, negotiation, task); thus, it means 'careful, elaborate, meticulous and considerate', depending on a given context. Due to its broader range of meanings, *teineina*, unlike *reigi tadashii*, can be used in a variety of situations. For example,

1 Because of this symbolic meaning (gods and goddesses), the left part of this *kanji* carries this sacred implication in other *kanji* containing this part; e.g. 神 (god), 社 (shrine), 祈 (pray), 禅 (zen), 祝 (celebrate).

| | | |
|---|---|---|
| (A) | *teineina ji* | (neat writing) |
| | *teineina tsutsumikata* | (wrapping carefully/beautifully) |
| (B) | *teineina sooji* | (thorough cleaning) |
| | *teineina shirabe* | (elaborate investigation) |
| (C) | *teineina kotoba-zukai* | (using kind/deferential/appropriate words) |
| | *teineina henji* | (heart-warming reply) |

*Teineina* can be categorised as three types of meaning: (A) beautiful outlook, (B) thorough and (C) considerate, which can be traced back to the implications the origin of this word bears. Although category (C) appears to be more closely associated with 'polite' in the English sense, the other categories can also fit the definition of politeness if the effects of the action of *teinei* are considered. *Teineina ji* (neat writing), for example, may give pleasant feelings to the reader. *Teineina shirabe* (elaborate investigation) may be appreciated by the chief inspector of police. Depending on what terms *teineina* combines with, it appears to change its contextual meanings. However, its basic effect remains the same, i.e. the result of an action is to make the other person feel appreciative.

The translated words, *teineina* and *reigi tadashii*, are complimentary, ranging from ritualistic formality to emotional up-lifting. Given the etymology of those terms in English and Japanese, how, then, are they interpreted by laypeople, and what associations do they have with those terms? The next section discusses this by examining previous studies on the term 'polite' in English and Japanese.

## 4.2 Sociological significance of 'polite' in English and Japanese

A number of studies have contrasted 'polite' in English with its translated words in Japanese (Dunn, 2013; Haugh, 2004; Ide et al., 1992; Obana and Tomoda, 1994; Pizziconi, 2007) and the translated word in Chinese (Tao, 2013). They employ different methods when extracting images, associative terms and subjective interpretations of 'polite' in different languages, as follows:

Ide et al. (1992) – Given scenarios in different situations, the subjects, native speakers of Japanese and American English, were asked to answer yes or no to listed adjectives that are assumed to be associated with the term 'polite'.

Obana and Tomoda (1994) – Interviews were conducted by asking the subjects (Japanese and Australian English speakers) about recent unpleasant experiences, and then asking why they felt like that, and how the other person should have behaved, etc., through which the researchers extracted possible relevant terms from their replies. They also directly asked the subjects what they associate with the terms 'polite' (to the English speakers), and *teineina* and *reigi tadashii* (to the Japanese speakers).

Haugh (2004) – Through dictionary definitions, the terms *teinei* and *reigi tadashii* were examined.

Pizziconi (2007) – The subjects were asked to freely create a map of associative terms of 'polite' in English, and *teinei* and *keigo* (honorifics) in Japanese.

Dunn (2013) – The researcher observed five business etiquette seminars in Japan, and extracted possible associative terms with *teinei*.

Tao (2013) – By using a questionnaire with native speakers of Chinese and Japanese, the researcher asked the subjects to provide associative terms with *teinei* in Japanese and *limao* in Chinese.

Ide et al. (1992) found that, while in American English, 'polite' and 'friendly' are readily correlated, Japanese *teineina* and *shitashigena* (friendly) do not fall into the same domain. Obana and Tomoda (1994: 40) extracted further associative terms to clarify different conceptualisations of 'polite' in the two languages.

English: friendly, kind, approachable, considerate, well-mannered, humble, appropriate use of language, respect, modest, attentive, indirect

Japanese: *keigo* (honorifics), *hikaeme* (reserved), *wakimaeru* (know what to do), *enryo* (discretion, hesitation), *jooge kankei* (vertical relationship), *tachiba* (standing place)

While both languages share certain features such as 'modest' and 'humble', Australian English speakers also chose 'friendly' and 'kind', which were not drawn out by Japanese speakers. This means that Japanese speakers maintained formal and reserved features, which are largely associated with the world of honorifics.

Haugh (2004) presents the following words from the dictionary definitions of *teinei* and *reigi tadashii*:

*hikaeme* (reserved), *teatsui* (warm, hearty), *shinsetsu* (kindness), *keii* (respect), *nengoro* (courteous)

It is interesting to see that dictionary definitions include *teatsui* (手厚い warm, hearty, hospitable) and *shinsetsu* (親切 kindness), which originate in the etymology of *teineina* as discussed earlier, whereas the other terms Haugh listed conform to Obana and Tomoda's (1994) interview result.

Pizziconi (2007) reached results similar to those of Obana and Tomoda (1994), although her map of associative terms is more elaborate and contains more examples. For example, the terms that were not found in Obana and Tomoda (1994) are:

> English: educated, distant
> Japanese: *seijitsuna* (sincere), *joohinna* (refined), *omoiyari no aru* (considerate)

Nonetheless, Pizziconi confirms that 'friendliness' does not fit the Japanese concept of politeness, and 'modesty' and 'restraint' are far less recognised in English. She then claims that English tends to code distinctions in politeness "in terms of the orientation to external protocol vs. spontaneous attitudes" whereas Japanese seems to distinguish between modes of 'reservedness' (or withdrawal) and modes of '*avance*' (direct, outgoing expressive modes)" (Pizziconi, 2007: 228).

Tao (2013) found similar traits between Chinese and Japanese. The top three associations with *limao* and *teinei* are:

> Chinese: honorifics and polite expressions, good breeding, ceremony and propriety
> Japanese: honorifics and polite expressions, ceremony and propriety, way of speaking

Interestingly, Japanese people also placed 'refined and cultured' in the top three,[2] which is equivalent to 'good breeding' in Chinese. Chinese and Japanese native speakers seem to associate 'politeness' with similar attributes, although Tao (2013: 162) notes that, "more Chinese than Japanese students think that if a person does not use polite language, he/she is uneducated or ill-bred", which is strongly associated with "one's reputation (*lian* and *mianzi* – face)".

Dunn (2013), by observing etiquette training in Japan, added the terms *kirei* (beauty) and *kanji no yoi* (pleasant) to those of the previous studies. She then concludes that "corporate manners classes reproduce wider Japanese understandings of politeness as encompassing both deference and kindness" (241). Her additions are understandable because her data source is the manners training programme for company employees. Naturally, employees are trained to be kind and considerate to their customers as well as to use appropriate words including honorifics. However, unlike the other studies (except Haugh [2004]), which attempted to understand how native laypeople conceptualise the term 'polite', Dunn's investigation captures an overall picture of how to achieve politeness in serving customers. Furthermore, Dunn extracted those words related to 'polite' herself by observing the seminars rather than asking

2 Tao's survey results conforms to those discussed in Section 6.3.2; honorific use today is more strongly associated with public presentations and individuals' social image.

laypeople through interview, map-making or questionnaires. Therefore, although her work itself is noteworthy in politeness studies, it should be differentiated from the other studies above.

In spite of applying different methods, the above studies commonly indicate that Japanese terms are more strongly associated with formality, reserve and humility, which are closely related to the world of honorifics. In spite of the dictionary meanings of *teineina*, which include consideration and appreciative judgements, laypeople upon hearing *teineina* readily relate it to its more formal domains. On the other hand, the English 'polite' encompasses a much broader scope of associative meanings, and its 'friendly and approachable' aspects contrast sharply with Japanese *teineina* and *reigi tadashii*.

## 4.3 *Keigo, keii hyoogen* and politeness

The previous section attempted to clarify how the term 'polite' is associated with different pragmatic interpretations across cultures. The translated words, *teineina* and *reigi tadashii*, in Japanese indicate much narrower ranges of pragmatic meaning than does the English term 'polite'. By the same token, the term 'politeness' in English, which refers to polite phenomena, is not isomorphic with its translations in Japanese. In fact, there is no umbrella term in Japanese that comprises a broader range of phenomena including actions of kindness, consideration and solidarity. *Teinei hyoogen* (丁寧表現 – lit. polite expressions), which is mostly used, may be close to 'politeness', but is limited to linguistic expressions and strongly associated with careful choices of words and formal situations. *Teinei hyoogen* may be at most related to consideration as a result of careful wording to the other person, but would never invite behaviour to express solidarity such as jokes, teasing and in-group terms (e.g. swear words, jargon), all of which are included in 'politeness' in English. Neither does it consider extra-linguistic features, although they are equally important in politeness.

*Kokugo gakusha* (国語学者 – national language scholars) have traditionally used *taiguu hyoogen* (待遇表現 – expressions of how to treat people), and *keigo* has been considered a part of this. However, *taiguu hyoogen* includes much broader varieties than (linguistic) 'politeness' in English because it ranges from politeness to impoliteness, from warm-hearted to cold-blooded approaches, and from deferential to scornful attitudes, as long as they demonstrate how the speaker treats the other person.

*Keigo* is surely associated with 'politeness', which typically includes *kenjoogo* (謙譲語 – lit. humble-language) and *sonkeigo* (尊敬語 – lit. deference-language) (see the classification of honorifics in Section 6.1). Due to the literal meanings of these terms, however, *keigo* appears to preserve vestiges of feudal times when social classes were rigidly distinguished. Perhaps because of this, the term *keii hyoogen* (敬意表現 – lit. respect-expressions, expressions of high regard) was officially introduced by *Kokugo shingi-kai* (国語審議会 – Japanese Language Council) in 2000[3], which is defined as:

> 敬意表現とは、コミュニケーションにおいて、相互尊重の精神に基づき、相手や場面に配慮して使い分けている言葉遣いを意味する。
>
> (平成12年度第22回国語審議会答申「現代社会における敬意表現」より)
>
> *Keii hyoogen* is based on the interactants' mutual respect in communication, referring to the way in which they differentiate expressions according to who they are talking with and where they are placed.
>
> ('*keii hyoogen*' in modern society' – one of the guidelines for Japanese language use, proposed at the 22nd meeting hosted by the Japanese Language Council in 2000)
>
> (Translation my own)

This definition seems to cover broader ranges of behaviour as long as they are respectful and appropriate in a given situation, although this term still eliminates teasing, joking and rude but friendly expressions that enhance solidarity between close 'mates'.

The definition of *keii hyoogen* is also problematic because it emphasises 'mutual respect', which does not appropriately apply to honorifics. This is because when juniors use honorifics with their seniors, honorific use here is not 'mutual' but 'one way' 'upward-respect'.[4] Juniors' use of honorifics is the linguistic evidence of the difference in their social status from their seniors, and when two senior members are involved in interaction, juniors often distinguish different levels of honorifics in accordance with those members' social rankings. In such circumstances, honorifics can never function to display mutual respect.

It is indeed possible to say that mutual respect can be achieved when a senior responds to his junior's honorific use in a kind and considerate manner. However, such *hairyo* (配慮 consideration) is mutually expected between the interactants, and irrelevant to differences in status, and thus cannot be balanced with or compensate for the junior's honorific use. Therefore, honorific use remains a one-way upward-respect. Furthermore, if a junior does not use honorifics with his senior, he will probably face a social sanction while, in contrast, his senior will not experience a social

3 This statement was criticised by a number of scholars (e.g. Fukushima, 2013; Hagino, 2001; Takiura, 2005; Usami, 2001). They state that the statement avoids the reality of social differences; it reflects only mental aspects rather than defines what *keii hyoogen* should look like; it shadows Brown and Levinson's strategic politeness, but lacks their rational principle which is the core of their theory (I suppose this principle refers to 'face').

4 However, honorific use between strangers and in public speaking may indicate mutual respect.

sanction simply because he does not display kindness to his juniors (simply, he is not popular with them).

It is ironic that, in spite of the Japanese government's attempt to counter the image of honorifics as representative of the obsolete class system, the term *keii hyoogen* has not come into wide use but remains an academic term, and *keigo* is still commonly used to specify deferential and humble styles in daily life (see further discussions on the ideological image of honorifics in the past and present in Section 6.3).

In this chapter, the conceptualisation of the term 'polite' in English and Japanese has been examined. While Japanese translated words for 'polite', *teineina* and *reigi tadashii*, are predominantly associated with formal and reserved images, 'polite' in English encompasses a wider range of associations, including positive images of interactions such as 'friendliness' and 'kindness'.

This chapter has also examined terms in Japanese equivalent to 'politeness' that should generalise polite phenomena. However, none of those Japanese terms can be equated with English 'politeness', and they offer different ranges of polite phenomena. Some scholars nowadays use *poraitonesu* (ポライトネス), directly translated from English, to encompass a wider range of polite phenomena (e.g. Sasagawa, 2016; Takiura, 2008; Usami, 2001), which seems to be a popular term used in current scholarship.

# 5 The origin of honorifics

## Distance begins

This chapter examines where Japanese honorifics come from and how their origin persists in modern honorifics. Japanese honorifics originate in *norito* (祝詞), a prayer for gods and goddesses in animism, which later developed into Shintoism (Asada, 2001, 2005, 2014). Ancient honorifics were created to appeal to gods and goddesses, indicating humans' awe of them because they caused natural disasters and controlled human fate, and showing gratitude to them because they blessed humans with rich harvests and family happiness. Although honorifics have undergone many changes in relation to their forms, types, targets and effects, their core feature, 'distance', persists in modern honorifics. On the other hand, unlike the origin of honorifics, which was fixed and exclusive to gods, honorifics today exhibit a variety of pragmatic effects and add dynamism to interpersonal communication.

### 5.1 The origin of honorifics as taboo?

As a result of observing the Ainu language, Kindaichi (1962[1959]) believed that honorifics started with terms expressing 'taboo', which aimed to avoid evil spirits and protect family members. The term 'taboo' originates in *tabu* in the Tongan language, meaning 'inviolable, sacred' and used for the purposes of social control or classification (Scott, 2014[1994]: 752). In Ainu, for example, women did not disclose their husband's name in public because doing so was taboo; instead they used a different term to disguise his real name. According to Kindaichi, the 'age of taboo' was the first stage in the history of honorifics. Indeed, by avoiding certain taboo terms (e.g. 'to die') and using euphemistic terms (e.g. 'to pass away'), for example, one can be considerate to the deceased and her family members. In this respect, taboo is somewhat related to politeness strategies. However, there is a fundamental difference between taboo and honorific use. Taboo words are called 'taboo' because their direct forms should be avoided for religious or superstitious reasons and replaced by other figurative forms. Therefore, the choice between taboo and figurative words is a matter of social strategy and, whichever is chosen, the same conceptual message is conveyed. On the other hand, honorifics are not the result of the replacement of different forms, but are mere 'markings' on the utterance that has already been structured strategically. Thus, the semantic content belongs to this original (unmarked) utterance before honorific marking; this means honorific markings do not contribute any semantic content. Therefore, honorific markings exist outside the information-based or goal-oriented utterance (see the detailed discussion in Section 6.2). On the basis of the different processes applied in linguistic construction, it is hard to accept the idea that taboo is the origin of honorifics. Taboo may enrich politeness strategies due to its metaphorical nature, but it is hard to accept that it laid the foundations for the honorific system.

Another problem with the taboo hypothesis is that it is questionable that the origins of Japanese honorifics can be traced in a different language. The Ainu language, which used to be widely spoken in the northern part of Japan but is now almost extinct, does not share basic terms (e.g. terms for kinship, basic human habits such as eating, drinking and sleeping) with Japanese (Nakagawa, 2003), and so typologically is classified differently from Japanese (Brown and Ogilvie, 2009: 15–16). These languages developed independently, although some terms from Ainu were imported into Japanese (e.g. 鮭 *sake* – 'salmon', トナカイ *tonakai* – 'reindeer', many place names in Hokkaido today) as this customarily occurs when two cultures interact because they are neighbours, experience cultural exchanges and/or are at war. However, there is no historical evidence in the literature illustrating how taboo words in Ainu were developed into honorifics in Japanese. Kindaichi's (1962[1959]) assumption of Ainu's taboo words as the origin of honorifics remains to be proven.

Kasuga (1977) investigated honorifics used in ancient literature such as *Kojiki*[1] (古事記) and *Nihonshoki*[2] (日本書紀) and concludes that honorifics were used exclusively to exalt gods and their messenger, the emperor, because the emperor oversaw Shinto ceremonies. In a similar way, Murakami (1977) examined how Shinto ceremonies used to be conducted and the role of the emperor in prayers, and claims that honorifics used in prayers or *norito* (祝詞 – lit. 'celebrating words') were meant exclusively for gods and goddesses. Following on from Kasuga and Murakami, Asada (2001, 2005, 2014) determined that honorifics originated in *norito*.

1 *Kojiki* (lit. *Records of ancient matters*) is the oldest book extant in Japan. It was written around the seventh century to claim that the emperor was a descendent of God. It contains a mythological account of gods and goddesses, legends and songs that werehanded down orally for centuries.

2 *Nihonshoki* (lit.*The chronicles of Japan*) was written in the eighth century and more elaborately describes Japanese history from mythological stories to imperial genealogy.

## 5.2 *Norito* as the origin of honorifics

### *5.2.1 The nature of* norito

*Norito* conducted in Shintoism is not a scripture like the Bible, Koran or Buddhist sutras; it does not contain God's teachings, rules or consolations. The priest creates a script according to the needs of supplicants (though the structure of *norito* is formatted) and chants it, appealing to gods and goddesses. The purpose of *norito*, the format of a *norito* and the way in which the prayer is delivered in today's Shintoism have changed little from ancient times. For example, a visitor to a shrine asks the priest to chant a *norito* when she has bought a new car, and the priest purifies the car by asking Shinto gods not to cause any car accidents. Before a building is built, a Shinto priest is invited to chant a *norito* to ask the god of land not to cause any disasters (e.g. earthquake, landslide); this is called *jichin-sai* (地鎮祭 'land calming ceremony'). New ships and aeroplanes also receive *norito* chanting before their maiden voyage or flight. For each occasion, the priest creates a *norito* based on its prescribed form as a model.

The oldest extant *norito* was written in the eighth century; however, according to Orikuchi (2009[2003]), Uryu (2017) and Toya (2016), *norito* already existed more than 2000 years ago, and indeed goes further back to *ju-shi* (呪詞 'magical rite') in animism. As the Japanese writing system was not well-established before the second or third centuries, those ancient *norito* were handed down orally, and thus we cannot tell how many *norito* existed or how long ago they were originally created. One of the oldest *norito*, *hifumi-norito* (ひふみ祝詞), is believed to have been created 1500 years ago, and has been handed down in the original form because it was recorded by using a type of hieroglyphic characters called *hotsuma-moji* (秀真文字), which some scholars (e.g. Ikeda, 2001; Ozora, 2002) believe, are the original Japanese characters before Chinese characters were adopted. Each character represents a meaningful expression, and was chanted in a slow and prolonged manner. The purpose of chanting *hifumi-norito* as well as other *norito* was to praise and show gratitude to gods and goddesses which were believed to reside in everything in nature, including mountains, rivers, land, rocks, animals and plants.

According to animist beliefs, gods and goddesses cause natural disasters, control human fates such as birth, death, and illness as well as recovery from it, and bless humans with abundant harvests. Therefore, *norito* was meant to appeal for their help, mercy and blessing, to express gratitude and even to request the cursing of a particular person (Asada, 2001: 185–186). Each *norito* specifies what human beings want, and gods and goddesses were believed to listen to the requests, provided human beings worshipped them with a special language used only for them (i.e. honorifics) and provided votive offerings (神饌 *shinsen* or 御饌 *mike*, usually food, *sake* and salt). Unlike other religions, such as Christianity and Buddhism, animist gods do not expect human beings to keep to rules or to be moral or kind to their neighbours. When they expressed wrath, causing inconveniences to humans, it was because humans were praying in an inappropriate manner (e.g. lack of deferential expressions) or because the quantity or quality of offerings was not satisfactory (Asada, 2014: 91–92). Asada (92–93) provides an example of *norito*, in which human beings negotiate with the god of wrath; it reads as "if you (= god) kindly move out of the place the village cherishes, (you) will receive a lots of offerings and be promised another place (you) can move into" (translation my own).

Most animist gods and goddesses were transferred to Shintoism,[3] which was established around the fourth century, and the emperor became the recipient of prayers and acted as the messenger of the gods; later the emperor was seen as the descendant of gods (cf. footnote 1). In modern Japan, though the concept of the emperor as equivalent to a god is no longer adhered to, Shintoism maintains a variety of gods and goddesses (*yaoyorozu no kami* 八百万の神 – lit. 'eight million gods' or 'myriads of gods and deities'), and the format and method of *norito* chanting remain the same.

### *5.2.2 Honorifics in* norito*: A language for gods and goddesses*

In ancient Japan, *norito* provided a linguistic bridge between humans and gods, and was believed to possess supernatural power to appeal to gods (Toya, 2016: 139). Therefore, abundant honorifics were used to place gods on a pedestal. No other historical record suggests that honorifics evolved in a different way. It is plausible that Japanese honorifics originate in *norito*. In fact, a few characteristics of honorifics, which are found in existing *norito* and other literature in the sixth to ninth centuries, may serve to prove that honorifics were created as a special language for gods/goddesses.

First, honorifics started as absolute honorifics (*zettai keigo* 絶対敬語) (Kindaichi, 1962[1959]; Nishida, 1995[1987]; Sakurai, 1983; Watanabe, 1974), and no addressee honorifics were used until the eighth century (Nishida, 1998: 47). Addressee honorifics, which are used in modern honorifics, aim to be polite to the listener in interaction or used as performative politeness in a given situation. Addressee honorifics (*desu/masu* forms attached to verbs) are not 'honorific' in a strict sense because they do not necessarily exalt the listener as do *sonkei* (尊敬 deferential) styles or degrade the speaker as do *kenjoo* (謙譲 humble) styles; these two main honorific styles, *sonkei* and *kenjoo*, are determined according to the interactants' differences in status, age and familiarity in modern Japanese. Addressee honorifics, or *teinei-go* (丁寧語 – lit. courteous terms) in Japanese, on the other hand, are used to enhance politeness

3 This is the reason why almost all Shinto shrines exhibit elements of nature, for example fox statues at Inari shrine in Kyoto, deer at Itsukushima shrine in Hiroshima, snakes at Shiroyama shrine in Niigata, which are now considered to be gods' servants. Kannokura shrine in Kumano, Wakayama, still worships a rock situated on top of the mountain where the shrine was built.

when attached to *kenjoo* or *sonkei* styles, or to be polite situationally, and used extensively with people from different social backgrounds to enable smooth communication. Or, as Moriyama (2011[2003]: 220) explains, *teinei-go* is the speaker's index of her interactional style; it does not indicate how the speaker is treating the listener, but rather expresses the speaker's style or stance.

Honorifics used in ancient *norito* did not aim at 'inter-actions', but directly appealed to gods/goddesses. They were absolute honorifics, and only gods and goddesses received honorifics, and no concern was paid to the (human) audience. Therefore, it is natural to find no addressee honorifics in ancient *norito*. In the fourth century, when the emperor began ruling the nation, he was the primary medium for Shinto prayers (Murakami, 1977: 49). Accordingly, honorific use was extended to the emperor and his family in the Imperial Court because the emperor was considered to be a messenger of gods.[4]

In a similar way, according to Moriyama (1996: 223), *kenjoo* styles until the eleventh century performed a different function to those in modern Japanese. Due to the nature of absolute honorifics, *kenjoo* styles were interpreted as 'lower-ranked' from the viewpoint of gods (and later from that of higher-ranked nobles). This means that the speaker (or the person offering the prayer) accepted herself as a lower-ranked soul in front of gods. In this way, absolute honorifics in old Japanese applied to something (or someone) supreme. In modern Japanese, on the other hand, *kenjoo* styles are situationally bound and relationally determined, and index a social distance whether vertically or horizontally, by degrading the speaker herself.

Another factor that may prove that honorifics originate in *norito* is that honorifics started only with *sonkei*-styles, in which some *sonkei* terms such as *tamoo* (賜ふ 'to give'), *matsuru*[5] (奉る 'to eat') and *masu* (坐す 'to exist') were used only to refer to the absolute deity, or gods. On the other hand, humans' existence was described as *haberi* (侍り 'to serve'), which originally means 'leaving votive offerings at a shrine' (Nishida, 1998: 49–50). Because

4 When honorifics were later extended to human beings, therefore, it is natural that absolute honorifics were maintained and adopted according to social ranking in the Imperial Court without considering the given situation or the nature of the interaction; thus, different social rankings received different levels of honorific (Sakurai, 1983; Watanabe, 1974). Because of this, a higher-ranked person customarily used *jikeigo* (自敬語 – lit. self-exalting language) when interacting with someone of a lower rank, behaviour prevalent until the end of the Nara period in the eighth century (Nishida, 2013[2003]).

Relative honorifics, or *sootai-keigo* (相対敬語), began to emerge around the eighth and ninthth centuries and spread rapidly as society became more complex as a result of the rise of regional clans with economic power and, later, *samurai* (侍 – lit. 'servant' or 'warrior'), who were originally hired as guards for the court and temples but then formed their own clans around the eleventh century. By then, honorifics were no longer only for nobles in court but also for rulers and the rich. By the end of the sixteenth century, relative honorifics were exercised to a greater degree than absolute honorifics (Nishida, 1995[1987]: 168), which established the basis for modern honorifics.

5 *Matsuru* in ancient Japanese means 'to eat offering served by humble humans'. Later this term was used as a *kenjoo*-style, meaning 'to serve to the higher ranked'.

of this, Nishida (50) concludes that honorifics were established based on the relationship between the absolute ruler (gods and later emperors) and the ruled (ordinary people). Therefore, I agree with Asada (2001, 2005, 2014), Kasuga (1977) and Murakami (1977) in that Japanese honorifics were originally created to appeal to animist gods/goddesses.

## 5.3 Characteristics of honorific use in *norito*

In this section, by examining how honorifics were used in ancient *norito*, I draw out some significant characteristics of honorific use to demonstrate that many of them are well-preserved in modern honorifics. I note in particular how motivations behind honorific use and their pragmatic effects in modern Japanese form an apt parallel with those in ancient Japanese.

*Norito* was and still is chanted in a rich and resonant voice. Ancient *norito* was chanted in the open air, especially before shrines were built as gods' houses, and recited in the manner of an operatic song (歌 *uta*), in prolonged tunes and special tones. Just as traditional Japanese poems, *waka* (和歌 – lit. 'Japanese song'), are read in a silvery and sonorous voice, *norito* was intoned like a particular song. Asada (2014: 74–75) explains that *norito* was chanted in a resonant voice with prolonged tunes because gods in nature were believed to reside at a distance. In a similar way, Toya (2016) refers to *haisei* (吠声 – lit. 'the howling of a wolf') used in chanting, a loud exclamation mark when praising gods or rejoicing over their blessings.

*Uta* (歌) in *kanji* (Chinese character) means 'singing', but its verbal form *utau* (歌う) originates in *utafu* (訴ふ pronounced 'utoo') (Asada, 2014; Kikkawa, 1965), which means 'to appeal to,[6], and so *norito* singing was meant to appeal to gods/ goddesses in ancient times (Asada, 2014: 71–73).

When appealing to gods and goddesses in chanting, certain words were repeated to indicate hesitation because humans were in awe of gods, and yet needed to appeal to them. Many *norito* songs were 'requests' to gods: requests to stop disasters, to bring about prosperity and to do good to humans. Therefore, requests were made tentatively. For example, *norito* typically ends with the repeated word, *kashikomi, kashikomi* (畏み、畏み), meaning 'in awe, in awe', which shows humans' tentative and hesitant approaches to gods (Uryu, 2017: 32). Asada (2001: 179) similarly interprets repeated honorific terms as 'carefulness' and 'faltering' resulting from humans' reverence by giving examples such as *tsudoi, tsudoi* (集ひ、集ひ – lit. [gods] gather) and *hakari, hakari* (諮り、諮り – lit. 'to consult [gods]').

*Norito* was also chanted to express gratitude to gods for abundant harvests, recovery from illness and childbirth. When praising and thanking gods, votive

6 In modern Japanese, *utau* is still used in a similar way, meaning 'whistle-blowing' in police jargon, especially when the organisation is denounced by a member.

offerings were carefully chosen and placed at the altar to please gods, and this caring solicitousness was explicitly expressed with lavish honorifics to ask gods to understand how grateful humans were.

Offerings were presented to show gratitude to gods for their blessings. They were also used as a tool for negotiation; for example, 'if the god of wrath can leave this place, more offerings will be presented' and 'if gods punish this particular person, nice and fresh offerings you (gods) like will be provided'. As Asada (2001: 186) describes, gods in ancient Japan did not distinguish right from wrong or virtue from vice, humans could negotiate anything with gods and goddesses as long as appropriate honorifics were used abundantly (i.e. placing gods on a pedestal) by presenting a sufficient amount of offerings. Unlike God in Christianity and Buddha in Buddhism, which are considered supreme deities and symbolised as absolute truth, gods in Shintoism were not interpreted as a model for morality or truth. Rather, they were believed to behave in selfish and wicked ways like humans, and when their actions were inconvenient for humans, *norito* was offered to calm their wrath. Orikuchi (2009[2003]: 310), as a result of investigating Japanese mythology, assumes that gods in ancient Japan were not separate from non-gods such as humans and thus when non-gods developed a high-quality 'soul' they could be promoted to gods. Humans were, therefore, believed to have some spiritual power like gods, but gods were more powerful and controlled the world. This is where *norito* came in as a tool for negotiation.

To summarise the above, honorific use in *norito* is characterised in the following way:

1. Gods are at a *distance*, existing outside in nature.
2. Gods are *placed on a high pedestal*, and humans stand in awe of them.
3. Gods are treated with awe and humans approach them *carefully* and *tentatively* because they cause disasters, unhappiness and other inconveniences, which are beyond humans' control.
4. Gods are *praised* and *thanked* when they bless humans with abundant harvests and family happiness.
5. When appealing to gods, humans *hesitate* and *falter* by repeating honorific words.
6. By serving votive offerings, humans attempt to show their *caring solicitousness*.

Note that these motivational factors, particularly those in italic, will be further discussed in Chapter 7, where a pragmatic parallel is observed between the origin of honorifics, conventional honorifics and honorific terms used in speech-level shifts. Simply put, the more intensely humans recognised the power of gods, the more abundantly were honorifics used in *norito*.

Honorifics started and developed as a language specifically for animist gods and goddesses. Initially, *sonkei*-styles appeared and later *kenjoo*-styles were developed, but human relationships were not recognised through honorific use in ancient *norito*. Even when honorific use was extended to human relationships, honorifics were 'absolute' in the sense that social rankings automatically determined honorific use. Thus, without referring to the agent of an action in literature, different levels of honorifics identified particular people involved in the context. Modern honorifics, on the other hand, are situationally determined, and prompted by the speaker's decision regarding what stance to take in relation to the other socially and/or psychologically. Honorifics have changed greatly; they used to belong to gods and then highly-ranked people, but are now used as social etiquette, and it is the speaker who determines when and how to use them. Yet, motivations for ancient honorific use, as listed above, are in many ways preserved in modern honorific usage. This will be further discussed in Section 7.3.4, where conventional honorifics and honorific terms used in speech-level shifts are compared to demonstrate a pragmatic parallel between them; ultimately, they both come down to the origin of honorifics.

# 6 Understanding honorifics

This chapter discusses an overall picture of the nature of the so-called 'conventional' honorifics. First, the traditional classification of honorific styles is briefly explained. Second, the concept of honorifics is discussed to identify their status in pragmatic principles. It has already been indicated in the previous chapters that honorifics function as the indexing of distance, whereby the speaker demonstrates his recognition of the social relationship that exists with the other person in an interaction. This indexicality is the main function of honorifics in spite of their complex system and numerous forms. They are not involved in semantic contributions to goal-oriented or information-delivery interactions. This will be elaborated on by reviewing previous studies on honorifics. Finally, the chapter refers to the socio-pragmatic significance of honorific use by examining the social image and ideological beliefs prevalent in Japanese society.

## 6.1 Classification of honorific styles

When it comes to studies on honorifics, traditional Japanese language scholars (国語学者) are more often than not concerned with the classification of honorific terms (e.g. Kikuchi, 1999[1997], 2011[2003]; Kindaichi, 1962[1959]; Minami, 1977, 1987; Oishi, 1975; Tsujimura, 1967, to mention just a few). They unanimously agree that *sonkei*-styles[1] (deferential styles) and *kenjoo*-styles (humble styles) are two main sub-categories of honorifics, but have different views concerning whether other styles such as formal styles and *bikago* (美化語 self-beautification styles; see below) should be included in honorifics or where honorific prefixes *o-/go-* should be categorised.

This section does not intend to settle these controversies, but provides a general idea of what forms and styles are involved to constitute the system of honorifics. To do this, I believe that the classification should be based

1 *Sonkei-go* (尊敬語 deferential-language) and *kenjoo-go* (謙譲語 humble-language) are common names in the traditional classification. However, since they are, strictly-speaking, 'styles' grammatically converted from their default linguistic units, I use *sonkei*-styles and *kenjoo*-styles throughout this book.

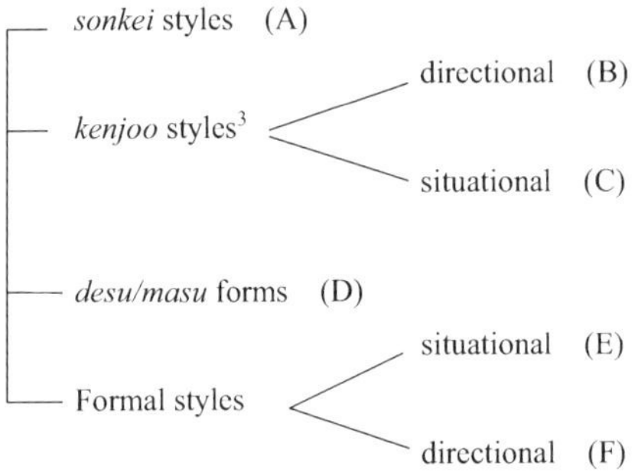


*Figure 6.1* Classification of honorific forms

on the basic nature of honorifics. That is, because the world of honorifics creates a formal atmosphere by exalting the other person, downgrading the speaker and performing ceremonial activities, *linguistic terms that are selected in accordance with those who are involved in an interaction and contribute to a formal milieu, should be categorised as honorifics*. This is because the so-called 'conventional' honorifics typically occur in the situations listed below, which are traditionally accepted by Japanese language scholars, and these situations require the speaker to recognise their social relationships with the other interactants (or referent persons); these situations in fact offer the basis of norms of honorifics (cf. Section 3.2). The situations also create a certain distance from the other(s), and distance in turn creates formality[2]:

1. *jooge kankei* (上下関係 vertical relationship) – status and age differences
2. *shinso kankei* (親疎関係 familiarity) – strangers, relatively not-close people
3. *kookyoo no ba* (公共の場 public-place) – formal public situations

Therefore, honorific terms are manipulated as the speaker's choice to display his stance or emotional state, or those which occur irrespective of the social relationship, are not included in the classification; e.g. *bikago* (self-beautification style) used by some women (see below), and honorific terms that occur on the spur of the moment (e.g. speech-level shifts) are not included in the classification shown in Figure 6.1 (also see Chapter 7, in which derivative uses of honorifics are discussed). The classification was based on Kikuchi (1999[1997]) and Kabaya et al. (2009), but I have added some features and altered others.

2 It should be noted that 'formality' itself cannot be equated with politeness though politeness does encompass formality. It is because formality can be achieved outside the world of politeness (or honorifics), for instance in academic writing in which formal terms are used to elicit dignified styles.

To explain the categories above, I use the ***uchi*/*soto* distinction** (see Endnotes 1 and 2 of this chapter), which determines who receives *sonkei*- or *kenjoo*-styles. *Uchi* (inside) refers to the speaker and his group members; however, his *uchi* group members may change depending on where he is situated. When the speaker is facing his senior in the same company, his *uchi* refers to his family members. On the other hand, when the speaker is interacting with someone from a different company, his *uchi* expands to everybody in his company; in this case, even the president of the speaker's company receives *kenjoo*-styles as the speaker's *uchi* member.[3]

Due to the terms 'inside' and 'outside', the *uchi*/*soto* distinction can be misleading. The speaker's *uchi* members have no psychological closeness between them; rather, they belong to the speaker's social territory, the borderline of which is drawn in relation to the social territory of the other interactant. In other words, the speaker determines which referent person should be treated as *uchi* in a given context by scrutinising the social relationship he has with the listener.

In the following, I briefly explain how each style shown in Figure 6.1 is formed and used:

(A) *Sonkei*-styles (deferential styles)

*Sonkei*-styles, by honorific-marking verbs and adjectives, are meant to exalt the addressee or a third person referred to (*soto* members) in a given interaction. For example,

*hanasu* (to speak) + *o_ninaru* (*sonkei*-marking) → *o-hanasi-ninaru*
*ryokoo-suru* (to travel) + *-nasaru* (*sonkei*-marking) → *ryokoo-nasaru*
*yasashii* + *o-* (*sonkei*-marking) → *o-yasashii*

*Note*. These *sonkei*-markings have no semantic meaning. The same is true of the other markings described below.

(B) Directional *kenjoo*-styles

'Directional' means that actions which belong to the speaker directly engage with or affect *soto* members. For example, the speaker's 'travelling somewhere for a holiday' and 'enjoying his hobby on a holiday' are a matter of his own concern, and not directed to *soto*. Thus, such actions cannot be *kenjoo*-marked. Examples of *kenjoo*-styles are:

*kaesu* (to return) + *o_suru* (*kenjoo*-marking) → *o-kaeshi-suru*
*annai-suru* (to act as a guide) + *go_*(*suru*) (*kenjoo*-marking) → *go-annai-suru*

3 In educational situations, however, office people use *sonkei*-styles to refer to the behaviour of teachers or professors even when they are interacting with those who belong to *soto* (e.g. visitors from different institutions). The same manner applies between academics and their colleagues; they do not treat each other as *uchi* members (linguistically, at least) even when facing *soto* people.

The speaker, when referring to his *uchi* members, treats them as if their behaviour were his own. For example,

(6-1) A: 私、大川商事の水本と申しますが、営業部の川田課長さんはいらっしゃいますか。
A: Watakushi, Ookawa shoji no Mizumoto to mooshi-masu ga,
I Okawa Co. of Mizumoto Quote say[Hon]-Polite but
eigyoo-bu no Kawata kachoo-san wa irasshai-masu ka.
marketing-division of Kawata sec.manager Top available[Hon]-Polite Q
'I'm Mizumoto from Okawa Trading Company. Is Section Manager Kawata available?'
B: 申し訳ございません。川田はただ今外出中でございます。戻りましたらこちらから お電話いたしましょうか。
B: Mooshiwakegozai-masen. Kawata wa tadaima gaishutsu tyuu
Sorry[Formal]-Polite Kawata Top now[Formal] being out[Formal]
de-gozaimasu. Modori-mashi-tara, kochira kara
Cop-Polite return-Polite-when this[Formal] from
o-denwa-itashi-mas-hoo ka.
Hon-phone-do[Hon]-Polite-MD Q
'I'm sorry, but Kawata is out right now. When (he) returns, (shall I tell him) to phone you?'

In this example, because Kawata is person B's *uchi* member as they belong to the same company, Kawata is referred to as *Kawata* without his title when person B is talking with person A from a different company. Furthermore, *odenwa itashi mashoo ka* is a *kenjoo* style of *denwa shimashoo ka*, which is Kawata's action in reality, but treated as if it were the speaker's (i.e. person B's) own. Kawata may be higher-ranked than person B, but in this situation, is treated as B's *uchi* and Kwata's behaviour is *kenjoo*-marked.

(C) Situational *kenjoo*-styles

Situational *kenjoo*-styles refer to a limited number of verbs and auxiliaries, and enhance formality in a given situation. They are not directed toward *soto* people, i.e. they do not distinguish between *uchi* and *soto*, instead they demonstrate situational politeness and courtesy to the listener. Examples in this category can be seen in formal situations; e.g. service industries, initial contacts in business and answering the phone at work. However, some are also used in personal interactions, particularly when the speaker is expected to be sensitive or tentative in approaching the matter concerned; e.g. asking a big favour, suggesting something that might antagonise the other and initiating a conversation on the phone.

*Verbs*

*yuu* (to say) → *moosu, mooshiageru*
*iru* (to be available) → *oru*

*Auxiliaries* either are added to non-directional verbs to create situational *kenjoo*- styles or can combine with directional *kenjoo* verbs to create higher levels of honorifics.

*-itasu* ← *-suru* e.g. *shusseki-**itashi**-masu* (I will attend to it.) →situational
*go-renraku-**itashi**-masu* (I will contact you.) → directional + situational

*-oru* ← *-iru* e.g. *gaishutsushite-**ori**masu* (He is out at the moment.) → situational
o-machishite-**ori**masu (I will wait for you.) → directional + situational

(D) *Desu/masu* forms: addressee honorifics

Addressee honorifics, or *teinei-go* (丁寧語 polite-language) in Japanese, refer to *desu/masu* attached to the verb ending; e.g. *iku* (go) → *iki-mau, ii* (good) → *ii-desu.* They are listener-based and the most fundamental level of honorifics. They also enhance formality when attached to *kenjoo*- or *sonkei*-styles. Unlike *sonkei*- and *kenjoo*-styles, which often emphasise social differences, addressee honorifics are used extensively with people from different social backgrounds to maintain a certain distance from each other, and so can be used to demonstrate mutual respect.

(E) Situational formal styles

Situational formal styles refer to nouns, verbs, adverbs, conjunctions and other formulaic expressions (e.g. greetings). They are contrasted with their default forms. For example,

*Nouns*

default → formal
kocchi → kochira (this, this person)

*Adjectives and adverbs*

sugu → sassoku (immediately)
ima → tadaima (now)

*Verbs*

wakaru → shoochisuru, kashikomaru (to understand, to accept)
kangaeru → kentoosuru (to consider, to contemplate)
kaeru → henkoo suru (to change)

*Greetings*

sayoonara → shitsureishimasu (Good-bye)

yoku shitekureta → gokuroosama, otsukaresama (You did a good job.)
saki ni kaeru → osaki ni shitsurei shimasu (I'm leaving ahead of you.)

As the term name implies, situational formal styles are not directly polite toward *soto* people, but polite in relation to the given situation. They are used when the situation demands a higher degree of formality, for example in business presentations or negotiations, or in service industries. In personal interactions, however, apart from the case of initial telephone conversations, situational formal styles are not frequently used.

(F) Directional formal styles
Directional formal styles refer to honorific prefixes, *o-* and *go-* (which are attached to nouns), and addressing terms such as titles (e.g. *shachoo* = president, –*sama*/*san* = Mr/Ms), kinship terms (e.g. *ojoosan* – your daughter, *musume* – my daughter) and special terms used in business (e.g. 当社-御社 *toosha* – *onsha*[4] = my company – your company). They are directional because the two types of term, conceptually meaning the same, refer to the distinction between *soto* and *uchi*. For example, *otoosan* versus *chichi* (your father versus my father) both refer to the same concept 'father', but they are distinguished according to which group, *uchi* or *soto*, the 'father' belongs to. There are also marked and unmarked terms referring to *soto* and *uchi*, respectively; e.g. *go-iken* vs. *iken* correspond to 'your opinion' and 'my opinion'.

In the classification of honorifics, I did not include *bikago* (self-beautification terms). *Bikago* is a derivative use of *sonkei-* or *kenjoo*-styles and honorific prefixes. It is typically used by women who want to achieve elegant and refined styles, and by service industries that attempt to impart an air of elegance to their customers. Although some scholars, such as Kikuchi (1999[1997]), Minami (1976[1973]) and Tsujimura (1977), include *bikago* in the category of honorifics, I do not consider it to be a part of the so-called 'conventional' honorifics. This is because honorifics index social relationships because the listener is higher in status, older in age, not familiar with the speaker or the interactants are situated in formal settings. On the other hand, *bikago* does not have such social indexicality, but is based solely on the speaker's intention to portray an elegant air or emphasise her femininity (in the case of women). *Bikago*, therefore, is a derivational use of honorific terms (see the discussion in Section 7.3).

4 *Onsha* is used in face-to-face interaction. *Kisha* (貴社) is normally used in writing or formal speech.

## 6.2 Status of honorifics in pragmatic principles

This section focuses on the so-called 'conventional' honorifics. Conventional honorifics mean that they are used to index the social relationship between the speaker and the other person, whether engaged in conversation or referred to as a third party. They typically occur in the situations described in the previous section: in *jooge kankei* (上下関係 vertical relationship), *shinso kankei* (親疎関係 familiarity) and *kookyoo no ba* (公共の場 public-place). On the other hand, honorifics, which are manipulated as the speaker's choice to show his style, stance and/or emotional state, are what I call **'strategic honorifics'**,[5] which will be discussed in Chapter 7.

### *6.2.1 Honorifics as* wakimae?[6]

Since Ide (1989) argued that Japanese honorifics cannot be categorised as a part of negative strategies as Brown and Levinson (1987) claimed, the term *wakimae* (discernment) has often been equated with the concept of honorifics, in contrast with 'volition' that applies to strategic politeness. According to Ide (1989, 2006), Brown and Levinson's strategic politeness originates in the speaker's individual choices, i.e. volition, while honorifics implemented by *wakimae* are social norms that are "the practice of polite behavior according to social conventions" or "the social rules of politeness" (Ide 1989: 230). Discernment means "social norms according to which people are expected to behave in order to be appropriate in the society" (Ide, 1992: 298). Honorifics are, therefore, "socially-agreed-upon rules" (Hill et al., 1986: 348). Later, Ide (2006: 116) adds that, "typical examples of *wakimae* are obligatorily required, which is determined by the given situation" (translation my own).

Ide's *wakimae* was questioned by Eelen (2001) and Kádár and Mills (2013) because *wakimae* is considered to be "an everyday concept" (politeness 1: Eelen, 2001) or "a second-order folk theoretic concept" (Kádár and Mills, 2013), which cannot be discussed on the same plane as 'volition', which is categorised as "an academic concept" (politeness 2: Eelen 2001) or "a theoretical concept" (Kádár and Mills, 2013). This leads to questioning whether it is valid to contrast between *wakimae* and 'volition', as Ide (1989, 1992, 2006) claims (e.g. Kádár and Mills, 2013; Pizziconi, 2003). I am of the same opinion as Pizziconi (2003) and Kádár and Mills (2013), but in the following discussion I look at the term *wakimae* itself to examine its precise meaning and how it is used when referring to human behaviour, and then to verify that the distinction between *wakimae* and volition cannot contrast honorifics with strategic politeness.

5 Although it appears that a distinction exists between conventional and strategic honorifics, the latter are derived from the former and both constitute two ends of a continuum (see Chapter 7 for details).

6 Sections 6.2.1–6.2.3 are excerpts from Obana (2017), amended to suit the flow of this chapter.

*Wakimae* is the noun form of the verb, *wakimaeru*. Its *kanji* (Chinese character) in modern Japanese is 弁, which is a simplified form of the three original (and now obsolete) *kanji*, 辨, 瓣, 辯: the first *kanji* meaning 'dividing or cutting with a sword', the second, 'cutting a melon to separate its flesh from seeds', and the third, 'distinguishing (something) with words' (Digital *Shin-Kangorin*). These archaic characters share a common feature: division or separation. In modern Japanese, *wakimaeru* is used more extensively to judge human behaviour. For example, in *zen-aku o wakimaeru* (善悪を弁える to distinguish between good and bad), and *koo-shi no kubetsu o wakimaeru* (公私の区別を弁える to know the distinction between public and private), the distinction between two opposing elements (good–bad, public–private) is observed, and *wakimaeru* implies not only 'to distinguish' but also 'to know (how to distinguish)' when referring to social actions and skills. Thus, *wakimaeru demonstrates one's ability to distinguish among different actions and to decide on and perform the most appropriate one in a given situation*. Some more examples are:

(6–2) *basho o wakimaeru* (場所を弁える to know where one is situated)
*kotsu o wakimaeru* (コツを弁える to have the knack of something)
*kihon o wakimaeru* (基本を弁える to know the basics)
*doori o wakimaeru* (道理を弁える to know the way things should be)

The examples in (6–2) show that *wakimae* portrays one's appropriate knowledge of social skills as gained by experience and learning; in short, *wakimae* is proficiency in know-how. Although such proficiency is internalised, it is not stored as a fixed or rigid set of directions or instructions; *wakimae in practice requires flexible and adaptable actions to be considered appropriate in each changing situation*. I briefly discussed this in Section 1.3 by providing the example of a woman climbing into the *sumo* ring, an action that violated tradition but was considered appropriate *wakimae* behaviour as a nurse in that particular situation. Another example is that *basho o wakimaeru* (to know where one is situated) displays one's behaviour adjusted to suit different situations; one behaves in a more friendly and casual manner at a friend's party, becomes formal in formal clothes at a ceremony and uses positive and persuasive language during business negotiations. Even in the same situation, there are moments that require more serious behaviour and others that allow jokes and mock-impoliteness; in each moment the evaluation of *basho o wakimaeru* changes. *Wakimae*, or knowledge of how to behave appropriately, therefore by no means refers to rigid rules, or "ritual patterns (*kata*)", as Ide (2006: 128) describes them; rather, it comprises the quality of flexibility and adjustability.

If *wakimae* is understood as 'knowledge of how to behave appropriately in a flexible manner', as discussed above, it is not unique to Japanese. As Pizziconi (2003) appropriately points out that "the need of *wakimae* is vital in communication, regardless of the language" (1500), *wakimae is prevalent in various interactions in different cultures*. That being the case, Brown and Levinson's (1987) list of strategies can also be categorised as a part of *wakimae* because those strategies, when used appropriately to achieve politeness, are the implementation of one's knowledge of how to behave by recognising the given situation and choosing the most appropriate action to suit it.

Furthermore, according to Ide (2006: 115), the difference between *wakimae* (honorifics) and volition (strategies) lies in the motivation for using certain linguistic forms; honorific use comes from the outer world, i.e. social expectations, while strategic use comes from the internal world, i.e. one's will. However, this distinction[7] is too simplistic to be accepted because politeness in general is a social action, which inevitably burdens one with social expectations, but at the same time is contextual and contingent, which requires one to devise and adjust one's behaviour. This applies to both honorifics and strategies. Strategies such as thanking, apologising and indirectly requesting in English, for example, are in many ways socially expected, and people follow social expectations assuming that doing so means they will be considered polite or appropriate ('social expectation' is one of the key features that define 'politeness', as was discussed in Chapter 2). Therefore, socially bound behaviour[8] is ubiquitous in both English-speaking and Japanese societies.

It seems that so-called 'conventional' honorifics can be seen as a set of fixed, rule-governed and obligatory terms . However, they can be manipulated by the speaker, although not as freely as honorific terms used in speech-level shifts as the latter give rise to more varied pragmatic effects. For example, a senior–junior relationship does not necessarily maintain the same level of honorifics throughout an interaction. When the interaction involves sensitive issues at work, such as a junior making a special request that he wants the senior to grant, the junior may *approach* the senior with more formal expressions and/or higher-level honorifics. When the interaction shifts to casual talk, such as a conversation about the next inter-company golf tournament, the junior may use the lowest level of honorifics. This shows that the speaker knows how to *manipulate* honorifics, and attempts to approach the senior with varied levels of honorifics to achieve smooth and effective communication. Therefore, honorific use is by no means "the socio-pragmatic equivalent of grammatical concord" (Ide, 1989: 227).

With this in mind, it seems clear that honorifics and Brown and Levinson's strategies cannot be differentiated in terms of the contrast between *wakimae* and 'volition', although I agree with Ide that honorifics are not a strategy.

7 I agree with Pizziconi (2003: 1480) in that "[f]rom a cognitive viewpoint, external (social) and internal (psychological) motives can be difficult to discriminate, and awareness of one's acts of volition can be commonly conceived in terms of commitment to an idealised norm of appropriate behaviour."

8 Eelen (2001: 126) regards Brown and Levinson's face and rationality as "standards people are expected to live up to – in simple terms, social norms". He also contends that "Brown and Levinson's 'individual wants' are actually 'cultural wants' just like Ide's rules of Discernment" (129).

### *6.2.2 Honorifics as a negative or positive strategy?*

Those who support Brown and Levinson's (1987) categorisation of honorifics as a negative strategy share a common view that the use of honorifics creates a certain distance whereby the speaker avoids intervening in the hearer's territory (Chinami, 2005; Fukada and Asato, 2004; Kumai, 2009; Moriizumi, 2009; Moriyama, 2010; Takiura, 2005, 2008; Usami, 2001). It is indeed true that a function of honorifics is to create distance, but it does not necessarily follow that they are categorised as a negative strategy, because between honorifics and Brown and Levinson's strategies is a fundamental difference in the process of linguistic construction. That is, honorifics are the grammatically converted (or honorifically-marked) forms that have already been strategically constructed; in other words, honorific forms contain a double layer in their linguistic architecture. Let us look at an example:

(6–3) (a) よかったら、映画見に行かない？
*Yokat-tara* *eiga* *mi-ni-ika-nai?*
good-if film watch-to-go-not

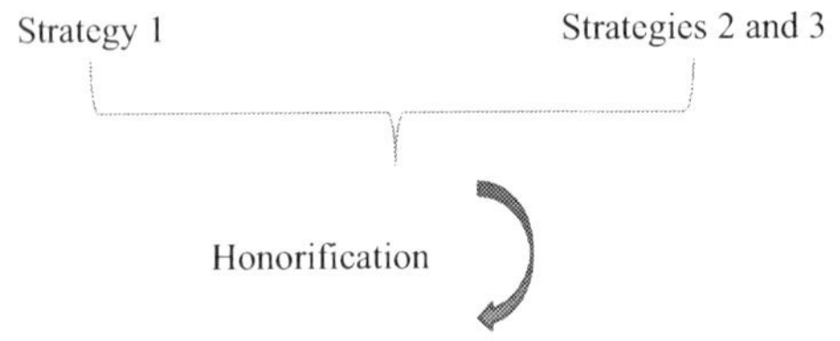


(b) よろしかったら、映画見にいらっしゃいませんか？
*Yoroshikat-tara eiga mi-ni irasshai-mase-n ka?*

'If you like, won't you watch a film (with me)?'
(Obana, 2017: 286)

Utterance (a) in example (6–3) is an invitation to a close friend to watch a film, using plain forms such as *mini-* (to watch) and *ika-nai* (not to go). It is strategically constructed with *yokattara* (if you like) as a tentative invitation (strategy 1), *-nai* (not) as a pessimistic hope (strategy 2), and an interrogative as giving options (strategy 3). Utterance (b), on the other hand, is an invitation to someone the speaker does not know well. Linguistically, it is the honorific conversion of utterance (a) with honorific markings on *yokattara* (changed to *yoroshikattara*) and *ika-* (to go) (changed to *irasshai-*), adding an addressee using a polite term, *mase-*. However, the content of utterance (b) remains the same as that of (a); that is, the speaker's goal (invitation), the strategies (tentative invitation, pessimistic hope and giving options) to achieve the goal, and the syntactic architecture of the utterance remain exactly the same between utterances (a) and (b). This means that utterance (b) has a *double-layered structure: a strategically constructed unit with honorific markings on it.*

Brown and Levinson's (1987) strategies focus on *how the content of an utterance may affect the hearer*, and how an appropriate strategy is employed *to avoid a potential FTA*. Negative strategies are, therefore, defined as strategies that mitigate potential FTAs because the content or the speaker's goal (e.g. a request) potentially threaten the hearer's negative face, i.e. the action to be implemented by the content of an utterance (e.g. to fulfil a request) may be imposed upon the hearer. On the other hand, honorifics, or precisely honorific markings, are not responsible for the content of an utterance, its potential FTA or a strategy for FTA mitigation. These arrangements are already completed when constructing the basic structure of an utterance. *Honorific markings occur when the speaker measures a social or psychological distance from the hearer*;[9] therefore, they function merely as 'marking' or 'indexing' such a distance (though both strategic planning and honorific marking are operated at the same time in reality).

Matsumoto (1988) regards honorifics as "relation-acknowledging devices", which is similar to the line I have taken above. To verify her statement, Matsumoto (1988: 415) argues that honorific use is triggered even "when the utterance would not be conceived of as an intrinsic FTA" by providing three utterances in plain, polite to super polite forms, all of which relate the innocuous content, 'Today is Saturday'. On the other hand, Chinami (2005), Fukada and Asato (2004) and Takiura (2005) maintain that honorific use is closely related to potential FTAs because "if people do not use honorifics when they are expected to do so, they could sound presumptuous and rude, and in effect, threaten the hearer's face" (Fukada and Asato, 2004: 1997). However, while this statement itself may be true in reality, it does not sufficiently rebut Matsumoto's (1988) argument. What Matsumoto emphasised is that *there exist honorific-marked utterances that would not predict any FTAs*. However, Brown and Levinson's idea of negative politeness means that the speaker's goal predicts an FTA and a certain strategy is employed to mitigate the FTA. On the other hand, honorifics occur irrespective of the prediction of FTAs. This is because they are not involved with the content of the speaker's utterance, but are triggered as the evidence of the speaker's indexing of distance from the other in a given situation. For example:

(6–4) 社長、今日は二時から会議です。
*Shachoo, kyoo wa ni-ji kara kaigi desu.*
president today two-o'clock from meeting Polite
'Sir, (we) have a meeting at two.'

9 This statement applies to both referent and addressee honorifics, as shown in utterance (b) in which the honorific conversion of utterance (a) prompts both types of honorific.

(6–5) 昨日雨がよく降りましたねえ。
*Kinoo,* *ame ga* *yoku furi-mashi-ta* *nee.*
yesterday rain Nom a lot fall-Polite-Past MD
'It rained a lot yesterday, didn't it?'

Example (6–4) concerns a company employee providing information to his president about the forthcoming meeting. Example (6–5) shows the sharing of information about yesterday's rain between neighbours. None of these examples anticipate any FTAs because the speaker does not impose upon the other to achieve his goal,[10] but delivers mere information. However, honorific markings occur because the speaker judges the other as a senior in status in example (6–4), and as psychologically distant in example (6–5). This shows that **honorific markings aim to solely index a social and/or psychological distance, and exist outside the domain of goal-oriented interactions in which FTAs are potentially extant and strategies to mitigate such FTAs are required** (although honorific terms can be manipulated as strategies, whether or not they are polite [cf. example [21] in Chapter 2; also see Chapter 7], we are talking about the so-called 'conventional' honorifics here). Therefore, due to the different motivation and function between honorifics and Brown and Levinson's (1987) politeness strategies, honorifics cannot be categorised as an element of negative politeness strategies in Brown and Levinson's sense.

We now turn to the view that honorifics may offer positive strategies. Pizziconi (2003: 1471) claims that, "the principles regulating the use of honorific devices in Japanese are not substantially different from those of English, both being similarly strategic". As an example to support her argument, she asserts that *yoroshiku onegaishimasu*, a greeting formula used at a first encounter,[11] does not impose a request as Matsumoto (1988) claims. The formula is equivalent to 'Nice to meet you', hoping to establish a forthcoming good relationship with a new group. It contains honorific terms such as *o-(negai)-shi* ('wish' + humble style, *o-suru*) and *–masu* (addressee honorific). By examining the nature of *yoroshiku* (the formal form of *yoku* [good, well]) and *negau* (to wish), Pizziconi (2003) concludes that the greeting formula is a positive strategy.

Pizziconi originally intended to oppose Matsumoto, who categorised this greeting formula as a welcome *imposition* on the senior: "deferent impositions

10 The speaker's 'goal' here means that the content of his utterance aims to achieve what he originally planned (e.g. request, agreement). Honorific use does achieve another type of speaker's goal, i.e. 'relation-acknowledging' (Matsumoto, 1988), but here we are concerned with how the content of an utterance influences the other.

11 Although the formula is used in more diverse contexts with different pragmatic meanings (Obana, 2012b), the discussion here is limited to its greeting function by following Matsumoto (1988) and Pizziconi (2003). See Endnote 3 of this chapter, in which the pragmatic functions of the formula are discussed.

can enhance the good self-image (that is, the 'face') of the addressee" (Matsumoto, 1988: 410). She then contends that, "the discourse function of this utterance [= the formula] as the opening of an encounter, can more intuitively be interpreted as an implicit – yet transparent – message of the speaker's appreciation of the hearer's social persona" (Pizziconi, 2003: 1485).

Obana (2012b), on the other hand, examined the original meaning of the formula and argues that the formula itself delivers the speaker's humble manner; it means 'With your permission, my wish would be accepted, which I'm humbly requesting' (see Endnote 3 of this chapter). Therefore, it can never be an imposition. However, it does not mean that the honorific markings used in the formula demonstrate positive politeness. The speaker may be joining a new group in a positive spirit and appreciate its welcome, but the occurrence of honorific markings originates in a different motivation (creating a distance, as is appropriate in public speaking) from that of Brown and Levinson's strategies. In this respect, Pizziconi (2003) seems to analyse honorifics, or more precisely honorific markings, by examining the content of the message itself (or more precisely, 'the speaker's wish' since the content itself is a humble request). Because honorific markings and strategic planning (i.e. motivations for strategy construction) occur at the same time, and honorific markings are grammatically encoded and completely embedded in a strategically-built construction, deciding whether we are talking about honorifics in terms of 'grammatical markings' or 'the content of a message' (or 'the speaker's willingness in his greeting situation') is often confusing. However, honorific markings themselves are not responsible for strategic planning in constructing a message. Whether the message is positive or negative, or potentially face-threatening or not, honorific markings take place as a result of the speaker's assessment of a social/psychological distance from the other.

### *6.2.3 Honorifics as ritual?*

Ide (2006: 108–109) states that, although there are certain variations of honorific use in reality, matching the situation and linguistic choice (honorific use) is automatic, which she calls the "super-system of *wakimae*". This leads Ide to compare honorifics to "consensual phatic communion" (117, translation my own), and consider them to be "a part of ritual" (127). Because Ide interprets 'ritual' as "patterns customarily used", she associates the ritualistic aspect of honorifics with "*kata*" (型[12] model, mould) because, according to her, the given situation (e.g. social ranking differences) requires particular honorific forms (125–127). However, ritual offers more than patterns customarily used, such as social solidarity, emotional involvement and communal

12 *Kata* in Japanese is often used in traditional sports such as *karate* and *judo* to refer to a fixed sequence of moves learners are taught as the basic skills.

participation. I doubt that honorifics accommodate such an affiliative drive (as discussed below).

Kádár and Mills (2013) and Kádár (2013) argue that one of the problems concerning Ide's (1989) *wakimae* is that she "places the interface between social ritual and politeness under the umbrella of discernment and contrasts this interface with non-ritualistic politeness" (Kádár, 2013:179). They, however, do not abandon the term completely, but instead acknowledge the cross-cultural differences the term captures (e.g. Kádár and Paternoster [2015] present a case study of Italian), and re-conceptualise the notion of *wakimae*. Their ultimate aim with the notion of *wakimae* is to use it cross-culturally by taking advantage of its ritual and conventionalised aspects. However, in the course of their argument, we can trace how they consider Japanese honorifics in terms of (their version of) *wakimae*.

Although Kádár and Mills (2013) and Kádár (2013) do not follow Ide's (2006) "super-system of *wakimae*" exactly, i.e. its automatic and inherent aspects, they basically employ the ritual aspect of *wakimae*, and claim that "ritual … does in fact represent discernment" (Kádár and Mills 2013: 145). By introducing examples of ritual interactions and comparing them with Ide's (1989: 227) example of honorific-marked utterance, Kádár and Mills (2013: 145–146) draw a parallel between ritual and honorifics because both meet "normative contextual expectations", and thus, the use of honorifics is "a ritualistic talk".

Kádár (2013: 6) defines 'ritual' as "a key social phenomenon because of its survival value, specifically its potential to enhance the establishment and reinforcement of interpersonal and/or intragroup relations". He also quotes Kertzer's (1988) definition: "What is important in ritual is our common participation and emotional involvement. … Thus, ritual can promote social solidarity" (Kádár, 2013: 7). This means that rituals, whether formal/ religious/ ceremonial or family/personal, such as patterned family jokes (93–98), or Sunday rituals (going to church and roast dinner afterwards), aim to achieve group solidarity and confirm communal bonds.

The idea of honorifics as ritual, however, cannot be accepted for the following reasons. First, unlike ritual which primarily aims at social solidarity, Japanese honorifics do not promote such a sense of communal bond. On the contrary, honorifics, as the implementation of a social/psychological distance, create a certain alienation from the other, which may be regarded as 'respectful distance', 'putting the other on a pedestal' or 'aloofness' depending on context and the relationship between the interactants. Because of this, the more honorifics are used, the more social/psychological distance is created between the interactants.

Second, while Kádár and Mills (2013) and Kádár (2013) correctly point out setbacks with which the term *wakimae* is associated in theorising it in politeness research (cf. Section 6.2.1), they take for granted the socio-cultural meanings of the term as defined by Ide (1989, 2006). For Ide, *wakimae* is conventional, consensual, ritualistic and even traditional (*dentooteki*: Ide,

2006: 76). However, as discussed in Section 6.2.1, *wakimae* is not a set of rules or ritualistic actions because people will be judged as having *wakimae* if they adjust their behaviour to different situations correctly, which requires flexibility to suit each moment in a given interaction. On the other hand, ritual is the "performance of appropriately patterned behavior to symbolically effect" (Rothenbuhler, 1998: 27). Indeed, there are moments in life when religious or ceremonial rituals are held and a certain *wakimae* is required to suit those occasions.[13] However, this is only a part of *wakimae*; *wakimae* prevails in a broad variety of social actions to show one's proficiency and skills in social interaction, including strategic manipulation to achieve goals in that interaction. In this respect, *wakimae* is so broadly utilized in everyday interaction that it cannot be dealt with only in the domain of ritual.

Third, even 'conventional' honorifics are not fixed or patterned behaviour like rituals; they are not a set of routine rules evoked by specific scenes like ritual, which is defined as "a series of actions according to a prescribed order" (*Digital Oxford English Dictionary*).

We saw the manipulation of honorifics in Section 6.2.1, whereby the same junior uses different levels of honorifics with the same senior in different contexts. Take another example. Two colleagues in the same age group do not usually use honorifics with each other. However, they use honorifics at a company meeting (cf. example [1–2] in Section 1.2). Obana (2016) explains this in terms of 'task-based roles', i.e. that honorifics in that situation are the implementation of their task-based roles as meeting attendees, while they are basically close colleagues according to their social role-identity (roles are multi-layered and the most suitable role to apply to each situation comes to the surface).

An interesting use of honorifics is reported by Ohkubo (2009), in which a wedding MC keeps changing honorifics from humble to deferential forms when referring to the same people. This is because the MC assumes different roles to suit the on-going situation. For instance, when talking to the guests, he takes a role on behalf of the bride and groom, using humble terms about the behaviour of the couple. When the MC asks the bride and groom to cut a cake, he uses deferential terms about their behaviour. This is an example of how dynamically honorifics change according to each different situation; the different roles the MC assumes prompt different honorific forms even when the same person refers to the same people (see Section 7.3.1 for a detailed discussion with examples).

Furthermore, ritual requires pre-settings and expects patterned behaviour accordingly; in other words, a certain pre-setting (e.g. Sunday) prompts a regular routine (e.g. church-going and roast dinner). On the other hand, honorifics are not as rigidly formulated as ritual. We may learn that honorifics

13 At funerals in Japan, for example, people wear black suits and women are limited to pearls in terms of jewellery. Attendees wear their *juzu* (数珠 a Buddhist rosary) when offering incense.

should be used in public places (公共の場 *kookyoo no ba*), however we often witness plain forms being used by performers on stage (e.g. musicians talking to the audience). We may learn that socially highly-ranked people should receive honorifics from their juniors (上下関係 *jooge kankei* = vertical relationship); however, in companies where all relatives and their sons and daughters work, workers use plain forms to their seniors.[14] We may learn that service industry employees should use honorifics with customers, while it is quite common to observe, for instance, small local restaurants (e.g. stand-up street stalls) serve dishes in a casual manner with very few honorifics.

For the reasons above, honorifics, even if our discussion has been limited to 'conventional' honorifics,[15] cannot be confined to the domain of ritual.

### *6.2.4 Honorifics as a social index and linguistic evidence of a social relationship*

In the previous sub-section, I suggested that honorifics are, strictly speaking, markings on the utterance that has already been constructed strategically, and do not bring any semantic contributions to the utterance. Therefore, honorifics are not strategies, but index a social distance, whereby the speaker linguistically indicates his social relationship with the other interactant (or a third person referred to). Therefore, the linguistic architecture of an honorific utterance is double-layered: an utterance strategically constructed and honorific markings on it. Despite their complex system and numerous forms, honorifics function merely as a social index.

Honorific use is often associated with social hierarchy, which appears to be in contrast to the ideal of egalitarianism in English-speaking societies. However, social differences exist in every culture and social power is witnessed in everyday life, although how awareness of such issues occurs may differ across cultures. In Japanese, it is implemented by means of honorifics. In English, on the other hand, such awareness may remain psychological in many ways, but a closer look at how individuals in different social positions interact shows that their choice of linguistic forms and strategies, and even extra-linguistic features such as tone of voice and speaking speed, verify their social differences. This is examined extensively by Holmes and Stubbe (2003) and Locher (2004).

Holmes and Stubbe (2003) provide examples of company situations in New Zealand in which various interactions occur between bosses and

14 Relational behaviour confirmed by the author through informal interviews at a few companies.

15 Because Kádár and Mills (2013) and Kádár (2013) limit their scope to 'conventional' honorifics, I have followed that here. However, I do not differentiate conventional honorifics from honorifics occurring in speech-level shifts (i.e. plus-level shifts) as the latter are derived from the former (see Section 7.2.4). If we include examples of plus-level shifts in the classification of 'honorifics', we find more dynamic, fluid and even ad hoc honorific uses with diverse socio-pragmatic implications.

junior members of staff. They argue that, while power may license the use of relatively coercive discourse strategies, "most workplace interactions provide evidence of mutual respect and concern for the feelings or face needs of others, that is, of politeness" (5), and collegial strategies are more often employed. However, this does not mean that juniors can use collegial strategies on the basis of egalitarianism. As social power is unavoidable in working situations, approaches to a senior inevitably involve the junior's awareness of the social power held by that person. Holmes and Stubbe provide an example in which a junior uses *hedging and attenuation devices* when negotiating with the boss. They also found that "another important resource for participants (= boss and junior) in handling confrontational interactions which threaten their face needs, is *to emphasise their own status and competence*" (146, italics added).

Locher (2004) also investigates how power is exercised in the workplace, among family and friends and during the US presidential election, and presents interesting findings. For example, *disagreement at meetings was often unmitigated*, which indicates that "a speaker wished to make a position clear" (212). This is because disagreement is "to restrict the addressee's action-environment because it creates a slot in which an answer to the subject of the disagreement is expected", which "often leads to the exercise of power" (84). This means that social power can be manifested by means of certain strategies in English.

The above examples show that, *in English speaking societies, too, social differences can be signalled linguistically*. However, there is still a fundamental difference between English power-related strategies and honorifics. In English, power-related strategies are employed *at times* when one needs to highlight social differences to achieve one's interactional goal. Thus, they are *a product of the discourse development*. The interactants may be constantly aware of their social differences when they are interacting, but only when such differences are required to be brought to the fore (e.g. in making a final decision, request from a junior, negotiation) are they linguistically manifested. Furthermore, *both juniors and seniors can highlight social differences by using certain linguistic terms and/or extra-linguistic features*. In Japanese, on the other hand, *honorific use is basically expected regardless of the discourse development* because honorifics are ideologically[16] put into

16 The term 'ideology' (more precisely, language ideology) is the belief/idea of an ideal state of affairs (e.g. linguistic use) that becomes a motivating force for society (my definition). This subjective definition means that ideology is not a reflection of reality, but often contradicts actual phenomena. Woolard (1998) suggests the existence of four strands of ideology, the first of which is taken "as ideational or conceptual, referring to mental phenomena" (5) and relates to the definition above. Another strand is "a direct link to inhabitable positions of power" (7). The Japanese government's language reformation discussed in the next section applies to this type of strand. However, as Woolard argues, these strands do not exist independently, but influence each other and are interwoven (together with the other types of ideology) into cultural beliefs.

practice in Japanese society, though the discourse development may allow the omission of honorifics every now and again, and influence the choice of honorific levels. Furthermore, honorifics are used only by the junior; they are a *non-reciprocal index*.

As a result of the indexical nature of honorifics, it is understandable that Ide (1989) claims that the use of honorifics is 'obligatory' just like grammatical concord, and Watts (1992) sees it as 'automatic'. However, as discussed in previous chapters, honorific use is not obligatory; in reality, honorific and non-honorific terms are mixed within the same discourse to create dynamic interactional exchanges, and peer language in certain contexts (e.g. at casual food stalls, rock musicians on stage, police being friendly with elderly people) seems to be more effective. Honorifics are not automatic, either because honorific levels and terms are carefully selected in accordance with the social relationships (speaker, listener and third person referred to), the stance the speaker takes, the topic, the given situation and the discourse development. These factors allow the speaker to manipulate honorific levels and choose different honorific terms. In other words, though social differences provide grounds for honorific use, actual uses of honorifics are dynamic, changeable and controlled by the speaker in each moment.

Brown (2011: 73) appropriately contends that the claims of Ide and Watts above "show clear examples of dominant social ideology being mistaken for linguistic reality" or "only explain the most ideologically-invested or canonical uses of honorifics and cannot account for a variety of honorifics usages at the politeness-in-action level". This does not mean, however, that Brown denies the language ideology behind Korean use of honorifics. On the contrary, he claims that, through education and the media, Koreans are trained "to pay attention to the hierarchical social structure and to attach importance to such modes of politeness" due to the "ideology of non-reciprocal and hierarchical social relationship" (81), and that Koreans use honorifics as a vehicle to verify this ideology.

Although language ideologies "are not exactly and solely based on the structure and distribution of linguistic facts" (Irvine, 1998: 62), they influence a society and its people over many years. Brown (2011: 71) explains that an inferior's use of non-honorific language provokes a severe social sanction for ideological reasons. Language ideologies are reflected in social changes and people's beliefs. In the next section, I examine how the language ideology the Japanese government attempted to impose for democratic reasons has changed the styles, images and effects of honorifics over the last 70 years. As I see it, the government's attempt has succeeded and the ideas or beliefs attached to the use of honorifics have changed to suit the socio-economic diversities of today.

## 6.3 Socio-pragmatic functions of honorifics: Ideology, image and reality

This section examines socio-pragmatic aspects of honorifics. We first look at the ideological statement concerning honorifics issued by the government after the Second World War as part of the democratic reformation of Japanese society, and examine how this ideology of honorifics has been accepted. Second, we turn our attention to how Japanese people in general regard honorifics today, and how the social values of honorifics have changed over several decades.

### *6.3.1 From hierarchical to democratic 'honorifics'?*

As discussed in Chapter 5, Japanese honorifics began as a language for animist gods and goddesses and was later extended to human beings, initially to the emperor, his family and nobles at court. As *samurai* (warriors) formed their own clans (called *goozoku* 豪族 regional clans) around the eleventh century, honorifics were more extensively used with rulers and the rich. Until the end of the Second World War, honorifics, though their forms and styles changed, were predominantly associated with social hierarchical positions as Japanese society was quite rigidly distinguished by class. Even after the Meiji Restoration (明治維新 *meiji ishin*), which started in 1868, superior government officials (who were mostly from the aristocracy), aristocratic ranks (originally from high-level *samurai* clans) and land-owning classes (*jinushi* 地主 originally from regional clans) occupied the upper echelons of society, and everyone else was called *heimin* (平民 ordinary citizens). Naturally, marriages between different classes caused social turmoil and controversy. Women were socially suppressed and expected to use honorifics with their husbands (women's right to vote was granted in December 1945, only after Japan was defeated in the Second World War and promised to build a democratic country[17]), and children in well-off families were trained to use honorifics with their parents.

When the war ended, Japan was controlled and subsequently changed by the Allies, particularly by the US's General Headquarters (GHQ). In order to prevent a new rise in militarism, Japanese labour, land and capital were reformed under the auspices of 'democratisation'. Social classes were accordingly abandoned and the emperor was now seen as a symbol in the new constitution. The Japanese language was also a target for reform; the

17 The women's movement began around 1900, towards the end of the Meiji era. A famous statement was issued by activist, Hiratsuka Raichoo (平塚らいてう), in 1911: *ganshi josei wa taiyoo de atta* (元始女性は太陽であったWomen were originally the Sun). She compared women to the Sun goddess, *Amaterasu oomikami* (天照大御神), the highest ranking of all gods and goddesses in Shintoism.

number of *kanji* was limited and *kanji* forms were simplified, written language was changed to more closely resemble spoken language, and the definition of honorifics was altered. The Ministry of Education issued the following statement in 1952:

> 「これからの敬語」
>
> これまでの敬語は、主として上下関係に立って発達してきたが、これからの敬語は、各人の基本的人格を尊重する相互尊敬の上に立たなければならない。
>
> "Honorifics from now"
>
> Honorifics so far were developed mainly based on *jooge kankei* (hierarchical relationships), but from now honorifics should be based on mutual deference which aims at respecting each person's individuality. (Translation my own)

Indeed, many of the aspects of democratisation the government was aiming for were quickly adopted throughout Japan, and honorifics were not an exception; they were greatly simplified, supreme honorifics used for the emperor in particular disappeared, and family members ceased to use honorifics between themselves.

A number of scholars, however, have questions and doubts about the governmental statement above. For example, Tsukishima (1976[1973]) doubts that honorific use would achieve mutual deference because "we live in the meshes of *jooge kankei*" (140, translation my own); for example, differences in status at work, age differences, the relationship between teacher and student (*onkei* 恩恵 intangible almsgiving) and *senpai* and *koohai* (seniors versus juniors) at school and in sports activities. Although the use of honorifics does not necessarily mean that the receiver of such is worthy of upward-respect, *jooge kankei* inevitably invites the use of honorifics, and in such circumstances, honorific use does not necessarily prove mutual deference (144–145). Therefore, "many uses of honorifics in reality have nothing to with respecting each person's individuality as announced in the above statement" (146, translation my own).

Watanabe (1994: 56) more strongly asserts that "Japanese language even today underlies hierarchical relationships", and in particular that honorifics "have historically represented Japan's hierarchical orders", and therefore, "by force of circumstance, express *jooge kankei*" (32, translation my own), in spite of the government's attempt to shift the image of "hierarchical honorifics" to that of "social honorifics" (58, translation my own). Tanaka (1999) is more extreme, suggesting that honorific use is a form of training to impose slavery and, because of this, Japan would fall behind the rest of the world.

Warabidani (2017) is not a Japanese language scholar, but a business consultant and has published books on honorifics for business people. He denies the existence of mutual respect demonstrated by means of honorifics because "honorifics in business are based on unequal treatment" (161, translation my own) because *jooge kankei* is self-evident in working situations. However, he adds that mutual respect emerges contextually when a senior shows consideration, kindness and tolerance in response to a junior's use of honorifics.

Hagino (2001, 2005) takes a similar but gentler line to those above by stating that, although honorifics are the expression of *jooge kankei*, the nature of *jooge kankei* has changed from a rigid social-hierarchical order to a situational hierarchy. For example, a teacher occupies a higher position than his students and customers are exalted when they interact with sellers and service people. Nonetheless, highs and lows take place in social life and honorifics are a means of expressing them.

Other scholars, on the other hand, attempt to remove the image of hierarchy associated with honorific use, and suggest different definitions. For example, Inoue (1999) asserts that modern honorifics in many ways demonstrate a horizontal distance, and thus should be called *sayuu keigo* (left–right honorifics or horizontal honorifics). Iritani (1978) and Tsujimura (1989) define modern honorifics as *aratamari* (改まり formal, ceremonial), and Watanabe (1974) as *hinkaku hoji* (品格保持 maintaining one's dignity). Fukushima (2013) goes a little further by defining modern honorifics as a linguistic tool to appeal to others to recognise what 'I' am like and how 'I' want to be treated.

Oishi (1984) describes modern honorifics as *shoogyoo keigo* (商業敬語 commercial honorifics) by observing more complex and elaborate honorifics used by service industries, despite the government's attempt to simplify honorifics for democratic reasons. However, Watanabe (1994: 59f) interprets this phenomenon as a re-production of the hierarchical nature of honorifics by replacing class-hierarchy with (economic) power; it is a capitalist production of honorifics.

The statements above, whether for or against the hierarchical aspect of honorifics, are not entirely wrong, but the reason for such diverse views is that each focuses too much on a particular part of modern honorifics, or attempts to bundle together all types of honorific use by means of a simple umbrella term. Honorifics today are used with a variety of motivations, and situationally offer different socio-pragmatic properties. As previously mentioned, conventional honorifics typically occur in three situations: *jooge kankei* (status and age differences), *shinso kankei* (familiarity) and *kookyoo no ba* (formal public situations). These situations differ in terms of motivational factors and present different pragmatic effects. First, *jooge kankei*. This has nothing to do with class distinctions determined by birth/family background. It is *situationally* higher or lower in status, power and intangible almsgiving (*onkei*). The president of a company may be more highly ranked in a situation with her employees (status), but is lower-ranked in the presence of her son's teacher since the son is indebted to the teacher in relation to education (*onkei*); the teacher may, however, use honorifics to demonstrate mutual respect. If she violates a traffic rule, she may use some honorifics with a police officer who has more power in this context, although nowadays the police do use polite forms with citizens. The president may be humble with her counterpart in another company, especially in negotiations in which she is seen to be in a weaker position. When talking with her mother-in-law, she may use some honorifics with her to show respect (age difference). In this way, *jooge kankei* changes in accordance with the speaker's situation and with whom she is interacting. This means that *jooge kankei* is situationally driven, and *almost all people in Japanese society use honorifics as a tool to manifest it in different social settings*. Watanabe (1994: 60) interprets honorific use in *jooge kankei* as "maintaining the public order" by explaining that "honorific use is the signal of one's awareness of the social order as well as one's respect for it".

While *jooge kankei* is a vertical distance, *shinso kankei* (familiarity) is a horizontal distance. Strangers use honorifics with each other (mutual respect) because creating distance makes both interactants feel comfortable. As they become closer, they use fewer and lower-level honorifics. If there is an age difference between them, the junior may maintain certain honorifics such as addressee honorifics, but non-honorific use occurs more frequently as a sign of intimacy, or depending on the nature of an interaction.

Third, in *kookyoo no ba* (formal public settings), speakers use honorifics regardless of social differences between them and the audience. Honorific use in this kind of setting displays *aratamari* (改まり ceremonial) as defined by Iritani (1978) and Tsujimura (1989), or *hinkaku hoji* (品格保持 maintaining one's grace and dignity) by Watanabe (1994). In *kookyoo no ba*, one's skillful use of honorifics is publically exposed, and a fluent command of honorifics is closely associated with a high-level education and good upbringing. For example, a school principal uses honorifics in his speech that are directed toward the students at a graduation ceremony. This is not because he shows deference to the students, but because he is being exposed to the public, in which other distinguished guests and most likely students' families are present (as by-standers) as well as the teachers, the principal shows a refined attitude as an educated person, which in turn represents the good image of his school.

Using honorifics to convey a public image seems to be quite common in Japanese society today. Oishi (1984) defines today's honorifics as *shoogyoo keigo* (commercial honorifics) and observes their high-level and excessive usage in service industries. Watanabe (1994) interprets this as 'power' entailment because customers have economic power to benefit companies. Therefore, it can be interpreted as manifesting *kookyoo no ba* because honorifics are utilised in the service industry and employees are trained to use them fluently before being allowed to serve customers. In a commercially competitive society, customers are highly regarded, but at the same time companies endeavour to maintain their positive social image and reputation. Training employees to use appropriate honorifics, to bow deeply, to smile and be attentive certainly aims to attract customers and get good business results. Because technologies and products are easily and swiftly shared, companies' success often depends on how they serve customers and the image they convey to the public.

The nature of honorific has changed considerably since the governmental reforms implemented just after the Second World War. Although honorifics maintain the indexing of *jooge kankei*, they are situationally driven and *jooge kankei* is experienced by almost everybody in all kinds of social setting. On the other hand, honorifics have been used to a greater degree in public presentations (cf. Koyama, 2011: 228), and, on the basis of egalitarianism, mutually between people. For example, doctors and public servants seldom used honorifics with patients and visitors 40 years ago, but today use them to show mutual respect. Recently, some restaurants refused to serve customers who did not use honorifics and spoke to waiters abruptly. Even in *jooge kankei*, seniors nowadays use honorifics with juniors to maintain their social dignity as highly-educated people. In many ways, the government's ideological statement about honorific use seems to have permeated Japanese society. How, then, do people in general consider honorific use today? The next sub-section examines this question by discussing recent survey results.

### *6.3.2 How the Japanese generally perceive honorifics today*

*Bunka-choo* (文化庁 Agency for Cultural Affairs) is an extra-ministerial bureau of *Monbu Kagaku-Shoo* (文部科学省 Ministry of Education, Culture, Sports, Science and Technology) and every year it conducts a poll to gain insight into people's opinions about their lives and daily circumstances. One of the sections of *Bunka-choo*, *Kokugo-ka* (国語課 Japanese Language Section), investigates how speakers of Japanese judge and use various aspects of the Japanese language. Questions about honorifics occupy a part of the survey, and the answers illustrate how speakers of Japanese grasp, feel and judge honorifics and their use. Similar surveys are conducted independently by NHK (日本放送協会 *Nippon Hoosoo Kyookai*, the Japan broadcasting corporation) on a regular basis, as well as by *Kokuritsu Kokugo Kenkyuu-jo* (国立国語研究所 National Institute for Japanese Language). In the following, some survey results relevant to this sub-section are illustrated.

Honorifics, though a part of Japanese language, are not naturally learnt and so never native to Japanese people. They are consciously learnt, memorised, practised and finally (or hopefully) used smoothly. School children at around 10 to 12 years of age start learning to use addressee honorifics, *desu/masu* forms, with their teacher. When junior high school students join a sports club, the *senpai/koohai* (seniors/juniors) relationship in club activities encourages them to learn a few *sonkei*-styles but it is rare to get to grips with *kenjoo*-styles, although on a few occasions they may learn how to approach their seniors in a humble way. At senior high school (age 15–18), more *sonkei*-styles and politeness strategies continue to be learnt, but they are used mainly with teachers, unless students work part-time in a shop in which case they memorise a manual of honorifics. Some *kenjoo*-styles may start occurring at university, though it depends on individual students and the degree to which they are exposed to the public (e.g. working part-time, organising group activities).

Learning honorifics more systematically (and quite seriously) only begins when people start working. One of the first things new employees face upon entering the company is *keigo* training, from how to answer the phone, welcome visitors and serve customers to formulaic expressions in business and even how to bow and smile.

In this way, honorifics are not instilled in native speakers of Japanese, and yet working situations and social interactions inevitably involve the expectation that honorifics be used appropriately and smoothly. One of the surveys conducted by *Bunka-choo* in 1995 revealed that only 15.1% of Japanese speakers regarded themselves as fluent in honorifics, 52.2% as just good at using them and 29.2% as not being able to use honorifics sufficiently while wanting to use them more. While feeling that they are not able to use honorifics, 95.7% of the respondents to the NHK survey in 1987 answered that *they consider keigo necessary*. Perhaps this explains why a huge number of books on *keigo* are published each year, with impressive titles such as '*Keigo* as a business weapon', 'Excellent businesspersons excellent in *keigo*', and 'Lead over others with *keigo*'. The dilemma is that people believe in the necessity of *keigo* in their social life and yet feel they cannot freely use it as 'natives' (though nobody in the world is a native speaker of *keigo*!), which drives them to purchase books on the subject and to make an effort to improve their *keigo*.

In spite of difficulties with honorific use, *Japanese people do not expect honorifics to be simplified or abandoned.* The 1995 *Bunka-choo* survey revealed that only 18.3% of the respondents agreed with the idea of *keigo* simplification. In the same survey, 78.3% of them supported the suggestion that honorifics should be differentiated according to where and who they are interacting with. The 2016 *Bunka-choo* survey also revealed that 65.1% of respondents supported the statement '*keigo* is a part of the traditional beauty of Japanese language, and so its rich expressions should be maintained', while only 26.1% agreed that '*keigo* should be simplified and easy to grasp, which will be suitable for our new age'. Asamatsu (2013[2003]), citing similar results obtained by the 1979 and 1985 NHK surveys, assumes that this finding is closely related to socio-economic diversity and the different values and lifestyles experienced in modern Japan; Japanese people are now appreciative and accepting of such diversity. According to Asamatsu, this attitude is now casting honorifics in a new role: *approval and recognition of individual differences*. This is an interesting assumption because when we encounter people from different backgrounds we often step back and keep a certain distance, not necessarily wanting to avoid them but rather trying to accept and respect our differences as they may hold different values and have a different background (e.g. overseas experience, employment by a university after a long career in industry). While appreciating differences, however, we tend to act more cautiously and this is where honorific use comes in. After all, honorific use creates a social or psychological distance, and the distance here serves to tolerate differences.

The above assumption is related to the following striking result revealed by the 1995 *Bunka-choo* survey; 71.4% of the respondents believed that *it is better to use honorifics with younger people in certain situations.* Kitahara (1995) assumes that this is because the seniority system is no longer a tradition in Japanese society as younger people may occupy senior positions at work; thus older people in junior positions are expected to use honorifics with younger people. However, even if *jooge kankei* is observed, many university professors now use honorifics with their students even when they are talking with them individually (while it is a norm to use honorifics in class as professors are exposed to the public). University administration staff also use honorifics with students at the enquiry desk whereas students in the 1970s were not treated in this way (as was my personal experience). This kind of change is reflected in the 1997 survey conducted by *Bunka-choo*, in which 74.7% of the respondents agreed with the idea that *doctors should use honorifics with patients to demonstrate mutual respect.*

All these examples may indicate that **Japanese society today is beginning to place more value on honorific use as a public performance rather than a demonstration of status and age differences.** In this regard, *keigo* is becoming a symbol of one's social image rather than a tool to display one's understanding of the social relationship with the other.

The 2017 *Bunka-choo* survey revealed that 73.9% of the respondents did not feel that honorific use works negatively when building up good relationships. In other words, *for a majority of people honorific use does not hinder them from forming good interpersonal relationships.* In spite of the belief that honorifics create a certain distance from the other, socially or psychologically, they seem to be well accepted as a tool for successful interaction. Perhaps a certain distance in interaction may be required to maintain a good social relationship, and abandoning honorific use does not necessarily achieve fruitful communication.

The survey results conform to the academic interpretations of modern honorifics as discussed in the previous sub-section. In spite of the difficulties in acquiring honorifics, in Japanese society today, from an ideological perspective, honorifics are seen as necessary for successful interaction, and more strongly associated with public presentations and individuals' social image. However, this does not mean that the relationship between junior and senior colleagues (particularly in business sectors) can be ignored. Even if some seniors use honorifics with their juniors these days, the latter are definitely expected to use honorifics with their seniors, otherwise, they may face severe social sanctions. In contrast, using honorifics remains a personal choice for seniors in terms of their public image.

## Endnote 1: *Uchi* as the extension of the speaker's viewpoint to differentiate honorific styles

The *uchi/soto* distinction is one of the most cited notions in sociology, referring to Japanese social behaviour to explain how Japanese society operates. However, I employ the distinction simply as the extended notion of the speaker's viewpoint that grammatically contributes to the arrangement of linguistic constructions. It is because the distinction is a convenient tool to determine whether the person the speaker is dealing with in a particular situation should receive *sonkei* (deferential) or *kenjoo* (humble) style, or neither.

Although *uchi* members are selected via social relationships between speaker and referent persons (thus *uchi* to this extent is a social concept), *uchi* is primarily linguistic-based, and shows where the speaker's viewpoint is anchored. Therefore, it is not derived from 'group-consciousness', 'dependence' or any other 'unique' aspect of Japanese psychology, as has often been discussed in sociology and social psychology (see Endnote 2 below).

The speaker's viewpoint usually refers to the way in which the speaker observes a phenomenon, and anchors its reference point on a particular object, by means of which the phenomenon is described. Deictic terms such as 'yesterday' (from the viewpoint of the time at which the speaker is talking), 'left' (on the basis of the speaker's body position) and 'here' (pointing at the place where the speaker is talking) are typical examples that indicate the speaker's viewpoint. Deixis is a relative viewpoint, and so changes in accordance with the placement of the reference point. However, another type of viewpoint is also intrinsically involved in sentence construction, a grammatical feature that I call the '**Speaker's view**' (Obana, 2000). For example:

(1) 昨日のりこさんが遊びに来ました。

| | | | |
|---|---|---|---|
| Kinoo | Noriko-san ga | | asobi-ni-ki-mashi-ta. |
| yesterday | Noriko | Nom | play-to-come-Polite-Past |

'Yesterday Noriko came to see me.'

The use of *ki-* (to come) in the verb phrase in example (1) shows that Noriko's action is described by placing the speaker's view upon the I-person (experiencer) because the action is directed toward the I-person. It may be argued that it is natural for the speaker to place his viewpoint on himself because the experience is the speaker's own. However, it is possible to separate the Speaker's view from the I-person (experiencer) in other languages.[18] For example,

(2) John helped me.
(3) Somebody stole my purse.

Both examples (2) and (3) are the speaker's own experiences, and yet the speaker observes the I-person (the speaker himself, the experiencer)

18 To the best of my knowledge, Japanese is exceptional in that the Speaker's view is placed upon the I-Speaker, and many other languages commonly place the Speaker's view outside the phenomenon the speaker is describing.

separately because the Speaker's view is not placed upon the I-person but outside the phenomenon. Therefore, whether the experiencer is the speaker or not, the grammatical structure is not changed in English, as illustrated in example (4).

(4) Susan helped me.
John helped Susan.
I helped John.

The utterances in (4) show that whether the experiencer (the receiver of the action, 'help') is the I-person, Susan or John or whether the giver of the action is the I-person, John, or Susan, the basic grammatical structure is not changed (i.e. somebody helped somebody else). This is because the Speaker's view is constantly placed outside the whole phenomenon, which is concealed behind the linguistic construction. Obana (1999, 2000) calls the English view the '**Isolation type**' because the speaker (or precisely the Speaker's view) and the I-person (the experiencer) are isolated, and the speaker views the I-person in the same way as Susan and John in example (4).

Japanese, on the other hand, does not isolate the speaker from the I-person in describing the I-speaker's own experience. Examples (2) and (3) can be translated as examples (4) and (5) respectively:

(5) ジョンさんが手伝ってくれました。
Jon-san ga tetsudat-te-kure-mashi-ta.
John Nom help-TE-receive-Polite-Past
'John gave help toward me (and I accept it).'
(the closest translation of the utterance)

*Note*. It is not acceptable to utter:
*Jon-san ga watashi o tetsudai-mashi-ta.
Nom myself Acc help-Polite-Past
'John helped me.'

(6) 本を盗まれました。
Hon o nusuma-re-mashi-ta.
book Acc steal-Pass-Polite-Past
'(I experienced) my book (had been) stolen.'

*Note*. It is quite unnatural to say:
*Dareka ga watashi no hon o nusumi-mashi-ta.
somebody Nom my book Acc steal-Polite-Past
'Somebody stole my book.'

In example (5), by using the auxiliary *-kure* (lit. give toward), the action 'help' is oriented toward the I-person; the Speaker's view is assimilated with the I-person. In example (6), the use of an indirect passive implies that the Speaker's view is placed upon the I-experiencer. This linguistic arrangement is called the '**Integration type**' (Obana, 1999, 2000) because the Speaker's view follows the I-person, and is assimilated with the perspective of the experiencer (the I-person).

In a similar way, 'I helped John' is translated as:

(7) ジョンさんを手伝ってあげました。
Jon-san o tetsudat-te-age-mashi-ta.
John Acc help-TE-(give away)-Polite-Past
'(I) gave help away to John.'

In example (7), the Speaker's view shadows the I-person, thus 'to help' is taken as an action given away by the I-person to 'John', which is entailed in the auxiliary *-ageru* (to give away).

The difference between English and Japanese is illustrated in Figure 6.2 (Obana, 2000: 145f). It should be noted that the Speaker's view has nothing to do with objective or subjective descriptions.[19] It is a grammatical feature that regulates how sentences are to be constructed, irrespective of the speaker's psychological state. Indeed, the Speaker's view placed outside the I-person in the case of English looks as though the speaker observed himself objectively by creating distance from the phenomenon. However, the Speaker's view is purely grammatical and intrinsically exists as a pivotal axis for linguistic architecture. Objective and subjective descriptions, on the other hand, are the speaker's free choice based on his psychological judgement. Both descriptions are possible whether the language is Isolation or Integration type by using particular expressions (e.g. 'a long speech' is more objective than 'a lengthy speech').

Japanese is speaker-oriented (though metaphorically) in constructing a sentence, and the Speaker's view follows the experiencer's or I-person's action. Therefore, when other people are described, the speaker must choose which person will be the one the Speaker's view is placed upon. This is the extension of the Speaker's view to another person. The view is first extended to people in the speaker's social proximity. For example, the speaker's family members are primarily selected as the target upon which the view is anchored. As shown in example (8), irrespective of the relationship between speaker and listener, the speaker's family members usually receive the Speaker's view as a focus:

19 See Morita's (1995) view in Endnote 2 of this chapter, in which he associates the Speaker's view with Japanese mentality.

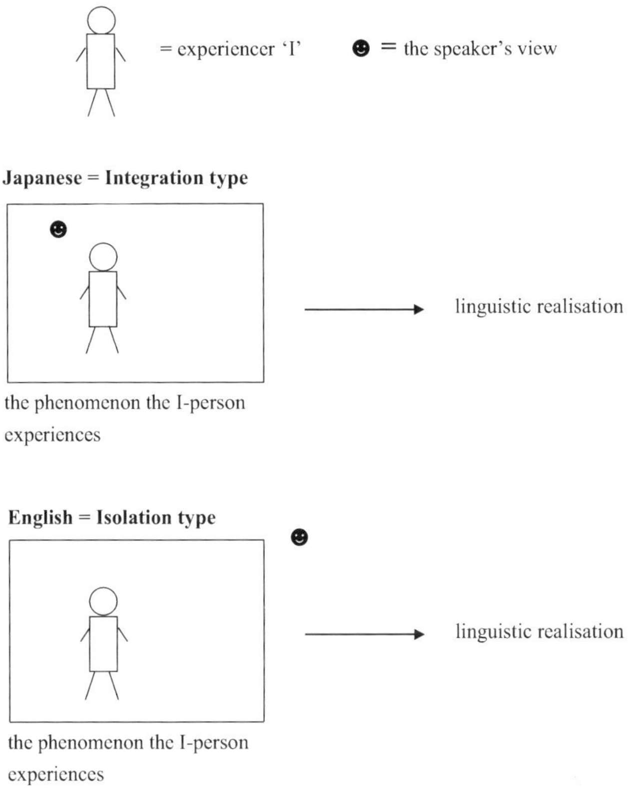


*Figure 6.2* The Speaker's view in Japanese and English

(8) 妹に英語を教えてやってくれませんか。

| | | | | |
|---|---|---|---|---|
| Imooto | ni | eigo o | oshie-te-yat-te-kure-mase-n | ka. |
| younger sister | to | English Acc | teach-TE-give-TE-give-Polite-Neg | Q |

'Could you please teach English to my sister?'

By using the auxiliary *-yat* (*-yaru* = to throw down to), the speaker is humble on behalf of his sister, and by using the auxiliary *-kure* (to give toward), the speaker treats his sister's reception of 'teaching' as if he were receiving it. **Family members are called the speaker's "absolute *uchi* members"** (Obana, 2000: 194) because they are treated as the speaker's *uchi* no matter where or when they are talked about.

Honorific use is largely determined by the speaker's *uchi/soto* distinction as the extension of the Speaker's view. Depending on the situation in which the speaker is placed, the Speaker's view follows a certain socially-categorised person, which results in the speaker treating that person's action as if it were the speaker's own. Therefore, as shown in example (6–1) in the text of this chapter, the Speaker's view is extended to her company staff when interacting with someone from a different company. Note, however, that whether or not the speaker is psychologically close to the other person is irrelevant to the choice of an *uchi* member. *Uchi* is a social categorisation, and a referent person is determined as *uchi* in accordance with where the speaker is positioned in relation to the other interactant.

## Endnote 2: The *uchi/soto* distinction as Japanese mentality?

### *The concept of* uchi

The *uchi/soto* distinction is well-known as a sociological term, and is used as a convenient tool to verify that Japan is a collectivist culture. For example, how companies are organised, traditions and other social behaviours in Japanese society are believed to be derived from the *uchi/soto* distinction, which is strongly associated with group-ism, differentiating between 'us' and 'others'.

According to Nakane (1970), the origin of the term *uchi* lies in the word *ie* (家 house), and *uchi* is portrayed in the household structure (the *kanji* for *uchi* is also read as *ie*). During the Edo period (1603–1867), those who belonged to the same clan (大名 *daimyoo*) called their clan *o-ie* (*o-* as an honorific prefix), meaning 'the household of one's lord', and were loyal to their *ie*. Because the Shogunate controlled all of the clans and could be quick to destroy them, *samurai* members of the same clan often sacrificed their own lives and those of their family members to secure their lord's family line as, if itended, they would be cast out from *samurai* society.

It seems that "the concept of this traditional institution, *ie*, still persists in the various group identities" (Nakane, 1970: 7) in modern Japan. Indeed, analysts of Japanese society from outside the country in particular argue that one of the major reasons for Japan's economic success is *uchi* consciousness in how companies are organised. For example, Vogel (1979) describes the systems applied in Japanese companies, and how individuals are related to their companies. He emphasises Japanese people's group behaviour in company organisation, information collection and technological development, which he believes has led to Japan's success. Reischauer (1977, 1988) asserts that behind the success story of the Japanese economy lies Japanese people's willingness to sacrifice themselves for their own group.[20] Employees are content with conformity to group rules and their work is not primarily for earning money but for seeking satisfaction from uniformity within their

20 However, as discussed in Endnote 2 of Chapter 1, survey results identify the contrary: American workers showed more loyalty to their workplace than did Japanese workers.

group. Zimmerman (1985) also discusses a similar mentality of the Japanese in his investigation of network systems in business.

Araki (1973) explains that the Japanese, as descendants of an agricultural society,[21] subscribe to group logic and standards (hunting societies, in contrast, resulted in an individualistic mentality). In contrast to Nakane's (1970) emphasis on the vertical organisation of Japanese society, Yoneyama (1976) cites the importance of its horizontal aspect that also signifies the group consciousness of Japanese people. Thus, collectivist characteristics seem to be derived from the *uchi* consciousness, a term that has been equated with group consciousness.

Those who advocate the *uchi* or group consciousness of Japanese people have sought further evidence from various fields, such as cultural heritage (how Japan has accepted outside cultures, e.g. Sofue [1976]), history (*mura* 邑 a small living group) and *uji* [氏 clan] in ancient Japan to the *ie* system in feudal times, e.g. Murakami et al. [1979] and Kawamoto [1982]), or fables and mythology (Kawai, 1982).

### *Weak ego boundaries due to the* **uchi** *consciousness*

The *uchi* consciousness has also been analysed from the perspective of social psychology. Doi (1981) uses the term *amae* (dependence), which originates in a child's dependence on his mother, and attempts to illustrate the Japanese *uchi* consciousness as the extension of one's *ego* to one's group. This is alleged to be due to weak ego boundaries in the psychology of Japanese people (e.g. Ide et al., 1986; Inetomi, 1963; Kogi, 1976); *ego* and *alter* are not clearly distinguished in the Japanese mind, which fosters the readily accessible extension of the ego to the other, forming a group consciousness. In contrast, a clear boundary is drawn between *uchi* and *soto*. A further claim is made that Americans (perhaps meaning 'white Anglo-Saxon Americans') exhibit a clear boundary between *ego* and *alter* but the boundary is not so clear between *uchi* and *soto*.

As such conjectures are purely speculative due to a lack of scientific evidence or statistical results, we can neither accept nor argue against them. However, I believe that *ego* and *alter* are basic elements of human psychology and so wonder whether they differ between societies. The clear existence of *ego* creates all sorts of social, cultural and historical phenomena, such as conflict, fear, consciousness of the other, all emotions and the will to live. The differentiation between my things and those of others is material evidence of

21 This view depends on how far back in the past one goes. Rice-farming skills were imported around 3,000 years ago but it was not until the third century that rice farming became common all over Japan. Until then, Japanese people were hunting in the mountains and sea. In Europe, the Romans initiated agriculture to feed their soldiers as their territories were expanding and around 3,000 years ago the agrochemicals needed for wine-making had already been introduced.

our *ego*. In this respect, the clear existence of *ego*, which differentiates the self from the other, exists in all cultures.

If weak ego boundaries exist in the psychology of Japanese people, does this mean that they accept and comply with group decisions without questioning? Why, then, are there so many stories about family crises, divorce, child abuse and children going against the wishes of their parents? If the *uchi* consciousness in a company is derived from such weak ego boundaries, why do we never cease to hear about conflict, competition and cheating between colleagues?

Group solidarity exists in every society. However, this has nothing to do with weak ego boundaries or the *uchi* consciousness that discards *soto* people. It is formed as a result of our need/want to be involved with society (our basic need as a social being; cf. Section 2.2.2). It is plausible that group solidarity may be stronger when groups face their enemies, a crisis coming from the outside or if their society enforces rigid and harsh rules on its members. For example, revolutionary groups have a strong sense of camaraderie, and sacrifice themselves to achieve their aims. However, this phenomenon has nothing to do with weak ego boundaries or dependence. The *ie* system during the Edo period is another example. It forced its members to prioritise their clan over their private life because the Shogunate was observing the clans (even using spies, or *ninja*) to seek a chance to destroy them, confiscate their fief and make all *samurai* members masterless (losing their jobs, land and houses). Therefore, those *ie* (clan) members inevitably developed a strong sense of solidarity in order to maintain their clan, their families and subordinate soldiers.

### *Is seeing the* **uchi** *consciousness as Japanese mentality justifiable?*

There is no shortage of examples of Japanese psychology; some attempt to be reasonably neutral, but others are so extreme as to emphasise the uniqueness of the Japanese. However, they commonly believe that the *uchi* consciousness, which forms groupism in various social situations, is an inherent, traditionally handed-down, deep-rooted element of the psychology of Japanese people.

The question here is whether such analyses are justifiable. Company systems in Japan, for example, may emphasise group cooperation but we do not know whether such cooperation derives from Japanese mentality or is a business tactic because group work is more efficient and creates greater profits. Furthermore, just because group work or cooperation is witnessed in certain areas of Japanese society, it does not mean that it prevails in all social activities.

It is more questionable whether Japanese groupism is derived from weak ego boundaries and whether dependence, based on this, is prevalent in Japanese social life. First, no experimental or statistical evidence has been presented to support the claim that Japanese psychology is unique, and so it is purely speculative. Second, it is easy to find examples to support this statement but it is equally easy to find counter-examples (for example, those cited by Sugimoto and Mouer [1995] below). This is because social phenomena are diverse, dynamic, volatile and situational, and a mere observation of certain phenomena in a limited way is not sufficient to describe a society as a whole.

It is true that we may be influenced by established social systems and may learn and try to conform to those systems as social beings. However, this does not mean that such systems can be used to predict every social behaviour of its members in various aspects of their social life. Japanese company systems may differ from those of their Western counterparts. However, just because they are organised in an apparently *ie*-system way, it does not necessarily mean that Japanese people's social lives are organised in the same way or that an allegedly group-oriented approach to business organisation is derived from the psychology of the Japanese such as dependence and weak ego boundaries. It is highly debatable whether this psychology is sufficiently inherent to characterise Japanese people.

In this respect, Sugimoto and Mouer (1995) approach the relationship between social systems and people in social life quite cautiously. They argue that, just because certain social behaviours are witnessed, they should not be generalised to represent a society as a whole. There may be other reasons for such behaviours, and they cite one possibility as ideological beliefs stemming from the upper echelons of society camouflaging a variety of social phenomena when presenting themselves as the archetype or embodiment of that society as a whole. Thus, social phenomena apparently converging into collectivism as the extension of *uchi* consciousness are often controlled by and moulded into those ideological beliefs.

Sugimoto and Mouer do not deny certain collectivistic features in Japanese society but they do object to the direct association of collectivism with the characterisation of Japanese people. They provide counterexamples to demonstrate a strong ego boundary or distinct individualism in Japanese traditional culture. For instance, traditional sports (such as *judo*, *kendo* and *karate*) are not intended to create group solidarity; rather, they are spiritual training for individuals. Hobbies such as *pachinko* (vertical pinball) and the growing of *bonsai* (a miniature potted plant) do not require another person to be involved. Japanese houses are surrounded by brick walls while houses and gardens in Australia are open to the public. Family members have their own chopsticks and rice bowl, whereas Western plates, knives and forks are shared. Sugimoto and Mouer do not mean to claim that Japan is an individualist society; rather, they warn that there is always danger in characterising a society based only on fragments of cultural phenomena.

### *The* uchi *consciousness implemented in linguistic terms*

More dangerous is making direct connections between social behaviour and linguistic construction by declaring that social behaviour is manifested in linguistic structure. (e.g. Araki, 1990, 1994; Ikegami, 2000; Makino, 1996; Miller, 1982; Moeran, 1998; Morita, 1995, 1998; Yamashita, 1986). For example, although Morita (1995) appropriately points out the idea of the speaker's viewpoint (or the Speaker's view in this book) as the central focus in sentence construction in Japanese, he extends this viewpoint to describe Japanese mentality. He assumes that Japanese people cannot observe phenomena in an objective way because the speaker's viewpoint is placed upon the speaker himself and this leads to his prioritising his own group *uchi* in his social life. He then extracts evidence of this mentality by referring to many sentence structures in Japanese in which the *uchi* consciousness is concealed.

Makino (1996: 11) defines the concept of *uchi* as *kakawari no kuukan* (関わりの空間 space of involvement, translation his own). First, he describes cultural phenomena that demonstrate this concept (e.g. social gathering, uniforms, *sekentei* [世間体 one's view of the outer world, translation my own]). He also connects this with linguistic examples (ellipsis, giving/receiving expressions such as *-kureru/ageru*, demonstratives, case markers). Furthermore, Makino talks about 'ambiguity' in the Japanese language as further evidence of the *uchi* consciousness.

Let us look at some of Makino's arguments. First, I do not see why *uchi* is equated with 'space of involvement'. Space of involvement exists in every society. How involvement is realised may differ from culture to culture but, as mentioned in Section 2.2.1, desire for 'involvement' is a basic element of human nature in every society. Does this mean that wherever involvement is witnessed lies the consciousness of *uchi*? When two baseball teams play a game, where is *uchi*? I suppose that 'my' team would be *uchi* members, but in reality both teams are involved with the same game. Social involvement is not unique to Japanese society but exists in every society, and does so without distinguishing 'my members' and 'the other members' (though supporting one's team is a natural thing to do in a game).

Second, his examples of social phenomena cannot be accepted as evidence of the *uchi* consciousness. For example, Makino compares barbeques in the West (held in open spaces: the individualists' way) with hot-pot parties in Japan (held inside the house with *uchi* members: the Japanese way). He also claims that uniform systems in Japanese society indicate solidarity. However, a closer examination of these examples raises a number of questions. Barbeques are indeed held outdoors but this has nothing to do with the individualist's social act. Barbeque parties are normally held with one's own friends (one's *uchi* members) whether they are held in the garden or a picnic area (*soto* people are not invited; they can just smell the food). Parties may be held in open spaces because the host's house is small[22] or the weather is inclement (in Britain, I seldom saw barbeque parties held outside because of the cold weather and frequent rain).

22 I am living in a rural area newly developed within the last 20 years. The houses are detached and have relatively large gardens. I often see barbeque parties in neighbours' gardens in spring and summer.

Makino also states that uniforms in Japan manifest the solidarity of the *uchi* group. However, uniforms are prevalent in many cultures. Police, doctors, nurses, security guards, shopkeepers and so on wear uniforms so that others can easily spot and approach them; their uniforms thus assist others. Factory workers' uniforms are worn for practical reasons. School uniforms may convey a school's identity or prevent children from skipping school.

Makino also talks about *sekentei* (one's view of the outer world), which he claims is prevalent in Japanese society. However, if a location consists of families who have lived there for generations, those residents may have a strong sense of community. On the other hand, communities comprised of more transient residents may not form such *sekentei*. This has nothing to do with the difference between Japanese and American psychology, even if Makino strongly believed this to be the case based on his own experience. Rather, it concerns the way in which one's own community is formed, irrespective of the culture; regional differences can also often be observed. Alternatively, each family's way of interacting with the community may create a different consciousness of the outer world.

As mentioned in this chapter, linguistic construction in Japanese is based on the Speaker's view. In this respect, some of the examples Makino provides may explain how this view is involved. However, those examples should not be equated with the Japanese *uchi* consciousness or the Japanese mentality that drives their behaviour according to the *uchi/soto* distinction (in other words, whether or not such Japanese mentality exists is not our concern here; the direct connection of linguistic phenomena with such mentality is to be questioned).

Ellipsis, for example, commonly occurs in Japanese and, according to Makino, is due to the *uchi* consciousness (so that information is known only to the speaker's *uchi* group and thus information well known to the group is not verbalised in actual interaction). However, Makino's assumption seems to result from confusion between grammatical conditions and the mental state of language users. In the Japanese language, ellipsis commonly occurs when an object is topicalised, focused on or spotlighted. For example, the omission of *watashi* (I) is quite common because the speaker's viewpoint is focused upon the speaker. A third person or any other object is omitted when the speaker's viewpoint is placed on it in the flow of conversation, which is called 'topic continuity' (Givón, 1983; Hinds, 1980, 1982, 1983, 1984); and ellipsis occurs no matter where the topicalised item is positioned in the grammatical construction (i.e. whether it occupies the object, subject or complement position). This is called 'zero anaphora in topic continuity'. When the topic is focused on, it is omitted in the subsequent discourse until a new topic is introduced or the speaker's attention shifts to something else (Obana, 2003). This is a grammatical phenomenon rather than the speaker's territorial psychology.

Ellipsis also occurs for other reasons. For example, certain auxiliaries (e.g. *-tsumorida* = intend to, *-yooda* = look like, *-garu* = showing a third person's action, such as *ureshi-garu* – [someone else]) is happy, verbs (e.g. *omou* versus *omotte iru*) and adjectives (emotive terms such as *ureshii, kanashii*) already indicate whether the grammatical subject is the first or third person:

Terms to indicate the agent is the first person:
-*tsumorida* (I intend to do), *omou* (I think)
*ureshii* (I am happy), *kanashii* (I am sad)
Terms to indicate the agent is the third person:
-*garu* (*ureshi-garu* = someone is happy)
*omotte iru* (someone is thinking)

These examples, in fact, can be counterexamples to Makino's claims because they distinguish between *ego* and *alter*, though I would not claim that Japanese people have stronger *ego* boundaries than English speakers on the basis of such linguistic fragments.

There may be other reasons for the use of ellipsis, but listing them all is beyond the scope of this Endnote (see Obana [2000: 271–331] for further discussion on ellipsis). The point to be emphasised is that ellipsis occurs for grammatical or pragmatic (contextual) reasons rather than as the result of the speaker's *uchi* consciousness or weak ego boundaries.

Language does indeed reflect culture, and culture influences language development (for example, the Japanese language reflects a Buddhist influence, with many words and expressions derived from this religion). However, language also presents a range of more contradictory, complex, diverse and dynamic features. Therefore, fragments of linguistic units (collected conveniently to support a certain hypothesis) do not necessarily involve or characterise a whole society and its people. The *uchi/soto* distinction as a grammatical feature indeed determines linguistic constructions in Japanese. However, it does not necessarily prove that Japanese mentality is created by such a distinction because other languages of allegedly collectivist cultures do not offer the same linguistic arrangements as those of Japanese. For example, in Chinese and Korean, although China and South Korea are categorised as collectivist cultures, the Speaker's view is foremost (cf. Endnote 1 of this chapter) in the same way as English and German, i.e. the viewpoint is placed outside the phenomenon the speaker observes. Social systems are not always reflected in language system because we find discrepancies between linguistic and social phenomena.

## Endnote 3: Functions of the *yoroshiku onegaishimasu* formula

The *yoroshiku onegaishimasu* formula has been analysed in a number of ways in the field of pragmatics (Matsumoto 1988, 1993; Ohashi, 2003; Pizziconi, 2003; Takekuro, 2005; Wierzbicka, 1991). However, in this Endnote, I discuss the functions of the formula in varied situations.

First, let us look at the original meaning of the formula. The word *yoroshiku* is an adverb derived from the adjective, *yoroshii*. This adjective is used when a more highly-positioned person gives permission for something or praises a lower-positioned person in a condescending manner. *Yoroshii* can therefore be used in an interrogative sentence, as in '*Yoroshii desu ka?*' (Is [it] okay with you?), to obtain permission from someone the speaker is obliged to be deferential to. This means that *yoroshii* is used when seeking a more highly-positioned person's consent. The *kanji* 宜 that used to be applied to this adjective is read as *mube/ube* in old Japanese, originally meaning 'order, affirmation, acceptance by a higher person', and used exclusively as Imperial decrees. Thus, by combining *yoroshiku* with *o-negai-suru* (the humble-marked verb *negau* = wish, hope), the formula originally means, 'With your permission, my wish would be accepted, which I'm humbly requesting.' This is a humble greeting in which the speaker implies that the decision is entirely left to the hearer.

The formula is typically used in the following situations:

Group1: Greetings in self-introductory speech, in the initial meeting and on ceremonial occasions, implying the commencement of a new relationship or activity
Group 2: Part of a request, i.e. the actual request form is replaced by the formula
Group 3: Request followed by the formula to confirm the request

In all of these situations, the formula reflects the speaker's Role-Identity (e.g. a newcomer to the group, pursuing jobs), which is also recognised and granted by the hearer. This mutual recognition allows the speaker to utter the formula for greeting, requesting and confirming the request. Without the recognition of mutual role-identities whether tacitly, visually or verbally, the formula does not occur; if it does, it sometimes becomes an imposition on the hearer (see example [4] below).

Group 1 is the use of the formula as a ritual greeting. For example,

(1) 群馬県から来ました、村上節子です。どうぞよろしくお願いします。

| | | | |
|---|---|---|---|
| Gunma-ken | kara ki-mashi-ta, | Murakami Setsuko | desu. |
| Gunma-prefecture | from come-Polite-Past | | Polite |

Doozo yoroshiku onegai shimasu.
'I'm Murakami Setsuko from Gunma Prefecture. Nice to meet you.'

The formula in example (1) is a greeting when meeting someone else (or the audience) for the first time, i.e. the situation is defined, which expects the speaker as a newcomer (identity) to greet with the formula (role-performance), and this behaviour is also expected by the audience. Since in a self-introductory speech the formula is used at the end, its function is to mark the closing of the speech while its pragmatic effect is to show the speaker's humble attitude to the audience, assuming a good relationship with the hearer(s). I provided the English translation 'nice to meet you' by considering the situation in which example (1) occurs. However, its literal meaning is 'I humbly ask you to accept me as a newcomer, and I leave the decision to you.' Example (2) is another greeting:

(2) これからインタビューを始めます。よろしくお願いします。
Kore-kara intabyuu o hajime-masu. Yoroshiku onegai shimasu.
from now interview Acc begin-Polite
'We start an interview now. Thanks for your participation.'

The formula is ritually used just before an event starts. Example (2) is the situation just before the interview starts (task-based roles as interviewer and interviewee). I provided the translation 'thanks for your participation', but the interviewee may reply with the same formula; pragmatically, this can mean 'thanks for this opportunity'. In other cases, two sports teams bow (with their caps off) just before the game starts and use the formula with each other. In a similar way, on New Year's day, relatives may become formal and bow with this formula (*Kotoshi mo yoroshiku onegaishimasu* = We will be good to each other this year as well). By deliberately creating a formal setting, the members intend to start everything anew (forgetting the past) on New Year's day, reasserting family ties.

Group 2 shows that the formula functions as part of a request. Instead of clearly stating what the speaker wants the hearer to do, *yoroshiku onegai shimasu* serves to indicate what needs to be done. It is a strategy whereby the speaker avoids a direct demand, implying that a subsequent action or response is left to the hearer. For example:

(3) ここは駐車禁止となっていますので、よろしくお願いします。
Koko wa chuusha kinshi to nat-te-i-masu-node,
this Top parking ban Quote become-TE-Prog-Polite-since
yoroshiku onegai shimasu.
'As this place is for non-parking, I appreciate your understanding.'

Example (3) is an announcement of the regulation followed by the formula that implicitly asks the hearer to follow it without directly referring to what the hearer should do (i.e. no parking here). The formula in this case can be used provided that the speaker is in charge of the job (traffic control: Institutional Role-Identity). Without mutual recognition of this role between speaker and hearer (e.g. another driver utters example [3]), the formula would sound imposing.

The formula in Group 3 functions as the confirmation of a request. For example:

(4) 社員 ：課長、報告書を作成したんですが、見ていただけますか。

Kachoo, hookokusho o sakuseishi-ta-n-desu ga,
section manager report Acc complete-Past-Nomi-Polite Conj
mi-te-itadak-e-masu ka.
look-TE-receive[Hon]-possible-Polite Q
'Employee: Ma'am, I have completed the report. Could you please have a look?'

課長：ええ、いいですよ。今日中に見ておきます。

Ee, ii-desu yo. Kyoo-juu ni mi-te-oki-masu.
yes okay-Polite MD today-within look-TE-done-Polite
'Section Manager: Yes, okay. I'll have a look by tomorrow.'

社員：じゃ、よろしくお願いします。

Ja, yoroshiku onegai shimasu.
then
'Employee: Right. Thanks a lot'

*Shain* (staff) is a junior to *kachoo* (section manager), and so uses honorifics with the latter. *Kachoo* is female and uses addressee honorifics *desu/masu* just to be courteous to her junior. Both recognise that *shain* can request his senior to do certain jobs such as checking the document he completed, and the senior will do the job: their institutional roles. After *kachoo* agreed that she will check the document, *shain* uses the formula, confirming his request. The formula should be used only after the other's consent to fulfil the job; otherwise, the formula would be an imposing request.

# 7 Variations and derivations of honorific use

## Strategic honorifics

This chapter discusses variations and derivations of honorific use, or what I call 'strategic honorifics'. In Chapter 6, I addressed the fact that honorifics index a social or psychological distance, and the appropriate measurement of distance achieves felicitous and pertinent communication as the speaker has astutely recognised the social relationship with the other person. This is a normative interpretation of honorific use, and we have focused on politeness achieved through the use of norms of honorifics. However, honorifics do not always conform to their normative practices. They can be manipulated to allude to the speaker's stance, attitude and psychological state. Honorific terms, when used in speech-level shifts (see Section 7.2), can be seen as indicators of a shift in the speaker's psychological stance as this shift takes place audibly and in real-time. Honorifics are also practised as a personal style to betoken a refined and cool image or to emphasise a woman's femininity. In spite of apparently diverse and varied interpretations of such honorifics, however, they are derived from the so-called 'conventional' honorifics (or norms of honorifics), and form a parallel with the latter due to common motivations for their use.

### 7.0 Introduction

This chapter discusses how honorific terms are manipulated and used for different purposes in varied contexts. As discussed in Section 6.2.4, honorifics, or more precisely honorific markings, function as the indexing of a social or psychological distance, and norms of honorifics largely conform to the standardised measurement of such a distance. However, if distance is manipulated as the speaker's choice, honorific markings render different pragmatic effects, and reveal how the speaker has interpreted the given situation (e.g. conflict, gratitude), or in what way the speaker wants to present herself to the public (e.g. personal style, femininity). Some effects are regarded as 'polite', others 'neutral', and still others as 'impolite' or even 'offensive'. I call such variations and derivations of honorific use '**strategic honorifics**' in this book.

This chapter looks first at examples of strategic honorifics. Some examples were introduced previously, especially when clarifying that norms of honorifics are not a set of static, fixed rules but anticipate flexible and contingent adaptations to the given situation. This chapter provides further examples and analyses them in detail. The chapter then compares those honorific variations with norms of honorifics (i.e. conventional honorifics) and with the origin of honorifics (cf. Chapter 5). This reveals that, in spite of their different purposes and effects, these three types of honorifics maintain their basic nature, 'distance', and a variety of pragmatic effects modern honorifics offer can be traced to motivational factors involved with the origin of honorifics. In other words, norms of honorifics and their derivations form a pragmatic parallel, constituting 'two ends of a continuum' (Obana, 2016, 2017) pivotal to the origin of honorifics.

## 7.1 Norms and contingencies: Bicchieri's (2006) 'grammar of society'

In Chapter 3, I claimed that politeness is a social norm. I use the term 'social norm' as it is defined in sociology; social norms emerge in interaction rather than being given, and are negotiable to suit the given situation, the climate of ongoing interactions and the nature of the group. I then introduced Bicchieri's (2006) 'grammar of society' that is analogous with social norms. Just as the grammar of a language is "implicit in a language and define[s] it, social norms are implicit in the operations of a society and make it what it is" (ix). Furthermore, the grammar of a language allows linguistic units to be manipulated, reoriented, twisted and even tailored to indicate individuality. We create unique language products in actual communication, e.g. complex structures, written and spoken styles as well as personal styles, deviated word orders and gender differences. Such an astonishing diversity of language use, however, does not exist at random but shadows grammar; the grammar of a language is implicit however uniquely we create a sentence, phrase, paragraph and text, and serves as a cornerstone in our language use. This is shown in Figure 7.1 (a reproduction of Figure 3.2 in Section 3.2).

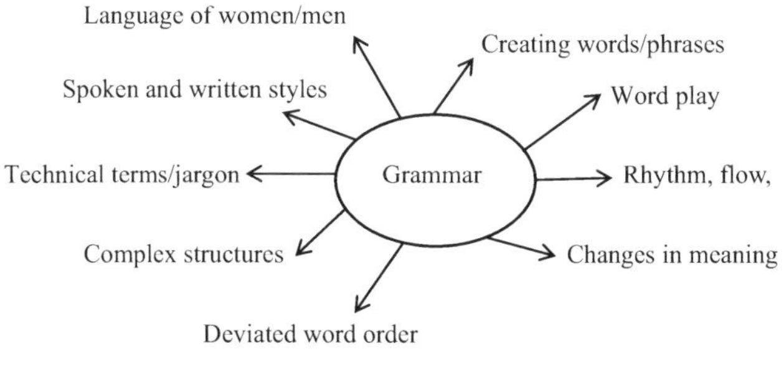


*Figure 7.1* Grammar and language use
(Obana, 2017: 305)

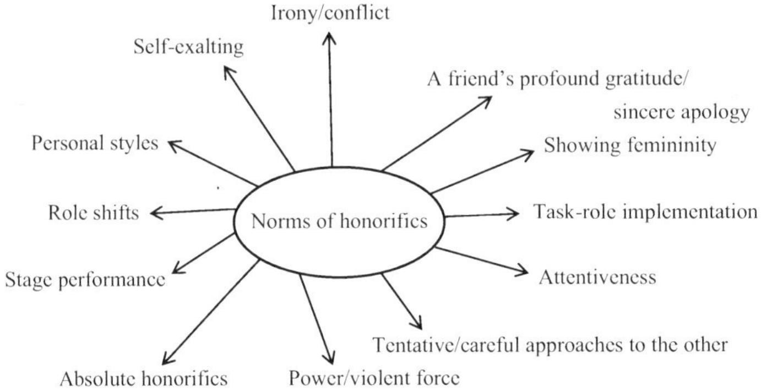


*Figure 7.2* Norms of honorifics and applications/deviations of honorific use (Obana, 2017: 306)

The correlation between the grammar of a language and linguistic realisations as such can apply to that between social norms and their practices in society. Social norms exist as the backbone of our social actions, but at the same time allow us to adjust and rectify social norms to suit the given situation. They may be manipulated to fit one's community or reshaped to benefit one's own social group. However, just as in the grammar of a language, so social norms are also inferred in the apparent diversity of social actions. Politeness, as a part of social norms, also works in a similar way. **Politeness as a social norm is implicit in our social actions while it is negotiable and adjusted to suit one's community as well as a given situation**.

The idea above can also apply to honorific phenomena. While conforming to norms of honorifics, we also act as creative creatures. We learn to take advantage of the nature of honorifics and manipulate them; we negotiate and re-define our interactional relationships, express our emotional states, and deliver subtle (situational or psychological) changes in dealing with the other. In other words, *norms of honorifics are implicit in these applications and derivations; they are a point of departure from which honorific terms are extensively applied to a variety of situations, giving rise to differing effects and diverse socio-pragmatic interpretations*. This is illustrated in Figure 7. 2 (a reproduction of Figure 3.3 in Section 3.2).

In Section 3.2, I briefly referred to some of the examples in Figure 7.2. In the following sections, further strategic honorifics are discussed together with examples.

## 7.2 Speech-level shifts[1]: The case of plus-level shifts

In Section 6.2.4, I stated that honorifics, or more precisely honorific markings, identify a social or psychological distance. Ikuta (1983) proposes that

1 This section is based on Obana (2016, 2017) and altered to suit the flow of this chapter.

politeness is basically a matter of social or attitudinal distance. The so-called 'conventional' honorifics are socially determined, which indicates that the measurement of distance is acceptable and so considered appropriate. On the other hand, honorific terms are often prompted in interaction between friends and close colleagues who normally do not use honorifics with each other. Seniors, who normally are not expected to use honorifics with their juniors, also might use honorifics with the latter for some psychological reasons. While maintaining the basic speech level with plain forms, the interactants may suddenly use honorific terms, and imply a different psychological stance at the moment of the occurrence of honorific terms. This phenomenon is a part of 'speech-level shifts'. Speech-level shifts occur because speakers are "active agents who strategically choose to use honorific or non-honorific forms to achieve their interactional goals" (Cook, 2011: 3658).

Speech-level shifts mean that honorific forms, especially *masu/desu* forms (i.e. addressee honorifics) as a part of the verbal form in the predicate, cease to be used at a particular moment of interaction and change to plain forms (minus-level shifts; see Endnote). Speech-level shifts also account for shifts from plain to honorific forms (plus-level shifts). Studies on speech-level shifts have lately drawn increasing attention as a part of discursive or situated politeness, and have demonstrated numerous dynamic and contextually sensitive examples of honorific use by presenting examples extracted from actual conversations, dramas and films (e.g. Barke, 2011; Chin, 2003; Cook, 1996a, b, 1997, 2008, 2011; Geyer, 2008; Ikuta, 1983; Ishizaki, 2000; Jones and Ono, 2008; Makino, 2002; Maynard, 2001, 2004; Mimaki, 1993; Okamoto, 1999; Saito, 2010; Shibamoto-Smith, 2011; Takeda, 2011; Yoshida and Sakurai, 2005).

In this section, we look at only plus-level shifts since this chapter examines derivative uses of honorifics, and so analysing why honorific terms suddenly occur while the interactants normally maintain plain forms with each other will lead us to understand what pragmatic effects honorific terms give rise to.

### *7.2.1 Distance as a psychological barrier: Irony, sarcasm and conflict*

Okamoto (1999) claims that plus-level shifts often indicate '**irony**'. Irony is traditionally defined as "an indirect speech act with a reversal of evaluation" or "an utterance with a literal evaluation that is implicitly contrary to its intended evaluation" (Burgers, 2011: 190). In a similar way, Kapogianni (2014: 601) claims that "meaning replacement" is characteristic with an irony utterance, and Attardo (2000: 797) states that irony means "saying something while meaning something else". In other words, irony is yielded when the meaning of an utterance is not congruent with the speaker's intention, i.e. the two propositions are in conflict. Let us call this type of irony '**propositional irony**'.

In the case of Japanese, however, not all types of irony are propositional. Especially when honorifics are involved, irony can be yielded even when the speaker's intention remains the same as the utterance meaning. This is because honorifics sometimes lead the utterance to produce irony as the result of a pragmatic imbalance between honorific use and contextual factors (including honorific strategies, the relationship between the interactants and the situation in which the utterance occurred). Obana (2020)[2] calls this '**non-propositional irony**'. Therefore, the traditional definition of irony does not always apply to ironies in Japanese.

Let us first look at an example of propositional irony with honorifics involved. In the case of propositional irony, honorifics serve to enhance the irony that has been generated through the incongruence between the speaker's intention and utterance meaning. The following example shows that in the drama serial *Hanzawa Naoki*, Ogiso, who is senior to Hanzawa, speaks to him in a sarcastic manner:

(7–1) 西大阪スチールの件ではえらくご立派な口をきいていたが…
Nishioosaka sutiiru no ken dewa eraku go-rippana
Nichiosaka steel of case in really Hon-praiseworthy
kuchi o kii-te-i-ta ga…
speak-TE-Prog-Past MD
'You said some damn praiseworthy thing about the case of Nishi Osaka Steel Company.'
(*Hanzawa Naoki*, Episode 3)

Since Ogiso is senior to Hanzawa, there is no reason for him to use honorifics with him. Furthermore, throughout the serial he makes every effort to humiliate Hanzawa in order to find a way to demote him, and naturally his speech style is authoritarian and insulting. Before his utterance in example (7–1), Ogiso talks about the case of Nishi Osaka Company, in which Hanzawa successfully recovered the lost 500 million yen for their bank, but tries to degrade Hanzawa by referring to the next case, which places him in trouble again.

With the background as above, Ogiso's use of an honorific prefix *go-* in *go-rippana* ('praiseworthy') in example (7–1) in describing his junior's attitude does not indicate appreciation but, rather, his intention to insult him. Sarcasm itself has been achieved with Ogiso's phrase *rippana kuchi o kiiteita* because *kuchi o kiku* (speaking: a set phrase), which is normally associated with the strong negative judgement of someone's impertinent remarks,[3] and this is Ogiso's true intention. However, it contradicts the word *rippana* (praiseworthy) as the latter is generally associated with positive appraisal. The contradiction here indicates sarcasm (propositional irony) because Ogiso is not praising with *rippana* but implies that Hanzawa is conceited or audacious. The honorific prefix *o-* in *go-rippana*, then, is not deferential but enhances

2 This paper was written based on the presentation co-authored with Michael Haugh at the 2018 American Pragmatics Conference. The term 'non-propositional irony' is credited to Michael.

3 The same set phrase has different meanings in other contexts, such as 'working as a mediator' and 'introducing someone as an agent'.

Ogiso's negative intention and thus intensifies the sarcasm Ogiso intends to deliver. In this example, the honorific marking itself does not yield sarcasm, but enhances the effect of the speaker's intention (sarcasm). Therefore, **in the case of propositional irony, honorific use enhances irony**.

Now let us look at an example of non-propositional irony:

(7–2) Here, the manager of the Second Investigation Section is talking to his subordinates.

ひまつぶしに特命の部屋に行ってはコーヒーを召し上がっていらっしゃる、それはどういうことだ！
Himatsubushi ni tokumei no heya ni it-tewa koohii o
pastime for special section of room to go-each time coffee Acc
meshiagat-te-irassharu, sore wa dooyuu koto da!
drink[Hon]-TE-Prog[Hon] that Top how thing Cop

'Every time you visit the Special Section to kill time, you (are honourably treated to) have coffee. Explain what that means!'

(*Aiboo*, Seacon 7, Number 10)

The protagonist Sugishita belongs to the so-called 'the Special Section' (特命係 *tokumei-gakari*), which does not belong to any of the investigation sections of the Metropolitan Police Department. However, it is Sugishita who solves various cases in this drama series. When the staff from the Second Investigation Section encountered problems with a financial crime, they sought advice from Sugishita on a couple of occasions. When they were consulting Sugishita, they were treated to coffee. The manager happened to hear that his subordinates were visiting Sugishita, and since he despises the Special Section (the place for dropouts with no identifiable role), he does not like the situation.

Example (7–2) involves the manager rebuking his subordinates. This manager never uses honorifics with his subordinates in the drama series, which is also a norm within the strict hierarchy of the police in reality. Therefore, the honorifics (the underlined part) here indicates something different from deference. Without honorifics, the manager's utterance is a simple rebuke. However, *honorific use causes a pragmatic imbalance with the social relationship between the manager and his subordinates, which results in achieving sarcastic irony*. The meaning of the utterance and the speaker's intention remain the same, i.e. a rebuke, and so there is no propositional element to yield irony. However, honorific use with juniors serves as a cue to achieve non-propositional irony.[4]

There are further studies on effects caused by speech-level shifts. For example, Barke (2011: 126) identified as a result of analysing television

4 Examples (7–18) and (7–19) in Section 7.3.4 also present non-propositional irony. In this case, honorific use itself is deviated from a norm, and twisted round to insult the other person.

dramas that plus-level shifts "assist the speaker in appearing *calm and in control* of his/her emotions in situations of conflict" (italics added). Interestingly, Maynard (2001) observed when analysing television dramas that the speaker's **weak and vulnerable psychology** is witnessed when plus-level shifts occur. Her finding appears to be opposite to that of Barke. However, they both point to the same psychological delineation, that is, a psychological distance due to one or the other possessing power, although Barke's example renders power in the speaker's hand while Maynard's places it in the listener's hand. Shibamoto-Smith (2011) presents the use of polite forms in political debates in which quite direct confrontations are observed. However, honorifics function **to protect the speaker** from unnecessary emotional reactions from the audience or opponent due to the certain psychological distance honorifics create.

The effects of honorific use illustrated in this sub-section share the same characteristic: **a psychological barrier temporarily created**. Not only do honorifics create a psychological distance but they also function as a shield against the other. While norms of honorifics to achieve politeness prove the appropriate measurement of distance, which protects both speaker and listener, deliberate use of honorifics, which is not expected in the non-honorific world, creates a barrier to protect the speaker from being counter-attacked by the other person.

### *7.2.2 The origin of honorifics: Gratitude, attentiveness and carefulness*

We now look at some examples of plus-level shifts that derive from the origin of honorifics. As discussed in Chapter 5, the origin of honorifics lies in *norito* (prayers for gods and goddesses) of animism and later Shintoism, and honorifics used with gods and goddesses were meant to praise, worship and exhibit humans' awe of them. For example, humans showed gratitude to gods for abundant harvests, family well-being and childbirth; their gratitude was expressed with ample honorifics. When asking gods for a favour (e.g. stopping disasters, causing rainfall), supreme honorifics were used, which indicate humans' tentative and cautious approach to gods. Ancient honorifics were a language used exclusively for gods and goddesses, and the more and higher-level honorifics were used, the more intense emotions (gratitude, awe, cautiousness) humans displayed in order to appeal to gods. Although modern honorifics are no longer the property of deity, they are not entirely alien to the origin of honorifics. Those intense emotions humans expressed with honorifics in prayers persist as motivational factors to trigger plus-level shifts in modern Japanese.

In the following, I examine mobile phone conversations between close friends that display occasional plus-level shifts revealing the speaker's emotional reactions.[5] The data[6] used to analyse plus-level shifts come from the

5 The discussion in this sub-section is taken from Obana (2016: 268–272).

6 The corpus comes from a part of the data collected by Mayumi Usami and her team at Tokyo University of Foreign Studies, compiled as 'BTS *ni yoru tagengo hanashi kotoba koopasu*' (Multi-lingual conversation corpus by Basic Transcription System).

*Table 7.1* Plus-level shifts in request and its related statements

| *Features* | *Number of shifts* |
|---|---|
| Preliminary to the request | 2 |
| Explanation of the request and its response | 9 |
| Post-request and its response | 24 |
| Total number of plus-level shifts | 35 |

mobile phone conversations of 18 pairs[7] of participants, in which one person requests the other to join him or her in recording 20-minutes of conversation and informs the other that each participant will receive a book token worth 500 yen as a reward. Each mobile phone conversation lasts 1 to 5 minutes. Participants comprise 10 male and 8 female pairs, aged between 18 and 26 years old; all are close friends (naturally their basic speech level is zero-honorific and they mainly use plain forms).

Plus-level shifts occurred most frequently when the conversation was related to the request situation, which accounted for 35 out of the 41 plus-level shifts in total. The other six utterances refer to different things such as a joke and a different enquiry. Table 7.1 shows the features involved surrounding the request situation.

In Table 7.1, 'Preliminary to the request' means preambles before the actual content of a request is detailed, which occurred twice in the data. They are:

(7–3) JFC05: お願いがあって電話したんですけど。
O-negai ga at-te denwashi-ta-n-desu kedo.
Hon-request Nom have-TE phone-Past-Nomi-Polite MD
'I wanted to ask you a favour and so contacted you.'

(7–4) JMC05: ちょっ、ちょっと、ちょっとすんません。
Chot, chotto, chotto sunmasen.
a little moment sorry[Hon]
'Sorry, just a second.'

NB: JF = Japanese female, JM = Japanese male,
C = correspondent (the person who initially contacted his or her friend)
05 = File number 5

Example (7–3) is a preliminary to the request, which occurred right at the beginning of the conversation. The use of an addressee honorific *-desu* is a

7 BTS states that there are 10 male and 10 female pairs, however two files are overlapped; thus, 18 pairs were obtained in reality.

plus-level shift because normally this speaker interacts with her close friend (call receiver) using plain forms. In the case of example (7–4), the interactants (JMC05 and his friend, JMR05; R = respondent) first talked about an air ticket to Thailand and the conversation was about to end. Then the speaker hastily interrupted with example (7–4) by using the polite form *sumimasen* (*suman* is its default form), implying that there was something else he wanted to talk about (the request, the main purpose of the phone call). In both cases, the speaker is tentative because the subsequent request may produce a threat, which gives rise to the speaker's **careful approach** to the other person, resulting in the occurrence of *desu/masu*.

'Explanation of the request and its response' in Table 7.1 includes the explanation of the request, the speaker's pressing of the other to reply and the other's responses concerning the request. For example:

(7–5) JFC02: 図書券が出るそうです。
Toshoken ga deru-soo-desu.
book token Nom be offered-I hear-Polite
'They say that a book token is offered.'

(7–6) JMC09: どうですか。
Doo-desu ka?
how-Polite Q 'What do you think?'

(7–7) JFR03: 何ですか、それは。
Nan-desu ka, sore wa?
what-Polite Q that Top 'What's that, please?'

(7–8) JFR03: 私でいいんですか。
Watashi de ii-n-desu ka?
I with good-Nomi-Polite Q
'Is myself all right?' (= Am I good enough to do that?)

*Note*. R = Respondent (the person who received a call)

Example (7–5) is a part of the request content, explaining how the requested job would be rewarded, which is similar to information delivery discussed by Ishizaki (2000). The speaker is **cautious** in conveying the message (reward) without antagonising the other because the subsequent request may inflict a threat, or the explanation might give rise to the tone of a demand. Example (7–6) shows that the speaker is pressing the other for an answer, but the plus-level shift indicates his **tentative** attitude to mitigate the imposition. Examples (7–7) and (7–8) imply that the speakers (respondents) are **stepping back** and guarding themselves before replying to the request. While examples (7–5) and (7–6), by creating a psychological distance, signal the speaker's consideration for the other person so that the latter has some space to think over the request, examples (7–7) and (7–8) steer 'distance' to safeguard the speakers themselves.

Plus-level shifts occurred most frequently in 'post-request and its response' in Table 7.1 and are demonstrated 24 times in the data. This category includes the speaker's confirmation of the request, his or her additional information about another contact to arrange the details, his or her expression of gratitude and the other person's responses to these statements. In this category, plus-level shifts are most frequently witnessed in the uttering of the formula, (*yoroshiku*) *onegaishimasu* (the underlined part showing a plus-level shift), as demonstrated seven times in the data. Three pairs never shift their speech level in the data except when uttering this formula to confirm the request before closing the conversation. This formula is a well-established ritual, meaning 'I wish to leave the decision (or the requested job) to you', showing the speaker's humble stance toward the other (Obana, 2012b: cf. Endnote 3 of Chapter 6). When this formula is used at the end of the request, it indicates the confirmation of the request and at the same time shows the speaker's gratefulness for the other's acceptance of the request. The latter is further enhanced by the occurrence of the plus-level shift, which creates a certain psychological distance. This implies that the speaker is approaching the other **cautiously but in gratitude**. Although honorific use creates a certain distance between the participants, this temporary distance in fact results in the speaker's careful admiration.

This kind of appreciative acknowledgement is more evident in the conversations of the other four pairs because additional plus-level shifts are tracked down surrounding this ritual formula. For example:

(7–9) JMC01: よろしくお願いします。
Yoroshiku o-negaishi-masu.
well [Hon]-request-Polite
'I leave it to you.' (I confirm my request, and I trust you'll do it.)
JMR01: はい、分かりました。
Hai, wakari-mashi-ta.
Okay understand-Polite-Past
'Yes, I accept (my job).'
JMC01: すみません。
Sumi-mase-n.[8]
sorry[Polite]
'Thank you.'

8 This is an apologetic expression, showing gratitude by demonstrating indebtedness (Coulmas, 1981). Its plain form is *suman* (male speech).

In example (7–9), both interactants use *masu* forms. Because JMC01 (Japanese Male Correspondent from File 1) utters the formula in a formal way, JMR01 (Japanese Male Respondent from File 1) responds likewise. Then JMC01 extends that politeness by uttering his gratitude (*sumimasen*) with the *masu* form.[9] Both speakers temporarily become formal and ritually confirm their consensus. A similar phenomenon was observed in File 2, as shown in example (7–10):

(7–10) JMC02: うん、じゃ、後日連絡しますので。
Un, ja, gojitsu renrakushi-masu-node.
yep then later[Formal] contact-Polite-Conj
'Yep, right, I'll contact you later.'
JMR02: うん、わかった。
Un, wakat-ta.
yeah understand-Past
'Yeah, I got it.'
MC02: はい、よろしくお願いします。
Hai, yoroshiku onegaishimasu.
yes well [Hon]-request-Polite
'All right, thank you very much.'

Example (7–10) shows that the first utterance contains a formal expression, *gojitsu* (later on), together with the verb accompanying *masu*, which illustrates that with his formal styles, the speaker becomes quite cautious when starting to confirm the request. Then the third utterance shows another formal term, *hai* (yes), and the ritual formula with *masu*. This means that the speaker is even more careful, at the same time showing his gratitude. Throughout the interactions in Files 1 and 2, the participants are casual and relaxed, showing their close friendship, and even the request was made quite casually and the respondent spontaneously accepted it. However, when closing their conversation, confirmation of the request was formally made, showing the speaker's **thoughtful acknowledgement**.

Examples (7–3)–(7–10) demonstrate that the origin of honorifics, i.e. reverence with awe shown in appreciation and gratitude, is evident in the use of plus-level shifts between co-equal friends. Because the main focus in conversation is a request, even close friends become hesitant, careful and yet attentive until completing the negotiation. Of course, other conversational fragments in the data such as hedges, apologetic comments (e.g. *gomen ne* – sorry) and direct acknowledgement (e.g. *arigato* – thanks) may also disclose the speaker's psychological states in request negotiation. However, it is interesting to

9 In other examples (e.g. female conversation files, 1 and 4; male conversation file, 1), *gomen ne*, which is an informal expression of *sumimasen*, is used to express their gratitude.

observe that, without expressing emotions directly, honorific terms used in plus-level shifts convey subtle nuances of the speaker's intention.

### *7.2.3 Mock stage performance*

The idea of 'public mode' or 'acting on stage' was introduced by Cook (1996, 2008, 2011) to explain certain phenomena of plus-level shifts. Cook explains that acting on-stage emphasises the speaker's institutional identity (e.g. professor) by raising speech levels. However, the following examples indicate that the speaker creates a different (interactional) role while acting on stage, and I call this '**mock stage performance**' in this book. For example,

(7–11) そのとおりだよ。だからこそ急げ、半沢。大和田常務がお前に興味を持っているうちに、何が何でも結果を出しなさいよ！聞いてんの？

Sonotoori-da yo. Dakarakoso isoge, Hanzawa. Ohwada joomu ga omae ni
exactly-Cop MD therefore hurry director Nom you in
kyoomi o mot-te-iru-uchini, naniganänndemo kekka o dashinasai
interest Acc have-TE-Prog-while at any cost result Acc produce[Hon]
yo! Ki-i-te-n no?
MD listen-Prog-TE-Nomi Q

'That's right. That's why you should hurry, Hanzawa. You should make it at any cost while Director Owada is giving attention to you! Are you listening to me?'

(*Hanzawa Naoki*, Episode 2)

This excerpt is from the scene in which Tomari, who is Hanzawa's close colleague in the same bank, is encouraging Hanzawa to hurry up and solve the fraud issue, which has caused huge monetary damage to the bank Hanzawa works for. Owada seems to be interested in observing how Hanzawa will solve the problem, and so has ordered his staff not to demote Hanzawa for the time being. Tomari obtained this information and phoned Hanzawa to tell him about the situation, as shown in example (7–11).

Tomari and Hanzawa are close friends of the same age, and so normally do not use honorifics with each other. However, *dashinasai yo* (get it, please) is a polite imperative as if Tomari were talking with someone he is not familiar with but has some power over at work. At this moment, Tomari is acting as if he were on a public stage; that is, mock stage performance. By creating a little psychological distance from Hanzawa, Tomari pretends to be somebody else so that he can *effectively offer his advice* since close friends of equal status would find giving professional advice difficult. It is also insinuated that Tomari avoids direct authoritative advice (e.g. *kekka o dase yo* = get it done!) by using an addressee honorific to imply his *cautious approach* to the offering of advice.

It should be noted that, although mock stage performance allows the speaker to play a certain role at a certain point in time, it remains the speaker's psychological decision. This is different from task-based role shifts (see Section 7.3), which occur when the interactants are situationally expected to change their roles to fit the given context; e.g. two close friends, who normally do not use honorifics with each other, start using honorifics when acting as interviewer and interviewee while their interaction is being recorded (see example [7–18] below). This is a socially-expected role-shift while mock stage performance is a strategy as the speaker's choice (an interactional role-shift; cf. Figure 2.3 in Section 2.3.2).

Mock stage performance also gives rise to **humorous effects** through playing a certain role. For example:

(7–12) 渡真利：おーい、生きているかい。<br>
Tomari: Oooi, iki-te-iru-kai?<br>
hey alive-TE-Prog-Q<br>
'Hey, are you still alive?'<br>
近藤：どうせ何も食ってないんだろう、へへっ。<br>
Kondo: Doose nanimo kut-te-nai-n-daroo, he heh.<br>
anyway anything eat-TE-not-Nomi-perhaps hehe<br>
'I bet you haven't eaten anything, ha, ha.'<br>
渡真利：はい、牛丼です。<br>
Tomari: Hai, gyuudon desu.<br>
here you are beef-bowl Polite<br>
'Here you are, a bowl of beef and rice for you, sir.'<br>
(*Hanzawa Naoki*, Episode 7)

This excerpt is from the scene in which Hanzawa is working hard late at night to solve the case of a hotel which is about to go bankrupt. Tomari and Kondo, who are both close friends of Hanzawa's, came to see him, and Tomari, in a little dramatic but playful way, takes a take-away meal out of the bag and gives it to Hanzawa. Tomari's addressee honorific with a formal interjection *hai* (here you are) creates a humorous air because he is behaving like a delivery person. Tomari, though he is a close friend of Hanzawa, is also a busy, elite banker, but in this particular moment, he is worried about his friend and went out to get some food for him. Pretending to be a delivery agent,[10] Tomari acts in a dramatic manner as if hiding his embarrassment about his mothering action. Tomari's use of honorifics creates an onstage mode, which allows him to play a role in a humorous way, but at the same time this stage acting hides

10 This kind of role, in which the speaker steps outside his basic role-identity (i.e. colleague) and acts like a different person, is also called a 'dissociative role' (Obana, 2016). Therefore, mock stage performance with plus-level shifts can be considered an element of dissociative roles. See further examples of dissociative roles in Section 8.2.3.

his real emotions (empathy and worry) toward Hanzawa by creating a little distance through his honorific use.

We have looked at examples of plus-level shifts. Plus-level shifts (as well as minus-level shifts; see Endnote) occur when the speaker's psychological state changes on the spur of the moment, or the speaker strategically manoeuvres the interaction to attain her goal. Some plus-level shifts achieve politeness, such as gratitude and consideration, some others impoliteness, such as conflict and irony, and others are neither of them, instead delivering the speaker's emotional states such as guarding herself and pretending to be a different person. Whatever effects are accomplished, however, plus-level shifts, just as norms of honorifics, share a common feature: distance. In the case of plus-level shifts, 'distance' is psychologically manipulated to yield a variety of pragmatic meanings under the influence of the surrounding context.

### *7.2.4 Norms of honorifics, honorifics used in plus-level shifts and the origin of honorifics: A pragmatic parallel*

It seems that speech-level shifts occur for various reasons and offer markedly diverse interpretations. Many of them appear to be far from the nature of norms of honorifics. However, a closer look at the examples of speech-level shifts introduced in Sections 7.2.1–7.2.3 reveals common traits between them and norms of honorifics. Furthermore, these two types of honorific can trace their shared attributes back to the origin of honorifics (cf. Chapter 5). To clarify this, let us examine what motivational factors trigger the occurrence of norms of honorifics (Honorifics 1), honorific terms used in plus-level shifts (Honorifics 2) and the origin of honorifics (the Origin). In Section 6.1, I explained that the so-called 'conventional' honorifics or norms of honorifics (Honorifics 1) occur mainly in the following situations:

1. *jooge kankei* (上下関係 vertical relationship) – status and age differences
2. *shinso kankei* (親疎関係 familiarity) – strangers, relatively not-close people
3. *kookyoo no ba* (公共の場 public place) – formal public situations

These situations require the appropriate measurement of distance, whether it is vertical (*jooge kankei*), horizontal (*shinso kankei*) or spatial (*kookyoo no ba*), in order to achieve politeness. They also serve as motivational factors to evoke social expectations for honorific use.

Now let us examine what motivational factors trigger the occurrence of plus-level shifts. The examples of plus-level shifts discussed in the previous sub-sections can be categorised as three groups according to their underlying psychological motivations:

(A) – *Creating a psychological barrier*
irony, weakness/vulnerability, cool/in control, conflict, self-defence

(B) – *Gratitude, attentiveness, carefulness*
careful/tentative approach, cautious in gratitude, appreciation, consideration/thoughtfulness
(C) – *Mock stage performance*
pretending to be a different role, announcement

In Chapter 5, I discussed the fact that honorifics originate in *norito* (prayer), a special language for deities. Honorifics were used a great deal when humans worshiped, begged, thanked and stood in awe of gods and goddesses. By observing motivations that evoke the occurrence of honorifics in *norito*, honorific use in ancient times can be characterised as follows (cf. Section 5.3):

1. Gods are in the *distance*, existing outside in nature.
2. Gods are *placed on a pedestal* and humans *stand in awe* of them.
3. Gods are treated with awe and humans approach them *carefully* and *tentatively* because they cause disasters, unhappiness and other inconveniences, which are beyond humans' control.
4. Gods are *praised* and *thanked* when they bless humans with abundant harvests and family happiness.
5. When appealing to gods, humans *hesitate* and *falter* by repeating honorific-marked words.
6. By serving votive offerings, humans attempt to show their *caring solicitousness*.

Let us now organise and draw up a table of those motivational factors that trigger the occurrence of honorific terms in Honorifics 1, 2 and the Origin, as shown in Table 7.2.

In Table 7.2, not all of the features in the three types of honorific use coincide with one another, but it is clear that many motivational factors for the origin of honorifics, a special language for gods and goddesses, persist in modern honorifics. The pivotal trigger for honorific use is 'distance', which is shared by all three types of honorifics. Gods were believed to reside at a distance in nature in ancient Japan, and humans' awe of Gods naturally created a safe distance from them. Modern honorifics, though they are situationally determined rather than absolutely fixed (i.e. targeting gods only), also show how the speaker has measured a social or psychological distance from the other interactant. In the case of Honorifics 1, only when the measurement of distance is judged as appropriate (by the receiver of honorifics) is honorific use accepted as 'polite'. Honorifics, or precisely honorific markings, themselves do not inherently possess 'politeness' or contribute any semantic features; rather, they are ideologically (thus conventionally) believed to function pragmatically as evidence of the speaker's awareness of her social relationship with the other. In reality, this results in signifying 'respect' to the other with a higher social status, 'solemnity' in public or 'avoidance of *narenareshisa* (overfamiliarity)' with unfamiliar people.

*Table 7.2* Motivational factors for Honorifics 1, 2 and the Origin

| Honorifics in *norito* <the Origin> | Conventional honorifics <Honorifics 1> | Plus-level shifts <Honorifics 2> |
|---|---|---|
| Trigger: gods exist outside in nature as a distant deity | Trigger: social distance | Trigger: psychological distance |
| Target: gods and goddesses | Target: socially highly-ranked people, strangers, the public | Target: peers deliberately higher-positioned or distance created |
| Distance due to humans' awe of gods | Social distance due to differences in status, age and familiarity | Psychological distance due to vulnerability/ weakness, self-defence, conflict, irony |
| *Norito* chanted in the open air, ritualistic ceremony | *Kookyoo no ba* (formal and public places), ceremonial occasions | Mock public performance, public announcement |
| More honorifics when showing gratitude toward gods for their blessings | | Profound gratitude, sincere apology |
| Showing hesitance by repeating honorific terms | | Tentativeness, cautiousness |

When 'distance' is manipulated as the speaker's choice, the speaker's psychological stance on the spur of the moment is revealed through the use of honorific terms. The speaker first perceives the nature of the given context (e.g. delivering sensitive information) and then decides on her stance (e.g. careful or tentative approach), which results in a plus-level shift. Depending on a given discourse-context, plus-level shifts bring about varied pragmatic effects; some polite (e.g. profound gratitude, tentativeness), some impolite (e.g. irony, conflict, coldness) and others neutral (e.g. mock stage performance).

Honorific terms used in plus-level shifts, though they seemingly yield diverse effects, do not exist independently from conventional honorifics. The former are derived from the latter, although the former are psychologically motivated and individually controlled while the latter are socially constrained and normatively activated. Therefore, **honorifics in plus-level shifts bear a parallel to conventional honorifics with 'distance' as the pivot, forming 'two ends of a continuum'** (Obana, 2017), **both of which then come down to the origin of honorifics**.

## 7.3 Other derivations of honorific use

This section examines further examples of derivations of honorifics. Unlike speech-level shifts, which indicate the speaker's psychological shift, the examples below are socially accepted styles (e.g. women's language and personal style) or socially expected job performances (e.g. task-based role shifts). In this section, I also examine examples of self-exalting. Self-exalting is obsolete in modern Japanese, but sometimes used in a humorous way (e.g. the speaker boasting about herself). The examples introduced in Section 7.3.4 further deviate from norms of honorifics; by repeating the other person's honorific utterance, the speaker ultimately exalts herself, and this twisted manoeuvre yields sarcastic irony.

### *7.3.1 Task-based role shifts*

Task-based role shifts mean that, in some cases, the same interactants, who normally do not use honorifics with each other, start using honorifics when they are assigned different task-based roles. As discussed in Sections 1.2 and 2.3.2, close colleagues, who normally do not use honorifics with each other, use honorifics when they are placed in a formal meeting. This is because the given situation (meeting) requires them to act as meeting attendees (a task-based role), showing that their task-based roles temporarily override their institutional role-identities as close colleagues. I also introduced in Section 3.2 an example of the two males in the drama series *Tsuri-baka nisshi* (*Diary of Fishing Fools*), in which at work one is superior to the other, but in fishing begs teaching from the other; their use of honorifics is reversed as their roles (power) are upturned.

In other cases of task-based role shifts, the speaker plays different roles and differentiates honorific styles while referring to the same referent. In Section 6.2.3, I briefly referred to an example of task-based role shifts that evoke different honorific styles while a wedding MC refers to the same newly-married couple[11] (Ohkubo, 2009). In this section, I examine some of Ohkubo's examples to discuss task-based role shifts in more detail:

(7–13) じゃ、これがんばって一口でお召し上がりください。
Ja, kore ganbatte hitokuchi de omeshiagari-kudasai.
Okay this with effort single mouth in eat[Hon]-please
'Okay, please make an effort to eat this in a single mouthful.'
(Ohkubo 2009: 166)

In this example, the MC directly asks the groom to bite a slice of wedding cake, using a deferential style with the groom. In this case, the MC is playing

11 Ohkubo uses the term *daiben* (代弁 speaking by proxy), and claims that the MC is speaking on behalf of the couple. However, I use 'task-based role shifts' instead mainly because it would be more appropriate to assume that the MC shifts from his social role as an MC to different situational roles from time to time. *Daiben* is limited to the use of humble styles, which the couple would have used with their guests, but in fact the MC's different styles deal with more than the couple, depending on what role he is assuming and to whom he is talking or referring.

his social role as an MC and exalting the groom, a central figure at the ceremony. On the other hand, example (7–14) shows the MC's temporary task-based role shift:

(7–14) これよりお二人、...すべてのテーブルにご挨拶に伺います。
Koreyori o-futari, ... subeteno teeburu ni go-aisatsu-ni
from now [Hon]-couple all table to Hon-greeting-to
ukagai-masu.
visit[Hon]-Polite
'Now, the couple will come to your tables to offer a greeting to you.'
(Ohkubo, 2009: 170)

In this example, the MC uses a humble style when talking about the couple's behaviour, indicating that he shifts from his institutional role to a different task-based role by assimilating himself with the couple,[12] and speaks to the guests with this stance. While the MC is aware of his (basic) social role as the MC, he momentarily shifts his attention to the couple and talks to the guests from their perspective.

Ohkubo (2009: 169) also provides an interesting example in which the MC, though apparently talking to the guests, uses honorifics to exalt the couple who are visiting each table to greet those guests:

(7–15) これより...各テーブルを回っていかれますが、皆さんの順番が来る まで、お二人いらっしゃいますまでは、お席にてお待ちいただきますように、どうぞよろしくお願いします。
Koreyori ... kaku-teeburu o mawat-te-ika-re-masu ga, o-futari
ga from now each-table Acc visit-TE-go[Hon]-Hon-Polite Conj Hon-two
Nom
irasshai-masu-madewa, o-seki-nite o-machi-tadaki-masu-yooni,
come[Hon]-Polite-until Hon-seat-at Hon-wait-receive[Hon]-Polite-so as to
doozo yoroshiku o-negaishi-masu.
please well Hon-request-Polite

'The couple are going to visit each table. Could I ask you to wait for them while remaining seated until they come to your table, please?'
(Ohkubo 2009: 169)

12 As discussed in Endnote 1 of Chapter 6, the sentence conceals the 'Speaker's view' in its construction. In the case of Japanese, the Speaker's view is placed first on the speaker and then shifted to someone else who is socially closer to the speaker as the next choice. The MC in example (7–14) shifts the view to the couple and speaks by assimilating his view with the couple.

In this example, the MC exalts both the couple (the single-underlined part) and guests (the double-underlined part). Although he talks about the couple's actions directed to the guests just as in example (7–14), he uses deferential styles about them in example (7–15). Ohkubo (2009: 169–170) explains that, in this particular situation, the MC is treating the couple as the centre of attention because their greeting at each table is one of the highlights of the ceremony, while he is equally showing respect to the guests as an MC (his social role) with appropriate honorifics.

This can be explained with the concept of task-based role shifts in the following way. In example (7–14), the MC takes a task-based role to assimilate himself with the couple, from this perspective he shows respect to the guests as if the couple were showing respect to them. However, in example (7–15), the MC goes back to his institutional role-identity (the MC) and, from this perspective, uses honorifics with both the couple and the guests. As Ohkubo explains, the scene in which example (7–15) occurs is differently interpreted because the MC is drawing the guests' attention to the couple as the central figure, and in order to subtly indicate this to the guests, the MC has carefully chosen deferential styles to describe the couple's behaviour.

The above examples show that the speaker differentiates honorific styles for the same referent by shifting from one role to another to suit the given context, which results in treating the same people in varied ways by placing and adjusting their situational positions to achieve the most appropriate ambience for all participants.

### 7. 3.2 *Women's language*

Women's language often contains honorific terms to emphasise their femininity, which is categorised as *bikago* (美化語 self-beautification terms; cf. Section 6.1). By using honorific terms to create a certain distance between the speaker (female) and others, the speaker achieves some gracefulness (i.e. a little aloofness creates an impression of class and displays elegance), which enhances her femininity together with her lady-like attitude. For example, the following excerpt[13] shows a female interviewee's response to a question, in which she uses *bikago* as well as conventional honorifics:

(7–16)

亜美: XXさんとはよく行き来なさいますか。英語学校以外に。
Ami: XX-san towa yoku iki-ki-nasai-masu ka. Eigo gakkoo igai ni.
with often go-come-do[Hon]-Polite Q English school except
'Do you often see XX outside the English class?'

13 The interviews were conducted by a female research assistant, who interviewed 23 people in different age groups (in their twenties to seventies) of both genders and asked about their family members, friends and people they respect. Some of the interviewees are the assistant's close friends and the others were newly introduced through her friends.

洋子: はい。お近くなの、ご近所なので、よくお顔を会わせますし、あの、何か
のおりには、お茶を飲んだりすることもあります。

Yoko: Hai. O-chikakuna-no, go-kinjo-na-node, yoku
yes Hon-near-MD Hon-neighborhood-Cop-since often
o-kao o awase-masu-shi, ano, nanika no oriniwa,
meet[Hon]-Polite-and well when something comes up
ocha o non-dari-suru koto mo ari-masu.
tea Acc drink-for instance-do occasion etc. exist-Polite
'Yes. (She lives) nearby. As (we are) neighbours, (we) often bump into (each other), and occasionally (we) have tea together.'
(Obana, 2019: 254–255)

In example (7–16), the single-underlined parts are conventional honorifics:

*iki-ki nasai masu ka* (do you see each other?):
*iki-ki nasai* – *sonkei*-style of *iki-ki suru*
*-masu* – addressee honorific
(*okao o*) *awase-masu* (bump into), *arimasu* (have): addressee honorific –*masu*
*ori* (opportunity): a formal style of *toki*

These honorifics conform to *kookyoo no ba* (公共の場 public situation). Although Ami and Yoko are close friends in reality, they are temporarily situated in public, playing a role as interviewer and interviewee (task-based role; cf. Section 7.3.1). On the other hand, the double-underlined parts are *bikago* as female language to enhance her elegant attitude:

*o-chikaku* (near), *go-kinjo* (neighbourhood), *o-kao* (face)

*O-* in *o-cha* (tea) is a *zettai joseigo* (絶対女性語 absolute women's language), which is used by all females wherever they are situated (unless pretending to play a male role). However, the other honorific prefixes are *bikago* as the speaker's choice to show her femininity or elegance, and can be used irrespective of the situation or social relationship with the other.

### *7.3.3 Personal styles*

We often observe that individuals have their own style of honorific use. Some professors use plain forms when talking with their students on the basis of egalitarianism while others use polite forms as their basic style by remaining a little aloof with their students (cf. footnote 4 of Chapter 3). Another example is that in the drama series, *Aiboo* (相棒 partners), the protagonist always uses polite forms with his subordinates, children and even criminal suspects, which is in direct contrast to the behaviour of the other detectives, who differentiate their speech levels in accordance with power, social status and age differences. The protagonist's personal style of honorific usage conveys to the audience that he is *cool, self-controlled and intellectual*,[14] and he acts accordingly throughout the drama (evaluations of this kind of honorific use may vary individually and contextually; one review of the series refers to him as 'sarcastic' and 'pompous'[15]).

Let us look at an example in which the protagonist (Sugishita) uses honorifics with his subordinate, Kai (nicknamed Kaito). After a phone call, Sugishita was contemplative and Kai asked him what had happened. Sugishita replies:

(7–17) カイト君、<u>お付き合いいただきたい</u>場所があるの<u>です</u>が。
Kaito-kun, o-tsukiai-itadaki-tai basho ga
Hon-accompany-receive[Hon]-want place Nom
aru-no-desu ga.
have-Nomi-Polite MD
'Kaito, there is a place which I would like you to come with me to.'
(*Aiboo*, Season 13, a special film)

It appears that Sugishita exalts Kai by using honorifics such as *o-tsukiai* ('coming-with-me' + honorific prefix *o-*), *itadaki-* ('receive': *kenjoo*-marked auxiliary) and *–desu* (addressee honorific). However, Kai is Sugishita's subordinate as a result of the age difference between them, like a parent and child, and so Sugishita would not be expected to use honorifics with Kai. The Japanese police maintain a strict and rigid hierarchy, and the use of honorifics and titles is invariably expected when juniors are talking with seniors. However, a closer look at utterance (7–17) reveals that the honorific terms underlined are Sugishita's personal style. It is because Sugishita's addressing of Kai as *Kaito-kun* means that Kai has a lower status because Sugishita as *kun* is used to address an equal or junior person. Furthermore, Sugishita utters *itadaki tai*; although honorific-marked, this expression is a demanding order ('I want you to do ~') and Kai has no choice but to follow Sugishita. It is because the auxiliary *-tai* (want) cannot be used in a request to a senior because it becomes an imposition on the senior. Thus, Sugishita's use of *-tai* indicates that he is expressing his higher position in the linguistic term. This means that Sugishita is fully aware of his position as a senior to Kai, which is proven by his choice of words (*-kun*, *-tai*). Therefore, Sugishita's use of honorifics does not mean

14 Numerous references to honorifics are published in Japan each year and it is felt that, if you can use honorifics properly and smoothly, you will be highly-regarded and judged as socially capable (cf. Section 1.1).

15 A scenario writer comments on the protagonist's pompous style which matches his sarcastic and extraordinary character (*Monthly Drama Scenario*, February 2014: 7).

to exalt the other person; rather, it displays his personal style, characterising him as the cool, refined and intelligent protagonist.

### *7.3.4 Absolute honorifics and self-exalting*

Honorifics used today are relative and heterogeneous. As explained in Section 6.3.1, the same person uses or receives honorifics, depending on where she is situated and who she is interacting with. The president of a company may be more highly-ranked than her employees (status), but lower-ranked in the presence of her son's teacher (*onkei* – benefit from a professional). If she violates a traffic rule, she may become humble with a police person (power). These are examples of *jooge kankei* (vertical relationship), but this relationship is *situationally* higher or lower according to the interactants' situational roles in status, intangible almsgiving (*onkei*) and power.

Absolute honorifics (*zettai keigo* 絶対敬語), on the other hand, were prevalent in feudal times when social classes and ranks were rigidly organised. More highly-ranked people constantly received honorifics even when they were not present in the interaction. In other words, the interactants' relationship did not count, and the situation in which they were placed was irrelevant, but honorifics were used to mark higher ranks and honorific levels were differentiated in accordance with different ranks. However, absolute honorifics are still preserved in modern Japanese, which are used toward and between Imperial family members, especially when they are facing the public.

Terms used in temples and shrines are also categorised as absolute honorifics to deify gods and Buddha. For example:

*haikan* 拝観: have the honour of seeing Buddha's images or visiting temples – *hai-* is a humble word meaning 'salutation' or 'praying'
*sandoo* 参道: an approach to a shrine or temple – *san-* is a humble term meaning 'visiting'
*sanpai* 参拝: worshipping – both *kanji* are humble styles, the combination of 'visiting' and 'praying'

Irrespective of the visitor, those humble terms are used as absolute honorifics to worship gods or Buddha.

Self-exalting by using *sonkei*-styles[16] about the speaker's own behaviour often yields a humorous or sarcastic effect, depending on where and how it is performed. For example:

16 Self-exalting honorifics existed in old Japanese to show differences in status between the speaker and the other who was lower-ranked as honorifics were historically the evidence of social rank. However, in modern Japanese self-exalting honorifics function only as humour or as the speaker's demand to be respected.

(7–18) Here, the junior members went to the murder site and found Kuraishi walking around there.

部下：倉石さん、来ていらしたんですか！
subordinates: Kuraishi-san, ki-te-irashi-ta-n-desu ka!
come-TE-Prog[Hon]-Past-Nomi-Polite MD
'Mr. Kuraishi, you are here!'

倉石：来ていらしてましたよ。現場百回っていうだろ。
Kuraishi: Ki-te-irashi-te-mashi-ta yo.
come-TE-Prog[Hon]-TE-Polite-Past MD
Genba hyakkai tte yuu-daro.
site 100 times Quote say-Aux
'I'm here, of course. They say the site should be visited 100 times, don't they?'

(臨場 *Rinjoo*, Number 8)

When Kuraishi's subordinates were looking for him, they found him walking around at the site where a murder had occurred. They were quite surprised to see him there because he had finished his tasks as a forensic examiner a few days earlier and no other jobs were assigned to him (but it is Kuraishi in this drama series who solves cases with his brilliant powers of reasoning). In response to their surprise, Kuraishi calmly repeats their honorific utterance, which converts it to a self-exalting utterance as shown in example (7–18). Self-exalting honorifics are seldom used in modern Japanese, and throughout the drama series, Kuraishi never uses honorifics even with his seniors (which characterises this protagonist as a lone maverick). Therefore, Kuraishi's utterance here is quite unusual because, first, he exalts himself and, second, he is polite to his juniors by using addressee honorifics.

Repeating the other person's utterance, unless it is for empathy or confirmation, is often considered teasing, ridiculing or even insulting the other (Perrin et al., 2003; see Section 8.2.2). Self-exalting honorifics may indicate humour, arrogance or disparagement of the other, depending on the given context. In the case of example (7–18), given that Kuraishi is normally close to his subordinates and looks after them well, his honorific utterance signals **ironic humour** to tease them because he wonders why they are so surprised to see him at the murder site. This is confirmed with the extra-linguistic features such as his facial expressions (his eyes a little too widely open and his mouth puckered) and tone of voice (calm but a rising inflection to demonstrate that he is pondering). Therefore, by repeating the same honorific utterance and turning it upside down, he is teasing his subordinates using irony because visiting the site is a matter of course in order to solve the case. *Genba hyakkai* (visiting the site 100 times) is a common belief among police because they may find a new clue by visiting the murder site many times. By quoting this, Kuraishi implies that they should not be surprised to see him at the site.

The next example of self-exalting is a sarcastic response to the other person:

(7–19) 杉下：森でなにをなさっていたんですか？
Sugishita: Mori de nani o nasat-te-i-ta-n-desu ka?
forest in what Acc do[Hon]-TE-Prog-Past-Nomi-Polite Q
'What were you doing in the forest?'
晋平：オレは森でなんか、なにもなさっちゃいねえよ。
Shinpei: Ore wa mori de nanka, nanimo nasatcha-inee yo.
I Top forest in such anything do[Hon]-not MD
'I didn't do anything in the forest at all.'
(*Aiboo*, Season 7, Number 19)

This excerpt is from the scene in which Sugishita suspected something had happened in the forest and that Shinpei must have been involved with it. Sugishita asked him a lot of questions, but did not get enough information. Shinpei initially responded quite abruptly with plain forms and distasteful words such as *ore* (the first person, male, in an arrogant way) and *shiranee yo* ('I don't know'; *nee* is an indecent form of *nai* [not]) because he was annoyed by Sugishita's persistent questions. Then, as in example (7–19), when Sugishita finally asks Shinpei what he was doing in the forest, Shinpei looks very nervous and does not want to answer the question because he was in fact involved with the death of a woman.

Given that Shinpei is hostile with Sugishita, repeating Sugishita's utterance like a parrot is far from humorous and is, in fact, intended to be insulting, and the self-exalting utterance in effect downgrades Sugishita. Furthermore, Shinpei's wrong use of honorifics is obvious and suggests his perverted intention to attack Sugishita indirectly; sarcastic irony is successfully achieved.

Note that both examples (7–18) and (7–19) are instances of non-propositional irony (cf. Section 7.2.1) because, while the speaker's intention is the same as the meaning of the utterance, irony is yielded by repeating the other's honorific utterance, which results in converting it to a self-exalting utterance.

## Endnote: Examples of minus-level shifts

Minus-level shifts mean that interactants basically use polite forms, but plain forms from time to time occur to index certain psychological shifts. Ikuta (1983) examined a television interview and identified that the participants normally use *desu/masu* forms, but the interviewer's use of plain forms demonstrates '**empathy**' for the interviewee. Maynard (2001) examined a television drama in which two people fall in love and style shifts indicate their emotional ups and downs, and concludes that *da* (plain form) indexes a '**sense**

**of familiarity, tolerance and indulgence**'. In a similar way, Takeda (2011) reports that minus-level shifts occur when speakers express their emotions, show empathy for the other and are **emotionally involved** with the other's story. Mimaki (1993) also refers to a minus-level shift by a female MC to her male guest, and concludes that it not only indicates the speaker's adopting a closer stance toward the guest but also her intention to **draw his attention to the topic**. Cook (1996a) finds in institutional talks that plain forms are derived from '**off-stage**' discourses (in contrast with 'on-stage' contexts where interactants are more aware of their institutional identity).

While the three studies above commonly identify the speaker's psychological closeness to the other, the following findings indicate impersonal or non-interactional features at the time of the occurrence of minus-level shifts. Makino (2002) examines the data from round table discussions to find that the plain form indexes the speaker's low involvement with the listener, directing the speaker's attention toward herself. He calls this the '**inward communication** direction' (Makino, 2002: 123). Takeda (2011) also finds that the plain form occurs when speakers give their own impressions as if they were speaking to themselves. This corresponds to Cook's (1996b) '**innate mode**' and Saito's (2010) 'inward thought'. Chin (2003) examines the conversation between newly-met young adults of the same age group and reports that the plain form often occurs when speakers are searching for appropriate words or trying to remember something while talking.

When examining the data of subordinates' plain forms toward their superiors in the workplace, Saito (2010) found that plain forms occur when highlighting information (e.g. providing opinions, clarifying superiors' directives).

The above findings can be categorised into three groups, as shown in Table 7.3.

*Table 7.3* Triggers of minus-level shifts: classification

| *Reasons for minus-level shifts* | |
|---|---|
| Group (1) | **Psychological closeness** |
| | Empathy (Ikuta, 1983) |
| | Attracting the hearer's attention (Mimaki, 1993) |
| | Showing familiarity, tolerance (Maynard, 2001) |
| | Off-stage (Cook, 1996a) |
| Group (2) | **Focusing on the current conversation** |
| | Stressing one's opinion (Takeda, 2011) |
| | Involved with the topic (Takeda, 2011) |
| | Information highlighted (Saito, 2010) |
| Group (3) | **Focusing on the speaker herself** |
| | Inward communication (Makino, 2002) |
| | Inward thoughts (Saito, 2010) |
| | Innate mode (Cook, 1996b) |
| | Attention to the speaker herself (Takeda, 2011) |

However, Obana (2016: 258) argues that most of the examples in group 3, 'focusing on the speaker herself' should be reconsidered, reclassified and placed in group 2. They are not really soliloquys but the speaker's attention is focused on the ongoing talk. Soliloquys do occur particularly when the speaker is trying to recall something, as Chin (2003) claims. However, if the speaker is giving information or telling a story, it is not an inward communication; rather, the speaker is interacting with the other, involving the other in her story. Moreover, given that the other participant responds to the original speaker, the examples in group (3) are not inward communication, but interacting communication. Therefore, minus-level shifts should be categorised into two groups, (1) and (2) in Table 7.3 (except for Chin's soliloquys).

While group (1) is characterised as 'the speaker psychologically stepping up to the other person' and group (2) as 'the speaker drawing the other into her world', both types of minus-level shift diminish a psychological distance between the interactants. Obana (2016: 260) calls this "an improvised role-identity", which is assimilated with the other participant (e.g. empathy) or with the proceeding topic (e.g. describing a scene) because the speaker temporarily steps outside her own role-identity (the basic stance with the other person in the honorific world), and creates an improvised role-identity.

## Summary of Part II

Chapters 4–7 have focused on presenting an overall picture of what honorifics are like by observing their concepts, diachronic meanings and pragmatic functions as well as their derivative uses that yield diverse pragmatic meanings in interaction.

Chapter 4 discussed the conceptual differences the term 'polite' evokes between Japanese and English. Although politeness is not a matter of honorific use (strategies and extra-linguistic features as well as situational interpretations count), the term 'polite' in Japanese is predominantly associated with appropriate use of honorifics. This is because the translated words for 'polite', *teineina* and *reigi tadashii*, encompass a narrower range of social actions than 'polite' in English. They are more readily related to formal, ceremonial situations and social differences, all of which the world of honorifics exhibit, while 'polite' in English is not limited to such formality but extended to 'friendliness' and 'kindness' and even 'solidarity' by means of in-group jargon (e.g. swear words among Australian 'mates'). In fact, there is no exact term in Japanese that equates to 'polite' in the English sense.

Chapter 5 examined the origin of honorifics. Honorifics originate in ritualistic prayers for animist gods and goddesses, which later developed into Shintoism. Thus, honorifics were used as a language for deities when humans appealed to them in prayers. The more sensitive or demanding the appeals, the more abundantly honorifics were used to demonstrate humans' awe of deities. The chapter also discussed the fact that motivational factors for honorific use in ancient prayers to a great extent persist in modern honorific use, although modern honorifics are situationally and relationally determined while ancient honorifics were organised as absolute honorifics and meant for gods and goddesses only.

Chapter 6 examined the status of honorifics in pragmatic principles. Honorifics are, strictly speaking, 'markings' on the utterance that has already been constructed strategically, and thus do not offer any semantic contributions. They index a social and/or psychological distance, indicating the speaker's recognition of the social relationship with the other interactant. Therefore, honorifics (conventional honorifics, in this case) should be differentiated from strategic politeness, which is a goal-oriented tool in negotiation with the other. Deference emerges by measuring distance appropriately, which is implemented in the grammatical conversion of an utterance that has been strategically built. The chapter also added how the socio-pragmatic effects of honorifics have changed since the Second World War; honorifics, which used to be strongly associated with differences in status, are now shifting to public and commercial images.

Chapter 7 moved on to examine strategic honorifics. Honorific terms used in plus-level shifts are prompted on the spur of the moment in interaction in which the interactants normally do not use honorifics with each other. They are manipulated as the speaker's choice to indicate her impressions, what stance she is taking or how she is trying to approach the other. Some of them achieve politeness (e.g. profound gratitude and apology), others aim at impoliteness (e.g. conflict, irony) and others remain neutral (e.g. mock stage performance). These effects appear to be diverse and far from the nature of the norms of honorifics. However, a closer look at plus-level shifts and norms of honorifics discloses that they all share a common feature: distance (whether social or psychological). Distance is measured, manipulated and interpreted in various ways in accordance with the nature of the given situation, and yet motivational factors that trigger honorific use, with 'distance' as the core, form a pragmatic parallel between norms of honorifics and honorific terms used in plus-level shifts. Furthermore, these two types of modern honorific converge into the origin of honorifics as the latter's motivational factors in many ways persist in modern honorific use.

# Part III

# Politeness strategies

# 8 Strategies as the implementation of one's Role-Identity

Although the Japanese language is one of the most frequently cited examples in politeness research, much of the work on Japanese politeness has customarily concentrated attention on honorifics. Because of this, politeness strategies in Japanese, in spite of their rich and diverse characteristics, have not adequately been explored to date (except Obana [2009] and Haugh and Obana [2011]). It is therefore worth examining how Japanese strategies are designed and the motivations (or '**strategic planning**' in this book) underlying strategy construction. As strategies in the non-honorific world are often different from those in the honorific world, this chapter first focuses on the former and the next on the latter. To explain politeness strategies in Japanese, I employ the concept of Role-Identity,[1] which was introduced in Section 2.3 as a tool for making linguistic choices to achieve politeness. In a similar way, choice of strategy also depends on what role-identity the speaker perceives in the given situation or decides on *making* (the term used in Symbolic Interactionism (SI), meaning 'creating') according to the interactional stance he assumes. In this chapter, the concept of Role-Identity in relation to strategic planning is further discussed, and then examples of (non-honorific) strategies are analysed by applying sub-categories of Role-Identity. I particularly focus on role shifts in the same discourse, which can trigger different strategies employed by the same speaker.

1 Obana (2009) and Haugh and Obana (2011) use the term *tachiba* (立場 – lit. standing-place) in analysing politeness strategies in Japanese. *Tachiba* refers to job categories (e.g. teacher, shopkeeper) and tasks and duties assigned (e.g. chairperson), but does not encompass improvised roles such as acting like a sister to one's friend or acting as though one were on stage. These interactional roles are equally important in analysing politeness strategies that are prompted contingently during the interaction. Therefore, I employ Role-Identity in discussing different types of strategy. Furthermore, unlike *tachiba*, Role-Identity differentiates identity from role since the same identity (e.g. teacher) may be implemented as different ranges of roles due to institutional policies as well as the beliefs of individuals.

## 8.1 The concept of Role-Identity[2]

In Section 2.3, I introduced SI to go a little deeper in defining the concept of politeness by explaining what processes are involved in achieving politeness. Here, I refer to some more characteristics of SI that are relevant to the occurrence of politeness strategies.

SI stresses interactional influences that create, shape and re-create identities[3] in the process of interaction; in other words, "interaction is … centrally a matter of negotiating identities and roles" (McCall, 2003: 329). This is because human beings always have a habit of interpreting things (objects or symbols) around them, and the meanings of symbols are created and changed through interaction. In interaction, a variety of symbols surrounding the interactants become a target for their subjective interpretation, including their social relationship, the situation in which the interaction takes place and the content of their conversation, which are all added to the interpretation process.

SI acknowledges both normative and contingent aspects of identity and role. Normative aspects of identity and role bear social expectations. For example, a school teacher is expected to behave as an educator ('Institutional Role-Identity' in this book), which loads her with a variety of duties and responsibilities. Customers in a restaurant behave in a certain way that suits the dining scene ('Task-based Role' in this book). These performances underlie shared expectations, based on which members of a community fulfil their roles. Therefore, expected roles are in their mind, and they behave based on a generalised role conception (or 'taking the role of the other', according to Mead, 1934). This is because, in our general life, "abrupt or radical changes in roles undermine predictability and provoke anxiety" (Turner, 2002: 235). However, an identity as a teacher, for instance, does not mean that its roles are rigidly enacted; school policies, class dynamics and personal interpretations of the 'teacher role' may give rise to different performances in reality, although the teacher-identity is commonly recognised at school and in society in general.

Contingent aspects of identity and role, on the other hand, reflect interactants' stance, psychological state, contextual interpretation and their attitude in response to each other. Social norms may provide a set of broad foundations but, in reality, interactants work out various improvised roles within the normative roles, or even shift their normative roles to completely different ones.[4] In other words, different roles may enter the interaction as

2 This section is an excerpt from Obana (2012a), and changed to suit the flow of this chapter.

3 SI claims that "identity is not equivalent to self but may be seen as a component self", and that identity is the most public aspect of self, which is "perceived and interpreted during interaction with others" (Vryan et al., 2003: 368).

4 For example, when an employed worker decides to leave the company, he may be expressive in insulting his employer. In this case, he is no longer taking his role-identity as an employed person, but is *making* a different role-identity.

More socially determined: more normative and predictable

↑

Institutional Roles – e.g. family members, job categories

Task-based Roles – e.g. chairperson, MC, organiser of an event, mentor, juror

Interactional Roles – e.g. acting as a consultant to a friend, mothering or nursing a friend, pretending to be someone else

↓

More psychologically determined: more individual and instantaneous

*Figure 8.1* Sub-categories of Role-Identity

it takes on different contextual features. For example, friends may have certain normative aspects: a bond of mutual affection as expected in society (Institutional Role-Identity). However, if one starts consulting the other about his problem with mathematics, for example, the other may employ the role of consultant (Interactional Role-Identity). If the other gives him a maths lesson, that person is playing the role of instructor (another Interactional Role-Identity). Their basic relationship as friends is not changed, but as the interaction develops into a different phase, the interactants recognise different role shifts, according to which they behave to suit their new (improvised) role. In this way, roles are subject to change in accordance with their interactional fluctuations. Such roles are *made* (improvised), which can be differentiated from normative roles that are *taken* ('taking the role of the other'; Mead, 1934).

Based on Turner's (2011) model, I sub-categorised Role-Identity in Section 2.3.2, as illustrated in Figure 8.1. The figure shows that role-identities range from more socially recognised roles to more individually improvised roles in interaction. As mentioned in Section 2.3.2, the so-called 'conventional' honorifics and formulaic expressions (e.g. greetings) are more socially practised role-identities in linguistic terms, and speech-level shifts are a typical example of the linguistic implementation of improvised role-identities, displaying different stances and psychological states of the speaker. In a similar way, *politeness strategies initially conform to social norms through the interactants' institutional role-identities, but as the interaction proceeds to a different phase, a particular interactional role may emerge, which is implemented as a different strategy to suit the ongoing interaction.* In this chapter, I focus on interactional-role shifts that prompt strategic changes in the same discourse.

## 8.2 Role shifts and changes in politeness strategies

### *8.2.1 Direct and indirect requests: Role shifts*

To argue against Brown and Levinson's (1987) principles of the face-threatening act (FTA), some scholars claim that request is not necessarily a FTA by classifying request types as benefit and burden requests because benefit requests in some cultures are somewhat directly made; for example, in Greek (Sifianou, 1992), Chinese (Oh, 2005) and Slavic languages (Wierzbicka, 1991, 1995). Oh (2005: 28f) explains that an indirect form (e.g. using a negation) in Chinese does not sound a positive invitation or offer and so the hearer would be more obliged to say 'no' because he would interpret the indirect approach as the speaker's hesitance in his offer. However, this does not mean that the same language maintains one or the other request type irrespective of the discourse.

In Japanese, initial invitations, or benefit-requests, take an indirect strategy even between close friends by using a negation and an interrogative form. However, in the same discourse with the same participants, the same invitation changes from an indirect to a direct form when the interaction starts assuming a different phase. For example:

(8–1) A1: ちょうど食事時だから、夕飯食べていかない？
A1: Choodo shokuji-doki dakara, yuuhan tabe-te ika-nai?
just meal-time because dinner eat-TE go-not
'It's almost dinner time, so won't you have dinner here?'
B1: え？なんか悪いなあ。もう失礼しないと。
B1: E? Nanka warui-naa. Moo shitsureshi-nai-to.
oh somehow bad-MD soon leave-not-Conj
'Oh, somehow I feel bad. I should be excusing myself, and so…'
A2: いいのいいの。ね、食べていってよ。
A2: Iino iino. Ne, tabe-te-it-te yo.
no problem you see eat-TE-go MD
'No problem at all. Surely you should eat (and go home), Okay?'
B2: そう？じゃ、遠慮なくごちそうになろうかな。
B2: Soo? Ja, enryo naku gochisooninar-oo-kana.
really okay reserve without have dinner-shall-MD
'Really? Okay, then, I shouldn't be so reserved. I suppose I'll have dinner.'

(Obana, 2012a: 7)

Example (8–1) is an interaction between close friends. Person B visited A and after some time A asked B to stay for dinner. In line A1, the invitation request is formed in an indirect way with a negation (*-nai*) and a question (by raising the tone). At this stage, a friend (Person A), no matter how close she is to her friend (Person B), has no prescribed roles to allow her to ask directly whether the request is a burden or benefit to her friend (a social norm). However, when B is hesitant to accept A's invitation, the interaction is tinged with a different phase. Because A perceives that B is hesitant from a sense of courtesy, A takes the liberty of *making* a role (interactional role) in order to be more persistent, which results in an imposing invitation, as in line A2. The utterance, *tabe-te it-te yo* ((You) should go home after eating), is quite a strong command and does not give any other option to the hearer. However, Person A's new role-making is successful in negating B's reserve, which readily allows Person B to accept the direct invitation, as shown in line B2.

Example (8–1) shows a successful example of Person A's role-*making*, i.e. stepping into the other's territory, imposing the invitation (as in line A2), because Person B accepts it in a positive way and welcomes the invitation (shown in line B2). However, it does not necessarily mean that in every interaction the reiterated invitation should be made in a direct way because many other pragmatic conditions count in making the imposing invitation successful; for example, how close the interactants are, how willing Person B is to stay longer and whether Person B recognises the invitation as genuine. Therefore, a strong invitation, like that in line A2, has the potential to offend Person B.

The argument above indicates that there is no one-to-one relation between a social act (e.g. invitation) and a politeness strategy (e.g. an indirect speech act) at the discourse level. Although indirect invitation may be a social norm in Japanese society, the interactants may take different routes in accordance with how the discourse develops. In other words, *the interactants' recognition of different phases of the discourse determines role-shifts and role-shifts invite different linguistic strategies*. In the case of example (8–1), the shifted role (line A2) takes priority over FTA considerations, which gives rise to a rather imposing invitation.

Haugh and Obana (2011) use the term *tachiba* (cf. footnote 1 of this chapter) and discuss how children make requests to their parents. They state:

> The *tachiba* of children in relation to their parents … enables them to make direct requests when they fall into certain categories. Since parents are supposed to raise, nurture and look after their children, requests from children which lie within the parents' responsibilities can be directly uttered. (166)

They give examples such as *are katte* (あれ買って Buy me that), *keeki moohitotsu choodai* (ケーキもうひとつちょうだい Give me another piece of cake) and *okawari!* (おかわり！ Refill [the rice bowl]). "These examples are direct requests, sounding almost like commands when translated into English" (ibid). On the other hand, when children want to join an activity (e.g. champing) or to go out with their friends, they need to get permission from their parents, and in such cases they use indirect requests; e.g. *kyanpu ni sanka shitain dakedo…*

(キャンプに参加したいんだけど I want to join the camp but…). Haugh and Obana (2011) explain the above as follows:

> The difference between the use of direct and indirect requests by children lies in their recognition of *tachiba*. Directness is afforded when the requests can be considered to lie within the scope of what parents are expected to do in raising their children. Indirect requests, on the other hand, occur when the parents' right (*tachiba*) to control their children's activities is recognised. (167)

*Tachiba*, here, is similar to Institutional Role-Identity in this book (but see their differences in footnote 1 of this chapter); the interactants *take* (the term used in SI) roles based on their institutional identity as 'parents' and 'children'. Children's direct and indirect requests come from which roles are brought to the fore by recognising the nature of requests. Therefore, **strategies in Japanese often consider Institutional (e.g. job categories) Role-Identity prior to FTA**, and direct requests can be made when the content of the requests remains within the domain of responsibilities or rights that are socially guaranteed by Institutional Role-Identity (or role entitlements).

Let us look at an example that demonstrates different strategies employed by the same speaker toward the same person due to the difference between the speaker's entitled and non-entitled roles. In the film *Okuribito* (*Departures*), Daigo, the protagonist, and Sasaki, his employer (and master encoffineer), arrive at a house to prepare a corpse for burial as *nookanshi* (納棺師 encoffineers who clean the body, apply make-up and change his or her clothes). Due to an accident on the way, they arrived a few hours late. Then the chief mourner shouts at them:

(8–2)

喪主：何時だと思ってるんだ。

Mourner: Nan-ji da to omot-te-ru-n-da.
what-time Cop Quote think-TE-Prog-Nomi-MD
'What time do you think it is now!'

佐々木：申し訳ありません。… このたびはまことにご愁傷さまです。

Sasaki: Mooshiwakeari-masen. …Kono-tabi wa makotoni
sorry[Formal]-Polite this-time[Formal] Topic indeed[Formal]
goshuushosama desu.
condolences[Formal] Polite
'I'm sorry. … My deepest condolences (for your loss) this time.'

喪主：いいよ、そんな挨拶は。… さっさとやってくれ。

Mourner: Ii yo, sonna aisatsu wa. … Sassato yat-te-kure.
no thanks MD such greeting Top quickly do-TE-for me
'No need for such a greeting. … Do it quickly now.'

The relationship between Sasaki and the chief mourner is that the latter is a paying customer. Furthermore, Sasaki and Daigo (assistant) arrived a few hours later than they promised, and so the mourner's words are demanding and almost rude, using abrupt forms and angry tones. It is obvious that the mourner takes advantage of his role-identity (customer) and feels entitled to be direct to the encoffineers. He also feels even more entitled to be rude because Sasaki and Daigo arrived late: a situational role as a superior stance. On the other hand, feeling guilty that he arrived late, Sasaki is apologetic, and also humble as an employed encoffineer.

The scene then moves on to the encoffineer's job, which impresses everyone in the house because of his affectionate and careful treatment of the corpse, and the skillful make-up on its face to make the dead person look alive. The mourner starts crying. When Sasaki and Daigo are leaving the house, the mourner comes after them with tears in his eyes, and speaks to them:

(8-3) あのう、よかったら、これ、もってってください。
Anoo, yokattara, kntvore, mottet-te-kudasai.
excuse me if you like this take-go-please
'Excuse me, if you like, accept this, please.'

The mourner offers a bag of home-made dried persimmons. He sounds tender and even humble probably because he was so impressed with Sasaki's work that he regretted having shouted at him earlier. However, another factor is involved with the mourner's humble offer. His offer in example (8–3) is outside the domain of his role as the employer of an encoffineer. It is unusual for a paying customer to give a gift to the person he employed. Furthermore, they are strangers and strangers normally would not give or receive gifts. The mourner's offer may be a token to express his apology as well as gratitude, but when he offers, he is obliged to utter in a hesitant way by adding *yokattara* (if you like) because his action does not belong to his role-identity (customer), but comes from his own personal decision.

The mourner's utterances toward Sasaki in examples (8–2) and (8–3) are quite contrastive in that the one is demanding and abrupt, and the other humble and hesitant. This cannot be explained as a matter of FTA considerations because the mourner's demanding request in example (8–2) is a dire threat whereas his offer in example (8–3) is not a threat at all and yet made in a humble manner. Rather, the contrast is brought out by judging whether or not the action belongs to the domain of role-entitlement; *direct requests can be made when the content of a request remains within the domain of the speaker's role-entitlement, and indirect requests come from outside his role-entitlement*.

### *8.2.2 Repetition as assimilating with the other's role: It takes two to complete it*

Interpersonal conversations sometimes observe one repeating the other's word, phrase or even whole utterance. This phenomenon is a part of mimicry that has been well investigated in psychology and social psychology. The macro definition of mimicry refers to the transmission of culture through generations by mimicking others' behaviour (e.g. customs, linguistic acquisition, gestures, how to behave in public). However, psychological experiments usually focus on mimicry in dyadic interactions in daily life in which one mirrors the other in gestures and facial expressions, or one repeats what the other says, in order to examine the effects of mimicry.

*Mimicry is largely accepted as a tool for "social glue"*; "it is an indispensable tool for binding individuals to their social groups" (Van Knippenberg and Van Baaren, 2008: 173). Many experimental results confirm the positive effects of mimicry, i.e. participants who were mimicked by the confederate showed more positive and cooperative attitudes toward the latter than those who were not. For example, Van Baaren et al. (2003) report that a waitress who repeated her customers' order in a restaurant received larger tips than when she did not. Van Baaren et al. (2009) also investigated how participants would engage with each other in discussing recent advertisements, and found that mimicry had changed their attitudes and opinions; they had an "assimilative mindset" and behaved "in a more prosocial manner" (2384).

Lakin et al. (2003: 145) assume that "mimicry played an important role in human evolution" for survival reasons. "Our ancestors lived in an environment in which individuals who were 'on their own' were not always able to survive and successfully reproduce". Therefore, individuals who were successful in achieving harmonious and cooperative relationships with their group members could continue to be included in the group. Mimicry has been one such strategy to establish rapport and group ties.

Though mimicry is largely associated with positive effects in communication, it is contextually driven because it can draw out negative effects due to the mimic's intention (e.g. giving warning, threatening), the nature of the ongoing interaction (e.g. police interrogation, hostile interaction) and the way in which mimicry is conducted (e.g. raising tones to show the mimic's doubt). Perrin et al. (2003), for example, provide an interaction between mother and daughter in which the mother repeats the daughter's word. Because the situation clearly reveals that the mother does not approve of her daughter coming home late at night, her mimicry of her daughter's utterance works retroactively, creating "a function of conceded authority" (1853). Liu et al. (2011) also report that mimicry can serve as a threat rather than enhance rapport if the interactants are reminded of money. They assume that, because reminders of money drive people to pursue their goals more eagerly and to act alone, maintaining their freedom, the mimicry of such reminders is likely to give the impression that their autonomy is threatened.

Regarding verbal mimicry, Perrin et al. (2003) summarise the following functions:

1. Taking-into-account function: the mimic's active listening
2. Confirmation-request function: the mimic confirming what he has heard is right
3. Positive-reply function: expressing agreement, implying that the mimic would have uttered the same as the other person
4. Negative-reply function: the mimic disapproving or denying the other's statement

Makino (1989[1980]) uses the term *kyookan* (共感 empathy) in analysing some examples of verbal mimicry in Japanese, which can be categorised as a hybrid between cases (2) and (3) above. This is further explained by Yokomori et al. (2018), who observed the repeated utterance with a mood marker *ne* attached to it. The mood marker *ne* indicates shared information; the information delivered by the first speaker is shared by the second speaker with *ne*. The mimic may already know the information imparted by the original utterance but, by repeating the utterance, indicates her empathy, or "a shared understanding with the prior speaker" (167), and the mood marker *ne* confirms or enhances this understanding.

The following two examples may be broadly categorised as empathy, but they seem to offer something more than just sharing; that is, **the mimic assists the other to sort out something or reach his decision**. The repetition of the other person's utterance allows the mimic to assimilate himself with the other (Interactional Role-Identity), and to encourage the other's thinking process. This kind of mimicry is often conduced in teaching situations when a teacher repeats a student's utterance fragments, trying to extract a complete answer from the student while the latter is in the process of answering the teacher's question. A similar use of mimicry is found in example (8–4) in which the mother is assisting her son in completing a jigsaw puzzle:

(8–4) A mother and her six-year-old son are playing with a jigsaw puzzle.

子供：んー、これは、
Child: N−, kore wa,
hmm this Top
'Hmm, this...'

母親：うん、うん、これは?
Mother: Un, un, kore wa?
yep yep this Top
'Yep, yep, this?'

子供：ここやな、お、お、
Child: Koko ya na, o, o,
here MD MD Intj Intj
'Here, surely, wow.'

母親：そうそう、ここやなあ、そうやそうや
Mother: Soo soo, koko ya naa, soo ya soo ya
good good here MD MD right MD right MD
'Good, good, here, surely, right, right…'
*Note*. *ya* (mood marker) in the utterances above is a mood marker of Osaka dialect, equivalent to affirmation, *da* (copula).

This is a part of the conversation I personally observed when I visited a friend of mine who is the mother in the interaction. As the child attempts to place pieces one by one while talking to himself, his mother repeats his utterances, especially when he is working out where to place each piece. Through mimicry, the mother is *making* (SI's term) an interactional role by assimilating herself with the child, and following his thinking process, which subtly encourages the child to succeed in placing pieces.

Mimicry to assist the other's thinking process is not limited to educational situations in the teacher–student or mother–child relationship. It also occurs between close friends; by showing empathy with mimicry, the mimic intends to make it easier for the other person to reach her decision, especially when the mimic can foresee a negative reply. This is shown in example (8–5).[5]

(8–5)

JSK01: 九時についてなきゃいけないの？
Ku-ji ni tsui-te-nak-ya ikenai no?
9 o'clock at arrive-TE-not-if must Q
'I should arrive there at nine o'clock, right?'

JBI01: 九時から三時間ぐらい。しかもボランティアなんですけど。
Ku-ji kara san-jikan gurai. Shikamo borantea na-n-desu kedo.
9 o'clock from three-hour about also volunteer Cop-Nomi-Polite MD
'(You work) three hours from nine o'clock. What's worse, it's voluntary work, so..'

JSK01: 交通費も？
Kootsuu-hi mo?
travel-expense too
'No travel expense, either?'

JBI01: 出ません、クー。
Demas-en, kuuu.
pay-not[Polite] oof
'No, unfortunately. Oooof!'

5 This excerpt is from the data collected by Mayumi Usami and her team at Tokyo University of Foreign Studies, compiled as 'BTS *ni yoru tagengo hanashi kotoba koopasu*' (*Multi-lingual conversation corpus by Basic Transcription System*).

<both of them laughing for a few seconds>

無理ならよろしいのよ。
Muri-nara yoroshii no yo.
not possible-if okay[Formal] MD MD
'If it is too much, that's okay, dear (you can say "no").'

JSK01: うん…
Un
right
'Right.'

JBI01: うん… ← Mimicry 1
Un

JSK01: ちょっときついなあ。
Chotto kitsui naa.
a little hard MD
'A little hard, indeed (hard to accept the job).'

JBI01: ちょっときついなあ。 ← Mimicry 2
Chotto kitsui naa.
a little hard MD
'A little hard, indeed (hard to accept the job).'

JSK01: うん…
Un…
yep
'Yep.'

JBI01: 分かりました。突然すみません。
Wakari-mashi-ta. Totsuzen sumimasen.
understand-Polite-Past sudden sorry[Polite]
'I understand. Sorry (I asked you this) unexpectedly.'

*Note.* J – Japanese, 01 – File number 1
(There is no explanation for what 'BI' and 'SK' stand for in the data.)

This is an interaction between two young female friends of the same age. JBI01 phoned JSK01 to ask her to take over the voluntary work JBI01 was supposed to do. First, JBI01 explained what the job involves and then, just before the interaction in example (8–5), states that the job is located near Akabane Station, which is quite a distance from their homes. Therefore, JSK01 is already reluctant to go because the job starts at nine in the morning, which means she has to leave home at seven. As she gets to know more about the job (no payment, no travel expenses), she is more hesitant about accepting it. Then the requester starts to help her friend turn down the request more easily without feeling guilty. First, in line 4, she throws in an interjection *kuu*, which is a sign of regret or disappointment, as if she were voicing her friend's emotion. Second, the requester is humorous in line 5: *Murinara yoroshii no yo* (If it is too much, that's okay, dear). This utterance uses an unusual style for a young adult toward her close friend; it makes her sound like an old-fashioned, upper-class, elderly woman. By pretending to be a different person like this (a dissociative role or mock stage performance; cf. Section 7.2.3 and also the next sub-section), she tries to ease her friend's mind because playing an old-fashioned and authoritative old woman creates a humorous air, implying that the requester is light-hearted about her request. The utterance also sounds as though the refusal of the request were granted by an authority, which further eases her friend's mind.

Third, when her friend starts uttering *un* (right) and *chotto kitsui naa* (it's a bit hard = I don't want to do it), she repeats these utterances as indicated as Mimicries 1 and 2 in example (8–5). Through the mimicries, the requester aligns or assimilates herself with her friend, and demonstrates to her that she is of the same mind as she goes through some agony in turning down the request. Furthermore, because the mimicries occur in the process of refusal, they serve to assist or even encourage the friend to reach her decision. Interestingly, Mimicry 2 is not just a repeated utterance, but ends up as voicing her friend's decision (refusal), and so uttering only *un* (yep) in line 10 is sufficient for her friend to indicate she has just turned down the request.

To refuse a request that has been made by a close friend requires a tactical approach in order to not jeopardise their friendship, and thus JSK01 utters *chotto kitsui naa* (it's a bit hard) at most to hint her reluctance. However, the requester is strategically more skillful at using humour in her speaking style to ease her friend's mind and mimicries to help her friend reach a decision. Furthermore, the second mimicry allows her friend to turn down the request without a word of refusal.

### *8.2.3 Pretending to be a different person: Dissociative roles*

The interactional roles shown in Figure 8.1 (Section 8.1), of all types of role-identity, are the most psychologically determined, individually-oriented and instantaneously created. We have seen a number of examples of interactional roles implemented in linguistic terms; for example, mock stage performances in the case of speech-level shifts (cf. Section 7.2.3), an insistant attitude in example (8–1) and the speaker's assimilation with the other person in examples (8–4) and (8–5) all show interactional roles that are prompted on the spur of the moment. This sub-section introduces another type of interactional role: dissociative role.

The term 'dissociation' is borrowed from psychology, defined as "a perceived detachment of the mind from the emotional state… the act of separating…" (MedicineNet.com). Phenomena of dissociation range from shifts in mood and self-observation as a third person to pathological cases of disharmony of the mind, the last of which is the foremost concern in areas of psychology.

The self is not composed of a unity but "made up of modules, and the modules are made up of modules themselves" (Erdelyi, 1994: 7). However, we normally do not recognise ongoing dissociations in our daily life, believing that we have a unified self. On the contrary, dissociations constantly occur whenever psychological shifts are witnessed; for example, absorption into film-watching and music-listening, day-dreaming and speaking to oneself as if two persons were on the scene.

A dissociative role in this book, however, does not mean that the speaker ignores the other interactant by going into his own world. Rather, through a dissociative role, the speaker is in a sense momentarily dissociated from his social role (e.g. teacher versus student as Institutional Roles), creating another role in relation to the other participant in interaction. Furthermore, unlike day-dreaming or total devotion to something, the speaker is fully aware of his social role in the given situation and conscious of the ongoing interaction.

Many examples of speech-level shifts can be categorised as dissociative roles[6]; especially, mock stage performances that allow the speaker to pretend to be a different role, as shown in example (7–12) of Section 7.2.3 in which a friend and colleague plays the role of a food delivery person when giving the other person a rice bowl with beef on top. By raising a speech level from the plain form to the addressing honorific, he acts as a different person as if he were on stage.

The examples in this sub-section also demonstrate dissociative roles through different linguistic manipulations, which allows the speaker to play a different role while intending to be strategically polite to the other person:

(8–6) 花： …あとは直樹に頑張ってもらうしかないから。難しいことは分かんないけどさ。
ぜってえ負けんじゃねえぞ！…

Hana: … Ato wa Naoki ni ganbat-te-morau-sikanai kara. Muzukashii koto wa
the rest for keep it up-TE-receive-only MD complex thing Top
wakan-nai kedo sa. Zettee maken-ja-nee zo!
know-not MD MD never lose-Nomi-MD MD

'After (some efforts on my side), I must ask you Naoki to keep it up, that's all I can do. I don't know the details (of your business), really. Never give up, buddy, got it?'

(*Hanzawa Naoki*, Number 2)

Example (8–6) is an excerpt from the conversation between Hanzawa Naoki, the protagonist, and his wife, Hana. Before the utterance of example (8–6), Hana explained that she makes an effort to be friendly with Hanzawa's bank members' wives, intending to gain some information useful for Hanzawa, who

6 Obana (2012a) provides an example whereby the protagonist in the film makes an embarrassing confession with his dance teacher by shifting his speech level down to abrupt forms. Because the confession shows "not just his feelings but the deep analysis of his psychology from the past to the present time", a dissociative role is created to confess as a third person in order to "avoid directly facing the humiliation caused by revealing his true emotions" (12–13).

is experiencing turmoil in the bank. Then, as in example (8–6), she says that after all it is her husband who must deal with the problem. To encourage her husband, she utters *zettee makenja nee zo* (Never give up, buddy, got it?). The style of this utterance is quite unusual for a woman who is well-educated and a banker's wife. It is a rough, coarse male speech style with a strong command *nee zo* (never, got it?). At the same time, Hana thumps her husband hard on the back to match her speech style.

The utterance underlined in example (8–6) could be rude and boorish unless the interactants are very close, feel a sense of solidarity and trust each other. Only then is it possible for the utterance to be interpreted as a good-will strategy. Hana pretends to be a big, tough and rough guy to imply her solid and fervent support, as if the support came from a powerful giant of a man. Hana *makes* (creates) a dissociative role and, by taking advantage of it, provides the maximum support for her husband.

**A dissociative role enables the speaker to act as a different person, and helps her achieve her purpose by maximising this characterisation (dissociative role).** In the case of example (8–5), the speaker pretends to be an old-fashioned elderly woman as if saying 'no' would be granted due to the authoritative speech style she uses, while creating a humorous air at the same time. By easing her friend's mind like this, the speaker implies that the refusal of her request would not jeopardise their friendship. In example (8–6), the dissociative role allows the speaker to act as a rough and powerful guy, through which the speaker provides the maximum support for her husband.

Although the dissociative roles above appear to be categorised as a different politeness strategy, they still conform to the way in which politeness strategies are defined by Brown and Levinson (1978, 1987). In the case of example (8–5), a request is an imposition on the other person, and its refusal may also pose a threat to the requester. The dissociative role (an authoritative old woman) then serves as a strategy to mitigate these potential FTAs. The imposition of a burden request is alleviated because the speaker creates a humorous air to imply that the request can easily be turned down. A potential threat via the refusal of the request is also mitigated because the refusal appears to be granted due to the authoritative woman's permission (I grant that you can say 'no'). Therefore, the dissociative role in example (8–5) serves as an equivalent to Brown and Levinson's negative strategies.

The dissociative role in example (8–6), on the other hand, works as enhancing a positive strategy. The content of the utterance underlined is an encouragement, a positive strategy that uplifts the hearer's spirit (though this particular strategy is not listed in Brown and Levinson's positive strategies; cf. Endnote 1 of Chapter 1). The dissociative role then enhances the encouragement by taking a ruthless step into the other's territory and by adopting a tough man's image to create a greater sense of support.

The next example is another dissociative role by which a third person is created to utter on behalf of the speaker. This strategy allows the speaker to readily turn down her friend's request by toning down the impact of refusal and by creating a humorous air. Example (8–7) is an excerpt from File 4 of the same data as example (8–5), which belongs to File 1. A different pair of female friends of the same age are situated in the context in which the one asks the other to take over the job at Akabane and the other refuses the request:

(8-7)

JBI04: 行ってくれよー(笑い)　行ってくれないとさ(笑い)
It-te-kure yoo <laugh> It-te-kure-nai-to sa <laugh>
go-TE-receive MD go-TE-receive-not-if MD
'Kindly go, please! If you don't, well…'

JSK04: 25日でしょ？
Nijuu-go nichi de-sho?
25 day Cop-Aux
'It's on the 25th, right?'

JBI04: うん、金曜日
Un, kinyoobi
yep Friday
'Yep, Friday.'

JSK04: うーーん
Uuuun
hmmm
'Hmm.'

JBI04: うーーん … (JSK04)さん、どうでしょう(笑い)
Uuuun (JSK04)-san, doo-de-shoo <laugh>
hmmm how is it
'Hmm… . Ms (JSK04), how is it (how does it sound to you)?'

JSK04: (JSK04)さん、(JSK04)さん、眠いです　(両者の笑い)
(JSK04)-san, (JSK04)-san, nemui desu. <both start laughing>
sleepy Cop[Polite]
'Ms (JSK04), she is sleepy (too early to get up).'

Before the interaction in example (8–7), the requester, JBI04, has been persistent in asking her friend to take over the job especially after she hears that her friend would be available on Friday. Her friend, JSK04, has indicated that she is reluctant, and even said that she would like to get a passport on that day. Then, in example (8–7), JBI04 (the requester) changed her strategy to approach her friend more formally (JBI04's last line) by calling her 'Ms JSK04 (her surname)' and with an addressing honorific *des-* in *deshoo* (*des* + MD) whereas, before this line, JBI04 was addressing her friend by her first name and using quite abrupt and demanding words (as shown in line 1 of the example).

To respond to JBI04, JSK04 in her last line took advantage of JBI04's formal addressing term, and repeated it to refer to herself. Addressing herself as 'Ms JSK04' (the surname + *-san*), she speaks as if she were talking as a third person, and provides a good reason ('she is sleepy') to turn down the request. In other words, JSK04 *creates a dissociative role as a third person, and lets this role speak on her behalf*. Especially because the utterance in the last line means a refusal, which may inflict a threat, *the dissociative role mitigates its negative impact on the other person* (JBI04). Moreover, the last two lines create a different world from their close friendship in reality, and both of them playfully act on stage, which generates a humorous effect without jeopardising their relationship.

## 8.3 Summary

This chapter has examined politeness strategies in the non-honorific world, particularly by focusing on shifts in strategic planning in the same discourse. During the interaction, the interactants experience constant changes in their psychological states, which may trigger different role performances, including politeness strategies. They do not necessarily follow social norms all the time, but may take a different route to be polite by considering the surrounding context. I assume that such strategic changes come from shifts in Interactional Role-Identity, and role changes are implemented as different politeness strategies. I have also argued that strategic planning is not just a matter of FTA considerations, but is often coordinated with Role-Identity considerations prior to those of FTA.

# 9 Honorific strategies

Strategies that are used specifically in the world of honorifics are called 'honorific strategies' (Obana, 2009, 2019). Since honorifics serve to reflect the social relationship between interactants in a given situation, honorific strategies follow the way in which they perceive their relationship. Therefore, honorific strategies often differ from strategies in the non-honorific world, especially when the interactants' duties and responsibilities, which are derived from their role-identities, are brought to the fore in a given context. In Chapter 8, we have seen some strategies in the non-honorific world as the implementation of Role-Identity, and in this chapter, Role-Identity is more extensively utilised to construct honorific strategies. This is because social differences (in age, status and familiarity), which are entailed in honorific strategies, are in fact an outcome of the interactants' role-identities. In this chapter, I focus on some particular honorific strategies that contrast with English strategies. Since honorific strategies are constructed based on the interactants' Role-Identity (cf. Sections 2.3 and 8.1), the consideration of Role-Identity often acquires a priority over that of Face Threatening Acts (FTAs; Brown and Levinson, 1978, 1987), while FTA considerations in many ways serve as an effective motive for English strategies. These different motives highlight the contrast between politeness strategies in English and honorific strategies.

## 9.1 Pragmatic transfer as a source for distinguishing Japanese from English

In the field of Second Language Acquisition studies, language transfer is one of the most discussed concepts in analysing learners' errors. 'Language transfer' is traditionally defined as *the influence of linguistic (e.g. word, phrase, sentence structure) or extra-linguistic features (e.g. socio-cultural norms, communication styles) of the first or native language (L1) upon the target language (L2)*. Pragmatic transfer is a transfer of extra-linguistic features, and politeness across cultures is often investigated based on pragmatic transfer made from learners' L1 to L2. (e.g. Blum-Kulka, 1982; Brown, 2011; Félix-Brasdefer, 2015; Garćia, 1989; Li, 2018; Olshtain, 1983; Olshtain and Cohen, 1989; Tanaka and Kawade, 1982, to mention just a few).

As Blum-Kulka (1982) and Olshtain (1983) demonstrate, learners may not transfer pragmatic features of L1 to L2 if they perceive them as language-specific. For example, set phrases such as *otsukaresama* (お疲れ様 'thank you' or 'good-bye') and *yoroshiku onegai shimasu* (よろしくお願いします the greeting when strangers meet or when a favour one asked has been accepted; cf. Endnote of Chapter 6) are seldom transferred incorrectly and, in spite of their complex socio-pragmatic interpretations, learners can safely handle them in a given situation.

Pragmatic transfer more often occurs when learners perceive L1 pragmatic features as universal. Learners may perfectly construct utterances in L2, and yet their L1 socio-cultural background may affect the way in which those utterances are built up. In the case of learning politeness, learners may well mean to be polite by adopting strategies from their L1, but may cause intercultural miscommunication. For example, Brown (2011) analysed English speakers' (learners') errors in Korean honorific use, and one of his claims was that "a Western mode of politeness ideology influences honorifics in L2 talk" because "Western politeness places more emphasis on 'modulation politeness' (the modifying of the propositional content or the force of an utterance) rather than 'indexical politeness' (the signalling of appropriate relationships to addressees, referents and bystanders)"[1] (259).

Félix-Brasdefer (2015) also argues for pragmatic transfer, as witnessed in errors made by US English speakers learning Spanish in the context of service encounters because learners tend to apply politeness strategies of their L1 (English) to those of L2 (Spanish). For example, indirect request strategies (e.g. 'Can I have…?), which are appropriate in English, are not customary in Spanish contexts because Spanish-speaking customers in general employ direct request strategies.

In a similar way, English speakers in learning Japanese tend to apply English strategies to honorific practices in Japanese.[2] For example:

(9-1) *先生、答えを黒板に書いていただきたいですか。

| | | | | | | | |
|---|---|---|---|---|---|---|---|
| *Sensei, | kotae | o | kokuban | ni | kai-te-itadaki-tai | desu | ka. |
| teacher | answer | Acc | blackboard | on | write-TE-receive[Hon]-want | polite | Q |

'Sir/Ma'am, would you like me to write my answer on the board?'

Example (9–1) is a typical error English speakers make by transferring the English politeness strategy into Japanese. In English, asking directly what

1 This also applies to the learning of Japanese honorifics. For example, English speakers tend to assume that, when one becomes closer to the other, one can stop using honorifics with the other. This comes from the confusion between psychological distance and social distance; while the former may trigger strategic changes (e.g. from formal to casual approaches), the latter maintains the use of honorifics.

2 All the Japanese errors exemplified in this chapter are extracted from the data I collected when I was teaching Japanese to university students in Australia between 1989 and 2003.

the other wants is a strategy to avoid a potential FTA (Brown and Levinson, 1978, 1987; cf. Endnote 1 of Chapter 1). In Japanese, on the other hand, such an enquiry sounds as though the speaker were reluctant to undertake the task (writing the answer on the board) because asking what the senior wants is equated with probing her thoughts (or true intention).[3] Both languages aim at the same target, i.e. the speaker wants to confirm whether she has correctly understood the teacher's instruction. However, in Japanese, this should be expressed by asking whether what the speaker is going to do would be approved of by the teacher, but not by directly asking what the teacher wants. Therefore, it is more appropriate to utter, for example:

(9-2) 先生、答えを黒板に書けばよろしいですか。
Sensei, kotae o kokuban ni kake-ba yoroshii desu ka.
teacher answer Acc blackboard on write-if good[Formal] Polite Q
'Sir/Ma'am, would it be all right if I write the answer on the board?'

This utterance comprises two strategies that conform to the world of honorifics. First, it is customary in Japanese to describe what the speaker should or can do rather than to ask the other person what is on her mind. Reading and verbalising the other person's mind is granted only between intimate relations such as family members and close friends, but seldom considered appropriate in the world of honorifics. Second, to confirm whether the speaker has understood the teacher's instruction correctly, the speaker employs a strategy to seek the teacher's approval. In this way, because the speaker as a junior cannot directly ask her senior (teacher) what the latter wants, the speaker must take two steps to achieve this aim.

Such an apparent periphrastic approach, however, does not mean that Japanese people are more FTA conscious than English speakers. Rather, Role-Identity is primarily considered in Japanese strategies, which often overrides FTA considerations. Just as honorifics are socially indexical, honorific strategies reflect the indexing of the social relationship between the interactants. This will be further clarified in the following sections.

Example (9–2) illustrates one of constraints imposed on a junior's role-identity, i.e. a junior cannot directly ask what her senior wants. A junior's role-identity, however, does not always mean imposing constraints on the junior. In other contexts, it entitles the junior to directly ask, instruct and negotiate with her senior, provided these actions are within the domain of the junior's roles (e.g. tasks, responsibilities and assigned duties). Let us look at

3 Example (9–1) also contains another error. The auxiliary *-tai* (want to~) is used either to describe the speaker's wish, or to ask what her absolute *uchi* member (e.g. family member) wants (cf. Endnote 1 of Chapter 6 regarding 'absolute *uchi* members'). Therefore, it can never be used to ask what a senior wants, which means that *-tai* never occurs with honorific terms.

the following example, which illustrates a common error made by Japanese speakers in learning English:

(9–3) I was absent last week. *Please give me a handout.

I often observe my students making this error. University students are capable of using indirect request forms such as 'Can I ~?' in other contexts[4] (e.g. when they want to go to the toilet), but for particular requests, they use direct forms, as in example (9–3). This is a pragmatic transfer from Japanese to English because the translation of the direct request in example (9–3) is perfectly natural in Japanese:

(9-4) 先週休んだので、配布プリントください。

| | | | |
|---|---|---|---|
| Senshuu | yasun-da-node, | haifupurinto | kudasai. |
| last week | absent-Past-because | handout | give please |

'I was absent last week, so please give me a handout.'

The direct request shown in example (9–4) is devised as a result of Role-Identity considerations. It is a reflection of the student's role-identity in relation to the teacher because the request content is within the domain of students' entitlements. At the same time, the content is the teacher's responsibility to fulfil. Their role-identities (teacher versus student) are mutually recognised and entail what entitlements and rights, duties and responsibilities are to be expected in their interaction.

## 9.2 Fundamental differences in strategic planning in English and Japanese: FTA based versus Role-Identity based

The examples we examined in the previous section suggest that English and Japanese honorific strategies are often different in strategic planning. By 'strategic planning' I mean 'the 'basic motivation behind the way in which one approaches the other'. In many ways, strategic planning in English involves FTA considerations; English strategies are based on the measurement of degrees of FTA, which determines how the speaker linguistically approaches the other person to mitigate a potential threat. This often precedes the speaker's social position, although higher-ranked people may issue orders to their juniors in certain circumstances (e.g. in the army, teaching instructions in class).

4 Japanese students tend to assume that indirect request forms should be used when they need their teacher's permission or approval for their action. This may be considered another pragmatic transfer from Japanese to English.

**Honorific strategies in Japanese, on the other hand, are the result of how the speaker perceives the social relationship with the other person, i.e. one's role-identity in relation to that of the other** (e.g. teacher–student, employer–employee, senior–junior). The responsibilities, duties, rights and entitlements involved with the interactants' role-identities are primarily considered and often assume **priority over FTA considerations**.

Although strategic planning in the world of honorifics appears to be a complex system (e.g. it is situationally changeable), it can be largely categorised into two types. First, **speaker's role-identity (e.g. junior in status) may have to use certain constraints when approaching the other (e.g. her senior)**. Example (9–2) falls into this category. Second, the **speaker's role-identity entitles or allows her to attempt to maintain her rights within the domain of roles assigned to her role-identity**. Example (9–4) demonstrates such an entitlement, which takes precedence over FTA considerations, and direct approaches are granted even if the other person is higher in status.

Having emphasised the difference in strategic planning between English and honorific strategies, I do not mean to claim that FTA is always a secondary consideration in Japanese, or that strategic planning in English is consistently based on the nature of an utterance, i.e. whether or not it is face threatening. For example, Holmes (2001: 268) claims that degrees of formality depend on the social relationship between interactants, and so the choice of formal styles primarily takes Role-Identity into consideration. We also observed in Section 6.2.4 that Holmes and Stubbe (2003: 5) provide an example in which a junior, when negotiating with the boss, uses hedging and attenuation devices as the junior is fully aware of his position and should leave the decision to his boss. Furthermore, Locher (2004: 212) provides an example that disagreement at meetings was often unmitigated because the speaker wished to make her higher position clear. In this way, in English, too, the speaker's role-identity (e.g. higher in status) is distinctively brought to the fore during the interaction, which may take precedence over FTA considerations.

In Japanese, too, FTAs do exist in social interaction and the consideration of FTA and Role-Identity occurs interchangeably even when the same interactants are involved. For example, Obana (2012a: 5–6) provides two different types of strategy: one based on Role-Identity and the other on FTA in spite of the same speaker interacting with the same tour group (a scenario presented below). As the tour guide's role entitlement, he talks to his group by using the direct imperative form though it is honorific-marked because the content of his request is accepted as the role performance (job entitlement) of his institutional identity (guide). This is illustrated in examples (9–5) and (9–6):

(9–5) 昼食の後、1時までにバスにお戻りください。
Chuushoku no ato, ichi-ji madeni basu ni o-modori-kudasai.
lunch of after one-o'clock by bus to Hon-return-please
'After lunch, please come back to the bus by one.'

(9–6) オプショナルツアーですが、お申し込みの時に代金をお支払いください。
Opushonaru tsuaa desu ga, o-mooshikomi no toki ni daikin o
optional tour Polite Conj Hon-application of time at fee Acc
o-shiharai-kudasai.
Hon-pay-please
'Concerning an optional tour, please pay the fee at the time of application.'
(If you choose an optional tour, please pay the fee at the time of booking.)

The guide's tasks, such as announcing schedules, rules and instructions and making requests of the group so as to conduct the tour smoothly are all tacitly recognised by both the guide and the group members. When the guide's role responsibilities are strongly expected to be fulfilled by both parties, the use of imperative forms as in examples (9–5) and (9–6) is appropriate, signifying the professional fulfilment of his (social) role as a guide; it also substantiates the fact that the requests fall into the category of his job entitlement. If the guide uses indirect forms in the requests above, he does not sound confident or professional.

If, on the other hand, a request does not clearly fall into the domain of the guide's job entitlement, he cautiously employs an indirect strategy to mitigate the imposing nature of the request. This may accompany the use of higher levels of honorifics. For example:

(9–7) こちらおひとりさまでいらっしゃいまして、あの〜、こちらのテーブルにご一緒に座っていただいてもよろしいでしょうか。
Kochira o-hitori-sama de-irasshai-mashi-te kochira no teeburu ni
this[Formal] Hon-alone-Hon Cop-Prof[Hon]-Polite-Conj this[Formal] of table at
go-isshoni suwat-te-itadai-temo yoroshii-des-hoo ka.
[Hon]-together sit-TE-ask[Hon]-if good[Formal]-Polite-Aux Q
'This person is (attending the tour) alone. Would it be all right (with you) if (I) ask (this person) to sit (with you) at this table?'

Example (9–7) is uttered in the situation whereby the guide has noticed that a customer who has joined the tour alone has been left out when the others are taking their seats for lunch. The guide is asking a group at a table with a vacant seat to let this lone customer join them. Although this kind of arrangement may be something the guide is obliged to carry out, he has no right to directly ask (or impose) the group at the table to act as he wants. In this type of request, the guide's role entitlement is not clearly recognised as he is acting as a mediator between the lone customer and the group at the table. His request is granted only with the group's consent. Therefore, an indirect approach to gain the hearers' permission is used (Obana, 2012a: 6). Furthermore, due to the nature of the request, the honorific levels used in example (9–7) are much higher than those in examples (9–5) and (9–6) because the guide is fully aware that this customer as well as the group at the table are all his customers and so is careful not to offend any of them. The request that is outside his role entitlement makes the guide become more careful of handling the situation, which results in triggering higher levels of honorifics.

Be that as it may, strategic planning in Japanese is very different from that in English, particularly when actions (e.g. requests, offers) are derived from Role-Identity considerations in Japanese. In the following sections, honorific strategies that are contrastive with English strategies are illustrated. As mentioned earlier, strategic planning in Japanese is of two types: constraints on a junior's behaviour and a junior's entitlement or right to pursue her assigned tasks. These two types of strategic planning are implemented in reality in the following way ('juniors' in this chapter, for convenience, refers to people 'lower in status', 'younger in age' or 'working in the service industry').

### *Constraints on a junior's behaviour*

1. Juniors cannot evaluate their senior's professional performances. Praising, permission (e.g. 'It's okay if you want to use it') and appreciation of the senior's work attitude (e.g. 'You are a hard worker') are all derived from evaluations of seniors' performances. Instead, it is customary that juniors refer to their own impression or how much they have learnt (in the case of praising), make a positive offer (permission) and show sympathy (work attitude). Judgemental enquiries concerning a senior's ability are also evaluative; thus, juniors generally take the approach of asking their senior's approval.
2. Juniors cannot ask or verbalise (based on their assumption) what their senior wants. Instead, juniors commonly utter what they can offer or ask whether their assumption is approved. The offer is to be imposed to indicate how willing the speaker is to act.

### *A junior's entitlement or right to pursue her assigned tasks*

3. When pursuing their duties and responsibilities, juniors can be direct in request, instruction and suggestion as long as the content of these actions remains within the domain of tasks assigned or socially expected.

## 9.3 Praising, recognition and checking: Evaluative statements are condescending

Praising is generally considered a positive politeness strategy. It is the result of the recognition of the other person's (H's) good performance or outlook (Positive strategy 1: 'Notice, attend to H' of Brown and Levinson [1978, 1987]) and then the verbalisation of the speaker's approval or positive judgement (Strategy 2: 'Exaggerate [interest, approval, sympathy with H]'). In both English and Japanese, praising is one of the most effective approaches to achieve solidarity, empathy and support. However, praising in fact stems from the result of one's *evaluation* of the other's presentation even if it results from a positive assessment. Therefore, praising can be judgemental and condescending in the honorific world depending on the given situation, and so should take a different route by avoiding evaluative expressions.

In working situations, seniors' role-identity generally includes their responsibility to guide and look after their juniors; juniors, meanwhile, learn and grow as a result of their seniors' guidance, advice and encouragement (though we are surely talking about an ideal working situation). In such circumstances, seniors do not expect their professional performances to be evaluated or their capabilities to be questioned by their juniors. For example:

(9-8) ＊社長の今日のスピーチはりっぱでした。
*Shachoo no kyoo no supiichi wa *rippa-deshi-ta.*
president of today of speech Top excellent-Polite-Past
'Your speech today was excellent, sir.'

Example (9–8) is not acceptable as an honorific strategy because the expression underlined alludes to an evaluation as a result of assessing how well the senior has performed. The adjective form *rippana* (splendid) delivers open praise when describing a third person's presentation; for example, *rippana hito* (りっぱな人 an outstanding person), *rippana seiseki* (りっぱな成績 one's excellent school record or achievements at work). However, when facing the senior, the junior cannot use this adjective, especially when intending to praise the senior's professional performance.[5] In fact, example (9–8) would not remain a simple error but could be misunderstood as sarcasm due to its condescending connotation. A simple solution to this is to replace *rippana* with *subarashii* (wonderful), which does not carry any condescending features. Alternatively,

5 The discussion here is limited to seniors' *professional performances*. In other cases, such as their performance in their hobbies and recreational activities (e.g. 'Ma'am, you have a nice collection of antiques', 'Nice shot, ma'am'), and their belongings (e.g. 'Sir, your new glasses suit you well', 'You are living in a nice house, sir'), direct appreciations with honorific terms can be freely expressed.

as shown in example (9–9), **praising commonly takes the form of demonstrating how the speaker has benefitted from the senior's performance**:

(9–9) 社長、今日のスピーチですが、感動しました。
Shachoo, kyoo no supiichi desu ga, kandooshi-mashi-ta.
president today of speech Polite Conj be impressed-Polite-Past
'Sir, I was impressed with your speech today.'

In a similar way, the appreciation of a senior's contribution needs to take a different route from that in English. Example (9–10), a learner's error, is a direct application of an English positive strategy to Japanese by specifying in what way the senior's performance has benefitted the speaker (junior). In Japanese, on the other hand, the appreciation of a senior's performance cannot be made with such a direct approach; it has to be expressed in a more roundabout way. For example, appreciation may be displayed by referring to what the speaker has received rather than what the other has contributed or how the other's contribution has been judged:

(9–10) ＊先生の講義は論文を書くときにとても役に立ちました。
*Sensei no koogi wa ronbun o kaku toki-ni
teacher of lecture Top thesis Acc write when
totemo yakunitachi-mashi-ta.
very useful-Polite-Past
'Your lectures were very useful when I was writing my thesis.'

Example (9–10) is acceptable if it is uttered to another student (and the teacher is not present). However, it is not acceptable when facing the teacher because *yakuni tatsu* (be useful) indicates a judgement of the effect of the teacher's lectures on the speaker. A more appropriate approach is:

(9–11) 先生の講義を受けたおかげで論文を完成することができました。
Sensei no koogi o uke-ta okagede ronbun o
teacher of lecture Acc have-Past thank to thesis Acc
kanseisuru koto ga deki-mashi-ta.
complete thing Nom can-Polite-Past
'Thanks to your lectures I attended, I could complete my thesis.'

Example (9–11) shows how much benefit the speaker has received and *okagede* (thanks to) adds the speaker's gratitude.

Judgemental expressions also include enquiries into the other's ability. It is almost a taboo to ask seniors questions that imply checking their ability. For example:

(9–12) ＊今の説明おわかりですか。 → 今の説明でよろしいでしょうか。
*Ima no setsumei o-wakari-desu ka.
now of explanation Hon-understand-Polite Q
'Have you understood what I explained?'
→ Ima no setsumei de yoroshii-desh-oo ka.
now of explanation with good[Formal]-Polite-Aux Q
'Is my explanation satisfactory?'

*Owakari desu ka* is a direct question regarding whether the other has understood the speaker's explanation. However, in reality it is not a simple question but an enquiry into the other's ability. Furthermore, the evaluative utterance, with honorific markings on it, turns into a sarcastic question; that is, whether the other (senior) person has enough intelligence to understand the explanation. It may even be interpreted as the speaker underestimating her senior's ability. On the other hand, the corrected utterance, *de yoroshii deshooka* (is [this explanation] acceptable?) takes the approach of asking the other's approval, which at the same time implies that if the other did not understand the explanation, it is not the other's fault but may be due to the speaker's insufficient explanation.

## 9.4 Direct enquiries into seniors' wants are intrusive: The case of offer

This section discusses another constraint imposed on the junior's role-identity. Juniors are not expected to directly ask what their seniors want or to verbalise what is on their mind. On the other hand, in English direct enquiries are logically plausible in order to offer precisely what the other wants. This is Strategy 9 in Brown and Levinson's (1978, 1987) positive strategies: 'Assert or presuppose S's knowledge of and concern for H's wants'. In Japanese, this strategy can freely be used in the non-honorific world, but more likely has the opposite effect in the honorific world. It is because direct enquiries are tinged with the following pragmatic effects, which do not match the nature of the honorific world:

1. Seniors are expected to look after and nurture their juniors. Juniors are expected to receive their seniors' instructions and advice. Being not socially equal and in the receptive position, juniors are not supposed to verbalise what is going on in their seniors' mind as this is either patronising or intrudes into their territory.
2. Probing into seniors' minds by directly asking what they want may diminish the effect of juniors' positive offers because such a direct enquiry is tinged with juniors' reluctance to offer or their hope that seniors will turn down the offer.

The honorific world by nature tenders a social distance, which erects a certain barrier that juniors are not expected to cross. Probing into a senior's mind by directly asking what they want, therefore, is interpreted as crossing such an invisible barrier. In Japanese, therefore, strategies are constructed from the speaker's perspective by referring to what she can do for the other, which I call a '**serving-attitude**' in this book. For example:

(9–13) ＊お手伝いが必要でいらっしゃいますか。
*O-tetsudai ga hitsuyoode-irasshai-masu ka.
Hon-help Nom necessary-Prog[Hon]-Polite Q
'I wonder if you need help, ma'am.'
→ お手伝いいたします。
O-tetsudai-itashi-masu.
Hon-help-do[Hon]-Polite
'I'll help you, ma'am.'

In English, asking whether or not the other person wants to accept an offer is an essential prologue to an offer. In particular, great care is needed when offering help because it may curtail or impede the other's independence, or the other simply may not need help. Therefore, an enquiry into whether or not the other person needs help is an appropriate strategy in English. However, such an enquiry has the opposite effect in Japanese because it sounds as though the speaker is reluctant to help the other. The corrected utterance in example (9–13) may sound imposing in the English sense, but it is a serving-attitude, promising the best the speaker can do and leaving the other (senior) to make a decision regarding whether to accept help or not. Let us look at another example:

(9–14) ＊のどがおかわきになりませんか。コーヒーショップに行きましょう。
*Nodo ga o kawaki ni nari-mase-n ka. Koohii shoppu ni iki-mash-oo.
be thirsty[Hon]-Polite-not Q coffee shop to go-Polite-Aux
'Aren't you thirsty? Let's go to a coffee shop.'
→コーヒーでもいかがですか。
Koohii demo ikaga-desu ka.
coffee like how about[Hon]-Polite Q
'How about coffee or something?'

Although *nodo ga okawaki ni narimasen ka* (Are you not thirsty?) itself is not grammatically incorrect, asking a senior whether she is thirsty is not common in the honorific world. As mentioned above, probing into seniors' minds is not a role juniors are expected to *take* (SI's term) as juniors are in the receptive position. Furthermore, an offer in Japanese is made directly without preamble because the offer is beneficial for the other person, and so a direct offer implies that it is genuine and the speaker is willing to fulfil it.

By the same token, the underlined part in example (9–15) is a superfluous preamble as it elaborates on what the other person (senior) should (or should not) do, and sounds as though the speaker (junior) were inducing the other to decline the offer (e.g. 'No, that's fine. I will get a taxi [at the airport].'). Therefore, the junior is expected to make a direct offer without referring to the senior's behaviour. This is another serving-attitude in constructing honorific strategies:

(9–15) ＊タクシーでいらっしゃらなくてよろしいですよ。私が迎えにいきます。
*Takushii de irasshara-naku-te yoroshii-desu yo.
taxi by come[Hon]-not-TE good[Formal]-Polite MD
Watashi ga mukae-ni iki-masu.
I Nom pick up-to go-Polite
'You don't have to catch a taxi. I will come and pick you up.'
→ 私がお迎えにいきます。
Watashi ga o-mukae-ni iki-masu.
I Nom Hon-pick up-to go-Polite
'I'll come and pick you up.'

In a similar way, service industries in Japan exercise a serving-attitude when assisting their customers. Osugi (1993) examines English politeness in various contexts and uses the term '**you-attitude**' in the case of an offer in English. You-attitude means that offering something beneficial to a customer (e.g. sending a pamphlet, offering a free service) is realised in linguistic terms that emphasise the beneficiary 'you'; e.g. '*You* will receive a voucher if you stay with us during the campaign.' However, this approach has the opposite effect in Japanese because it is likely to be interpreted as the speaker boasting of an offer or implying that customers should be happy about being offered the benefit. For example:

(9–16) ＊当社のパッケージ旅行にお申し込みの方は、ホテルのサービス券がお受け取りになれます。
*Toosha no pakkeeji-ryokoo ni o-mooshikomi no kata
our company[Formal] of package tour to Hon-apply of person[Formal]
wa, hoteru no saabisu-ken ga ouketorininar-e-masu.
Top hotel of service-voucher Nom receive[Hon]-can-Polite
'If you apply for one of our package tours, you can receive a hotel voucher (with which you can use their facilities free of charge).'

The underlined part, which is not acceptable as an honorific strategy, is directly translated from the English strategy (you-attitude). Example (9–16) should be changed to the utterance that is furnished with the travel agent's serving-attitude, as shown in example (9–17):

(9–17) 当社のパッケージ旅行にお申し込みの方に、もれなくホテルのサービス券を差し上げます。
Toosha no pakkeeji-ryokoo ni o-mooshikomi no kata
our company[Formal] of package tour to Hon-apply of person[Formal]
ni, morenaku hoteru no saabisu-ken o sashiage-masu.
to without exception hotel of service-voucher Acc give[Hon]-Polite
'To all customers who have applied for a package tour with us, we will give away a hotel voucher.'

It should be noted that *ouketori ni naremasu* (you can receive [it]) in example (9–16) is not wrong if it is used in other contexts where the customer receives something that is expected as her right, such as something purchased or something previously arranged. For example:

(9–18) 航空チケットは空港カウンターでお受け取りになれます。
Kookuu chiketto wa kuukoo kauntaa de o uketori ni na-re-masu.
air ticket Top airport counter at receive[Hon]-possible-Polite
'You can collect your air ticket at a [check-in] counter at the airport.'

(9–19) ミールクーポンはチェックインの際にお受け取りになれます。
Miiru kuupon wa chekku-in no saini o uketori ni na-re-masu.
meal voucher Top check in of when[Formal] receive[Hon]-possible-Polite
'You can receive a meal voucher at the time of check-in.'

In both cases, what is to be received is what has been expected or arranged. The speaker has made an arrangement for the customer to receive a ticket or voucher at a certain place. These cases, then, are not offer but merely explanations telling the customer where he can pick up a ticket or meal voucher.

## 9.5 Direct request: One's role entitlement prior to FTA considerations

This section discusses role-identity (whether junior or senior) that allows one to uphold rights or fulfil assigned tasks as long as these belong to the domain of one's role-identity entitlements. Role-identity entitlements derive from the interactants' institutional as well as task-based role-identities. Requests based on such role-identity entitlements are made directly (in the imperative form) though they are honorifically-marked. English speakers (learners) make errors in Japanese because they may assume that burden requests are potential FTAs and therefore should be made in an indirect way or through laying down preambles to temper potential threats. However, in Japanese, role-identity entitlements often take precedence over FTA considerations, and direct requests as the fulfilment of such entitlements are generally judged as professional performances.

Institutional Role-Identity allows juniors to make a direct request to their seniors provided the request content is something seniors are institutionally expected to fulfil; e.g. a request to check a junior's document, provide advice on the next project or supply the agenda for next week's meeting. For example:

(9–20) ＊部長、もしお時間がおありでしたら、来週提出する企画を見ていただけないでしょうか。
*Buchoo, moshi o-jikan ga o-ari-deshi-tara,
division manager if [Hon]-time Nom [Hon]-have-Polite-Conj
raishuu teishutsusuru kikaku o
next week submit plan Acc
mi-te-itadak-e-nai-desh-oo ka.
look-TE-receive[Hon]-possible-not-Polite-Aux Q
'Sir, if you have time to spare, would it not be possible for you to have a look at the plan I'll submit next week?'

→部長、来週提出する企画なんですが、ちょっと見ていただけますか。
Buchoo, raishuu teishutsusuru kikaku na-n-desu ga,
division manager next week submit plan Cop-Nomi-Polite Conj
chotto mi-te-itadak-e-masu ka.
a little look-TE-receive[Hon]-possible-Polite Q
'Sir, [this is] a plan I will submit next week. Could you have a look?'

In example (9–20), the asterisked utterance contains two inappropriate honorific strategies. First, the preamble *moshi ojikan ga oarideshitara* (if you have time to spare) is an unnecessary preliminary to the division manager (unless a junior is talking to a terrifying senior) because checking the junior's project plan is one of the senior's responsibilities; thus, the junior is entitled to directly ask her senior to check it. Another inappropriate strategy is the use of a negation *-nai* in the request: *~itadakenai deshoo ka* (would it not be possible ~?) because the use of a negation in the request provides options and so the other person can say 'no'. Unless a junior intends to be sarcastic (implying 'You are so mean not to do it') or is terrified of her senior, she is entitled to request directly and her senior is expected to meet the request. **As they both**

**mutually recognise their social relationship, and the duties and responsibilities involved in it, requests that fall within the tasks assigned to those roles are made directly.**

Task-based Role-Identity similarly authorises a junior to make a direct request to her group members, who she is assigned to look after. For example, when a university student is assigned to act as organiser of her seminar group's tour, her requests to her group (including the professor responsible for the seminar group) are made directly as long as the requests belong to the domain of her tasks as an organiser; e.g. asking the group to turn up at 8 o'clock at the train station, to bring their laptop with them and to inform her of special dietary needs so that she can pass them on to the hotel at which they are staying. Requests like these are strategically constructed with polite but imperative forms, which may sound authoritative if translated into English. For example:

(9–21) セミナー旅行の出発は大阪駅西コンコース、8時です。＊時間までにお集まりくださいませんか。
Seminaa ryokoo no shuppatsu wa oosaka eki nishi konkoosu,
seminar travel of departure Top Osaka station west concourse
hachi-ji desu. *Jikan made ni o-atsumari-kudasi-mase-n ka.
eight-o'clock Polite time by Hon-gather-please-Polite-not Q
'To those who join our seminar tour, we are to leave at eight. Could you not please gather at the West Concourse of Osaka station by then?'

→ 時間までにお集まりください。
Jikan made ni o-atsumari-kudasai.
time by Hon-gather-please
'Please gather by then.'

Example (9–21) is an announcement made by a student tour organiser for her seminar group. The announcement is meant for her peers, *senpai* (senior students) and even her seminar professor. A student has been appointed as an organiser and her assigned job (task-based role) continues until the tour ends. Her task-based role is recognised by all members of her seminar group and, until the tour is completed, she is entitled to make direct requests to the group including her seniors and professor as long as the request content remains within the domain of her task-based role. Example (9–21) involves one of her task-based roles, and the request is directly made.

Tentative requests in some circumstances may sound as though the speaker is not professional, especially when those requests are in accordance with official rules or institutional principles. For example:

(9–22) ＊スーツケースをお開けになってお見せになってくださいませんか。
*Suutsu keesu o o ake ni nat-te o mise ni nat-te-kudasai-mase-n ka.
suitcase Acc open[Hon]-TE show[Hon]-Te-please-Polite-not Q
'Could you not please open your suitcase, and kindly show [the inside to me]?'
→スーツケースの中を拝見します/ スーツケースを開けてください。
Suutsu keesu no naka o haikenshi-masu.
suitcase of inside Acc look[Hon]-Polite
'I will have a look at the inside of your suitcase.'
Suutsu keesu o ake-te-kudasai.
suitcase Acc open-TE-please
'Please open your suitcase.'

This example involves a situation at airport customs. The officer has authority to check passengers' suitcases, therefore the request should be made in a polite but imperative form. This attitude may sound authoritarian to English speakers, but the officer's role-entitlement is linguistically entailed in the imperative form, which is accordingly judged as professional. On the other hand, the utterance identified with an asterisk in example (9–22) takes a rather indirect approach and may sound fawning to the passenger; alternatively, it may be interpreted as sarcasm by alluding to the passenger's possible criminal activity (e.g. smuggling).

## Summary of Part III

Chapters 8 and 9 focused on politeness strategies. Although I do not deny that potential FTAs are considered in constructing strategies in Japanese, the speaker's social position, stance and/or relationship with the other interactant (i.e. the consideration of Role-Identity) may often be prioritised over FTA considerations. One of the reasons for this is that the context of the discourse goes through different phases, in each of which the interactants experience a different psychological state and take a different stance to suit how the conversation develops. I call this phenomenon 'role-shifts', and role-shifts invite different strategies. The shift from indirect to direct requests discussed in Chapter 8 falls into this category. In Japanese society, indirect requests that incorporate a negation and an interrogative are quite common even between close friends: a social norm. However, as the interaction proceeds, the speaker may employ a direct approach to obtain the other person's consent; the speaker is now *making* a different role to achieve her goal.

Chapter 8 also discussed a type of verbal mimicry, in which the mimic encourages or helps the other person to achieve his goal. In this case, the speaker *makes* an interactional role that allows him to assimilate himself with the other person.

Chapter 9 discussed honorific strategies that are particularly contrastive with English strategies. Role-Identity considerations are more extensively utilised in constructing honorific strategies. This is because, as honorifics are a social index, indicating the social relationship between the interactants, so too are honorific strategies, which inevitably consider the interactants' role-identities. The chapter discussed constraints on juniors; for example, praising seniors' professional performances requires a different route so that they are expected to express what they have learnt from or how impressed they are with their seniors' performance rather than praising seniors directly. This is because direct praising is a result of evaluation, and so evaluative comments are not socially appreciated. The chapter also focused on enquiries into seniors' needs/wants. In the process of making an offer to satisfy the other person's needs/wants, Japanese strategic planning takes the speaker's perspective, i.e. the best the speaker can offer or suggest is linguistically realised, rather than direct enquiries into what the other person wants. This is another constraint on strategic planning in the honorific world. Finally, the chapter illustrated direct requests made by juniors to seniors, which are a junior's entitlement to maintain her rights in an institutional environment or when she is assigned a certain task until the task is completed.

# Concluding remarks

## What this book has offered

This book presented varied aspects of Japanese politeness by examining extant studies on politeness, discussing some issues that have been raised in and outside Japan and introducing a few new assumptions. Furthermore, technical terms were carefully introduced, and those illustrated in previous studies were re-examined in order to understand them more appropriately. As a concluding remark, I summarise the following three points that form the core of this book:

1. What constitutes politeness
2. Contingencies and discursiveness of politeness
3. Role-Identity as a process to determine polite behaviour

### *What politeness constitutes*

In this book, I enquired into what constitutes politeness. While many previous studies take a synchronic approach to define politeness or to extract elements of politeness (e.g. evaluations, rapport, face-work), I took a diachronic route to reach what constitutes politeness. As politeness emerges in social actions, the relationship between man and society is the first step to understanding what motivate us to require politeness in our society. First, the basic human needs, 'involvement' and 'independence' (terms borrowed from Scollon and Scollon [1995] but interpreted as the 'basic human needs' in this book), are both opposite and contradictory and yet everybody in society has these needs and attempts to pursue them in social life. However, because our constant consciousness of other people constrains us from pursuing them freely, we make an effort to strike a balance between involvement and independence. For this, negotiations and adjustments are essential to satisfy our own as well as others' need for independence and involvement.

Second, negotiations to satisfy the basic human needs in social life are based on certain standards that have been established (but not prescribed) in society. Such standards originate in another element of human nature that we evaluate

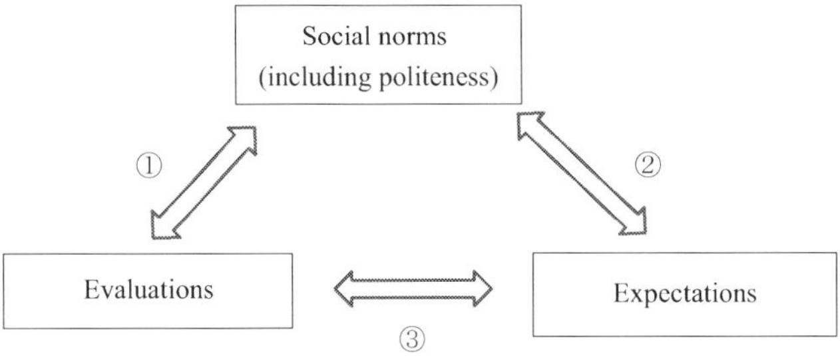


*Figure C.1* The mechanism of social norms, expectations and evaluations

almost everything in our daily life. Evaluations may be historically handed down and eventually prevail in society, thereby becoming social standards or social norms. Socially prevalent evaluations are called 'social evaluations' (Li, 2014; Abdai and Miklósi, 2016). Social evaluations presuppose the existence of social norms because social norms are socially and historically constructed evaluations (① in Figure 3.1, Chapter 3, and reproduced here as Figure C.1). Evaluations, once socially accumulated, yield expectations, which in turn assist or affect evaluations (③). Furthermore, as defined in sociology, social norms, for their existence, rely on shared expectations, and expectations contribute to stabilising social norms as a more reliable resource for determining social behaviour (②). Therefore, 'social norms', 'social evaluations' and 'expectations' form a triangular mechanism in which they evoke and control one another.

This mechanism closely related to the way in which politeness is diachronically borne out. I then claimed that politeness is a social norm. Just as a social norm is strongly "supported by shared expectations" (Bicchieri, 2006: 10), so too is politeness substantiated by expectations. Just as a social norm is closely related to 'social evaluations' as a collective, socially-prevalent tool for the judgement of social actions, reflecting the values, needs and interests of the society to which people belong, so too politeness presupposes evaluations in a similar way. Therefore, the triangle mechanism shown in the figure also corresponds to what constitutes politeness and how politeness (social norm), evaluations and expectations feed and condition one another.

### *Contingencies and discursiveness of politeness*

A diachronic approach, as discussed above, allows one to explore how the constituents of politeness, social norms, evaluations and expectations, are borne out and sheds light on how they are intertwined. The concept of 'social norm' is a convenient tool in politeness research because social norms implemented in social life have an adjustable, negotiable and contingent nature. Social norms as defined in sociology are not rigid or prescribed rules

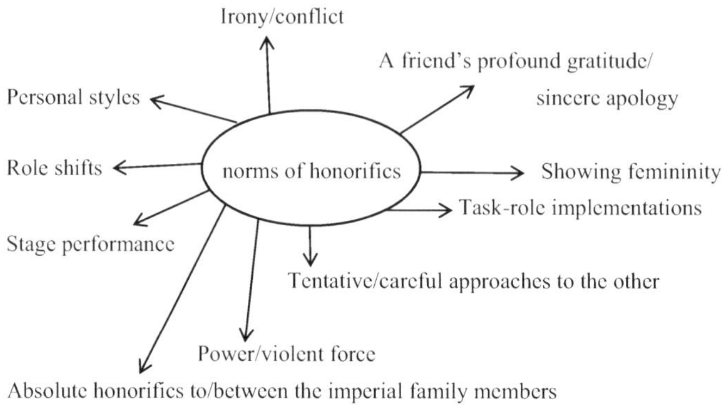


*Figure C.2* Norms of honorifics and applications/deviations of honorific use

as has often been believed in pragmatics (e.g. Eelen, 2001; Ide, 1989). They emerge rather than are given, and are constructed and re-constructed as the societal climate changes. Thus, social norms can be negotiated and adjusted to suit a particular community or a given situation, which Bicchieri (2006) compares to the 'grammar of society'.

Just as the grammar of a language functions as a point of departure, based on which we manipulate our language to create unique linguistic products (e.g. complex structures, written and spoken styles, deviated word orders), social norms of politeness are a cornerstone, whereby their derivative, adjusted and rearranged performances are witnessed in varied situations. However, just as the grammar of a language is implicit in actual linguistic realisations, social norms of politeness are implicit in such apparent diversities.

As an example of the relationship between politeness as a social norm and its contingencies and discursiveness, I provided Figure 3.3, Chapter 3 (reproduced here as Figure C.2), in which norms of honorifics serve as a cornerstone for the application and derivations of politeness. I analysed these variations in Chapter 7.

As discussed in Section 6.2.4, honorifics (or the so-called 'conventional honorifics') are markings on an utterance that has strategically been constructed, functioning as the indexing of distance whether it is vertical, horizontal or psychological. They have no semantic contributions but index the social relationship the interactants recognise in a given situation. The concept of distance is normatively entailed in the following three situations (or motivations):

1. Social status and age differences
2. Formal situations
3. Familiarity

These three situations lay the groundwork for norms of honorifics or conventional honorifics. However, as creative creatures, we manipulate, take advantage of and even twist honorific terms to indicate our emotional state (e.g. profound gratitude to a friend, conflict) and interactional stance (e.g. mock stage performance), or to present how we want to look to the public (e.g. personal style, femininity). And yet, norms of honorifics are implicit in these variations of honorific use.

### *Role-Identity as a process to determine polite behaviour*

In Sections 2.3 and 8.1, I introduced the concept of Role-Identity based on Symbolic Interactionism (SI), a significant role theory in social psychology. Role-Identity is a useful tool to explain the processes involved in achieving politeness. Indeed, politeness is implemented based on social norms (or local norms of one's community). However, polite behaviour is not directly extracted from norms of politeness; rather, it goes through some processes in interactants' minds to determine the most appropriate behaviour in the given context. This is because interactants first 'define the situation' (SI's term) by observing the actual place of their interaction, other participants, the nature of an interactional topic and how it is going (and perhaps more, such as common ground, atmosphere, likes and dislikes). Once the situation is defined, the interactants' identities emerge, which formulate their behaviour (role-performances); "identity emerges and is acknowledged in situations – we live in the identity process" (Altheide, 2000: 4). Or, "identity is a product" (Bucholtz and Hall, 2005: 585) and "identity is the social positioning of self and other" (586) and is implemented in role performance.

Just as politeness has normative aspects, roles have normative forces; roles carry shared behavioural expectations. This kind of role performance is called 'role-taking' in SI, and roles are constructed in relation to and relevant to other participants' positions (e.g. a teacher's role is recognised only in relation to the role of students: 'Institutional Role-Identity'). The so-called conventional honorifics and honorific strategies are the implementation of role-taking by indexing the social relationship recognised by the interactants in a given situation. I also created the term 'Task-based Role', another role-taking, which explains, for example, why the same interactants may or may not use honorifics in different situations.

SI equally emphasises flexible and improvised aspects of roles. This is called 'role-making' by adjusting our behaviour to fit the on-going situation or to fit with the performance of other participants. I used the term, 'Interactional Role-Identity', which is equivalent to role-making, to explain, for example, why speech-level shifts occur within the same discourse. Role shifts trigger linguistic changes, whereby the speaker signals his stance, psychological state or intention to achieve his goal.

SI's Role-Identity is a convenient tool, especially for the investigation of Japanese politeness. It is because Japanese politeness in many ways entails the

| Subcategories of Role-Identity | Examples of roles | Examples of the application of Role-Identity to politeness |
|---|---|---|
| <more socially determined><br>Institutional Role | family members, job categories | honorifics used due to social differences in age, status and familiarity, formality in ceremony or public, honorific strategies |
| Task-based Role | chairperson, MC, organiser of an event, mentor, jury | direct request as a task role performance, honorifics used as meeting attendees |
| <more psychologically determined><br>Interactional Role | the speaker's stance, emotional state, pretending to be someone else, | plus-level shifts to show profound gratitude, apology and attentiveness, to encourage the other by pretending to be a different person |

*Figure C.3* Sub-categories of Role-Identity

indexing of the social relationship between interactants. The so-called conventional honorifics are 'indexical politeness' (Brown, 2011), and honorific strategies, as they occur in the world of honorifics, also reflect this indexical nature. We have seen that honorific strategies impose certain constraints on the junior's side when approaching her senior. Some of the interactants' task-based roles, on the other hand, entitle them to use direct approaches so long as the content of the approach is recognised as one of the tasks assigned to the interactants. Therefore, when dealing with indexical aspects of Japanese politeness, Role-Identity comes into play to explain why particular linguistic forms are required in a given situation.

Since SI generally focuses on individuals' identity in relation to a large network of social actions, the domain of identities SI deals with is limited to social identities (e.g. racial, ethnic, gender and national) and Role-Identity (equivalent to Institutional Role-Identity in this book, such as job categories). However, because politeness often reveals subtle, contingent role performances during the interaction, I provided further sub-categories of Role-Identity such as Task-based roles and Interactional roles (including 'dissociative roles'). Sub-categories of Role-Identity are shown in Figure C.3 (which is an adaptation of Figure 2.3, Chapter 2). Here, I add some examples of the application of Role-Identity to politeness.

## What this book has left out

In writing this book, I made every effort to illustrate diverse phenomena of Japanese politeness with ample examples from conversations, films and television dramas. However, I admit that the book did not cover other types of politeness, such as regional varieties and gender differences. Discussing honorifics, for example, I focused on standard Japanese which learners of Japanese generally encounter. However, regional varieties are enormous due to dialectal influences, and many regions do not practise 'honorifics' as described in standard Japanese and many dialects do not offer the equivalence of honorifics. For example, in Osaka city, it is quite common to use V' + *hari-masu* in place of *sonkei*-styles (deferential forms); e.g. *itsu iki-hari-mashi-ta?* (when did you go?) in Osaka dialect instead of *itsu irasshai-mashi-ta?*

An extreme example is observed in the southern part of Osaka prefecture where the so-called *senshuu-ben* (泉州弁 Senshu dialect) does not include deferential or humble styles; their communal politeness is practised with much more intimate expressions than in other places of Osaka. I once had an encounter with a person from Senshu who offered me sweets when we were attending a seminar, uttering *omee, kore iru-ke?* (do you want this?). First, as a woman I never use *omee* (you) unless I intend to be humorously rude by pretending to be a tough guy; I would never use it to someone in a formal situation such as a seminar. Second, I would add at least addressee honorifics when offering something because we met at the seminar for the first time. Finally, the mood marker *ke* is beyond my imagination; I understand it is equivalent to the question marker *ka*, but it is very difficult to accept it as a polite expression. Initially, I was shocked to hear the utterance made by an educated-looking woman in formal business wear. However, I later learned that, because we got along so well, the woman perhaps felt close to me, and so wanted to be *polite* to me by using her dialectal expression. For her, intimacy is more polite than maintaining a distance (she was initially using standard honorifics). 'Politeness' is, therefore, perceived differently in different regions, especially when dialectal expressions are involved since their pragmatic meanings are different from those of standard Japanese. Regional differences, then, would not be mere variances, but can constitute independent systems of politeness.

Politeness is not just a matter of linguistic expression, however. It also comprises extra-linguistic features, such as gestures, facial expressions and physical distance. Although studies on such extra-linguistic features are beyond the scope of this book, I admit that they are important in achieving politeness in social life. In this book, I occasionally referred to some extra-linguistic features when analysing some examples discursively. For instance, example (1–4) of Chapter 1 appears to be an appreciative exchange between a senior and his junior when looking at the apparent thanking and appreciative expressions inherent in the junior's appropriate honorific use. However, the senior's hostile expression matches the implications extracted from the previous negative context, and so convinces viewers of the drama that example (1–4) is a sarcastic rather than an amicable exchange; linguistic politeness on the surface is actually sarcasm.

Another example of a facial expression, in example (7–18) of Chapter 7, helps interpret precisely the effect the speaker achieves by delivering a self-exalting honorific. Self-exalting can be interpreted as arrogance or disparagement of the hearer but, in this example, it is interpreted as ironic humour because of the speaker's wondering look.

The dramatic gesture shown in example (7–12) of Chapter 7, in which someone gives a take-away meal to a friend and colleague by using an addressee honorific and pretending to be a delivery person, is playful. The speaker acts dramatically as if hiding his embarrassment about behaving in a motherly way because he is worried about his friend's problem. Laughing during the interaction in example (8–7) of Chapter 8 also indicates that the requester's attitude is amicable in spite of her friend's reluctance to accept the job. In this way, extra-linguistic features are an important tool for analysing the discourse context, and play a significant role in polite behaviour.

Politeness, therefore, is a field that is ripe for further exploration. More varieties of politeness are expected to be found by examining, for example, regional dialects and gender differences. More new features that entail politeness may be discovered by probing into extra-linguistic features discursively. Given the scope of this book, I have described only a part of Japanese politeness. Therefore, upon completion of this book, I could not help but feel that it is not the end but the beginning of my research on politeness. I find it thrilling as a researcher that there remains a lot more to be investigated.

# References

Abdai, J. and Miklósi, A. (2016). The origin of social evaluation, social eavesdropping, reputation formation, image scoring or what you will. *Frontiers in Psychology*, *7*(1772), 1–13.

Altheide, D. L. (2000). Identity and the definition of the situation in a mass-mediated context. *Symbolic Interaction*, *23*(1), 1–27.

Araki, H. (1973). *Nihonjin no koodoo yooshiki – Taritsu to shuudan no ronri* [*Behavioural patterns of the Japanese: The logic of their dependence on others and groupism*]. Tokyo: Kodansha.

Araki, H. (1990). *Keigo no japanorojii* [*The Japanology of honorifics*]. Tokyo: Sotaku-sha.

Araki, H. (1994). *Nihongo ga mieru to eigo mo mieru* [*Seeing Japanese in depth enables one to see English clearly*]. Tokyo: Chuoo koron-sha (Chu-ko shinsho series).

Asada, H. (2001). *Keigo de toku nihon no byoodoo • fubyoo*doo [*Equality and inequality in Japan deciphered with honorifics*]. Tokyo: Kodansha gendai-shinsho.

Asada, H. (2005). *Keigoron – Uta kara keigo e* [*On honorifics – from poetry to honorifics*]. Tokyo: Bensei Shuppan.

Asada, H. (2014). *Keigo no genri oyobi hatten no kenkyuu* [*Studies on principles of honorifics and the development of honorifics*]. Tokyo: Tokyo-dō Shuppan.

Asamatsu, A. (2013[2003]). *Keigo no genzai o yomu* [*The Observation of Honorifics Today*]. In Y. Kikuchi (ed.), *Keigo – Asakura Nihongo Kooza* (5th ed.). Tokyo: Asakura Shoten, 93–116.

Asch, S. E. (1956). Studies of independence and conformity – 1. A. minority of one against a unanimous majority. *Psychological Monograph – General and Applied*, *70*(9), 1–70.

Attardo, S. (2000). Irony markers and functions – Towards a goal-oriented theory of irony and its processing. *Rask*, 12, 3–20.

Barke, A. (2011). Situated functions of addressee honorifics in Japanese television drama. In B. L. Davies, M. Haugh and A. J. Merrison (eds), *Situated politeness*. London: Continuum International Publishing Group, 111–128.

Barnlund, D. C. and Yoshioka, M. (1990). Apologies – Japanese and American styles. *International Journal of Intercultural Relations*, *14*, 193–206.

Baurmann, M., Brennan, G., Goodin, R. E. and Southwood, N. (2010). Introduction. In M. Baurmann, G. Brennan, R. E. Goodin and N. Southwood (eds), *Norms and values: The role of social norms as intruments of value realisation*. Munich: Nomos, 7–15.

Berger, P. L. (1966). *Invitation to sociology*. Harmondworth: Penguin Books.

Bernstein, J. H. (2010). Folk concepts. In H. J. Birx (ed.), *A reference handbook – 21st century anthropology*. Thousand Oaks, CA: Sage, 848–855.

Bicchieri, C. (2006). *The grammar of society – The nature and dynamics of social norms.* Cambridge: Cambridge University Press.

Bicchieri, C. (2009[1997]). Learning to cooperate. In C. Bicchieri, R. Jeffrey and B. Skyrms (eds), *The dynamics of norms*. Cambridge: Cambridge University Press, 17–46.

Bicchieri, C. and Chavez, A. (2010). Behaving as expected – Public information and fairness norms. In M. Baurmann, G. Brennan, R. E. Goodin and N. Southwood (eds), *Norms and values: The role of social norms as instruments of value realisation*. Munich: Nomos, 151–172.

Blumer, H. 1969. *Symbolic interactionism – Perspective and method.* Berkeley, CA: University of California Press.

Blum-Kulka, S. (1982). Learning to say what you mean – A study of speech act performance of learners of Hebrew as a second language. *Applied Linguistics*, *3*, 29–59.

Bourdieu, P. (1977). *Outline of a theory of practice* (translated by R. Nice). Cambridge: Cambridge University Press.

Bourdieu, P. (1984). *A social critique of the judgement of taste*. Cambridge, MA: Harvard University Press.

Brislin, R. and Yoshida, T. (1994). *Intercultural communication training – An introduction.* Thousand Oaks, CA: Sage.

Brown, K. and Ogilvie, S. (eds) (2009). *Concise encyclopaedia of languages of the world.* Oxford: Elsevier Science.

Brown, L. (2011) *Korean honorifics and politeness in second language learning*. Amsterdam/Philadelphia: John Benjamins Publishing Company.

Brown, P. and Levinson, S. (1978). Politeness – Some universals in language usage. In E. N. Goody (ed.), *Questions and politeness – Strategies in social interaction*. Cambridge: Cambridge University Press, 56–289.

Brown, P. and Levinson, S. (1987). *Politeness – Some universals in language usage*. Cambridge: Cambridge University Press.

Bucholtz, M. and Hall, K. (2005). Identity and interaction – A sociocultural linguistic approach. *Discourse Studies*, *7*(4–5), 585–614.

Burgers, C. (2011). Finding irony: An introduction of the verbal irony procedure (VIP). *Metaphor and Symbol*, *26*, 186–205.

Chang, H. C. and Holt, G. R. (1994). A Chinese perspective on face as inter-relational concern. In S. Ting-Toomey (ed.), *The challenge of facework*. Albany, NY: State University of New York, 95–131.

Chin, B. (2003). Doonendai no shotaimendooshiniyorukaiwanimirareru ‘da-tai’ enoshifuto – shookisiyasuijookyoo to sonohindo o megutte [Shifts to *da*-style observed in conversations between new people of the same age group – Concerning their occurrence circumstances and frequencies]. *Kokuritsu Kokugo Kenkyuujo, Nihongo Kagaku*, *14*, 7–28.

Chinami, K. (2005). Nihongo no poraitonesu – Sono seido-teki sokumen to goyooron sokumen [= Japanese politeness – its institutional and pragmatic aspects]. *Kyushu University Korean-Japanese Language and Culture Studies*, *6*, 35–66.

Cook, M. H. (1996a). Japanese language socialization – Indexing the modes of self. *Discourse Processes*, *22*, 171–197.

Cook, M. H. (1996b). The use of addressee honorifics in Japanese elementary school classrooms. In N. Akatsuka, S. Iwasaki and S. Strauss (eds), *Japanese/Korean Linguistics* (5th ed). Stanford, CA: CSLI Publications, 67–81.

Cook, M. H. (1997). The role of the Japanese *masu* form in caregiver–child conversation. *Journal of Pragmatics*, *28*, 695–718.

Cook, M. H. (2008). Style shifts in Japanese academic consultations. In K. Jones and T. Ono (eds), *Style shifting in Japanese*. Amsterdam: John Benjamins Publishing Company, 9–38.

Cook, M. H. (2011). Are honorifics polite? Uses of referent honorifics in a Japanese committee meeting. *Journal of Pragmatics*, *43*, 3655–3672.

Coulmas, F. (1981). Poison to your soul – Thanks and apologies contrastively viewed. In F. Coulmas (ed.), *Conversational routine*. The Hague: De Gruyter, 69–91.

Cousins, S. (1989). Culture and selfhood in Japan and the US. *Journal of Personality and Social Psychology*, *56*, 124–131.

De Fina, A., Schiffrin, D. and Bamberg, M. (eds) (2006). *Discourse and identity*. Cambridge: University of Cambridge Press.

Deckert, K. S. and Vickers, H. C. (2011). *An Introduction to sociolinguistics – Society and identity*. London: Continuum.

Doi, T. (1981). *The anatomy of dependence*. Tokyo: Kodansha.

Drew, P. and Sorjonen, M.-L. (1997). Institutional dialogue. In T. A. van Dijk (ed.), *Discourse as social interaction*. London: Sage, 92–118.

Dunn, C. D. (2013). Speaking politely, kindly, and beautifully – Ideologies of politeness in Japanese business etiquette training. *Multilingua*, *32*(2), 225–245.

Dunbar, R. (1988). *Grooming, gossip and the evolution of language*. Cambridge, MA: Harvard University Press.

Edmonds, B. (2014). Three barriers to understanding norms – Levels, dynamics and context. In M. Xenitidou and B. Edmonds (eds), *The complexity of social norms*. Heidelberg: Springer, 189–197.

Edmondson, W. (1981). *Spoken discourse – A model for analysis*. London: Longman.

Eelen, G. (2001). *A critique of politeness theories*. Manchester: St. Jerome.

Erdelyi, H. M. (1994). Dissociation, defense, and the unconscious. In D. Spiegel (ed.), *Dissociation – Culture, mind, and body*. Washington, DC: American Psychiatric Press, 3–20.

Esfeld, M. (2003). What are social practices? *Indaga. Revista internacional de Ciencias Sociales y Humanas*, 1, 19–43.

Félix-Brasdefer, J. C. (2015). *The language of service encounters – A pragmatic-discursive approach*. Cambridge: Cambridge University Press.

Fine, G. A. (2005[2001]). Enacting norms – Mushrooming and the culture of expectations and explanations. In M. Hechter and K.D. Opp (eds), *Social norms*. New York: Russell Sage Foundation, 139–164.

Foley, W. A. (1997). *Anthropological linguistics – An introduction –*. Oxford: Blackwell.

Fraser, B. (1990). Perspectives on politeness. *Journal of Pragmatics*, *14*(2), 219–236.

Fukada, A. and Asato, N. (2004). Universal politeness theory – Application to the use of Japanese honorifics. *Journal of Pragmatics*, *11*, 131–146.

Fukushima, N. (2013). *Gensoo no keigo-ron* [*Illusion of theory of honorifics*]. Tokyo: Chikuma Shoin.

Garćia, C. (1989). Apologizing in English – Politeness strategies used by native and non-native speakers. *Multilingua*, *8*, 3–20.

Gecas, V. and Burke, J. P. (1995) Self and identity. In K. S. Cook, G. A. Fine and J. S. House (eds), *Sociological perspectives on social psychology*. Boston, MA: Allyn & Bacon, 41–67.

Geyer, N. (2008). *Discourse and politeness*. London: Continuum.

Givón, T. (1983). Topic continuity in discourse – An introduction. In T. Givón (ed.), *Typological studies in language*, Vol. 13: *Topic continuity in discourse*. London: John Benjamins Publishing Company, 1–41.
Goffman, E. (1959). *The presentation of self in everyday life*. New York: Doubleday Anchor.
Goffman, E. (1963). *Stigma – Notes on the management of spoiled identity*. Englewood Cliffs, NJ: Prentice Hall.
Goffman, E. (1967). *Interaction ritual – Essays on face-to-face behavior*. New York: Garden City.
Goffman, E. (1971). *Relations in public – Microstudies of the public order*. New York: Penguin.
Grice, H. P. (1975). Logic and conversation. In P. Cole and J. Morgan (eds), *Syntax and semantics*, Vol. 3: *Speech acts*. New York: Academic Press, 41–58.
Gu, Y. (1990). Politeness phenomena in modern China. *Journal of Pragmatics*, *14*(2), 237–257.
Hagino, S. (2001). *Minasan kore ga keigo desu yo* [*Everyone, this is* keigo]. Tokyo: Riyonsha.
Hagino, S. (2005). *Hontoo no Keigo* [*True honorifics*]. Tokyo: PHP Shinsho.
Haugh, M. (2004). Revisiting the conceptualisation of politeness in English and Japanese. *Multilingua*, *23*(1/2), 85–109.
Haugh, M. (2007). The discursive challenge to politeness research – An interactional alternative. *Journal of Politeness Research*, *3*, 295–317.
Haugh, M. and Obana, Y. (2011). Politeness in Japan. In Z. D. Kádár and S. Mills (eds), *Politeness in East Asia*. Cambridge: Cambridge University Press, 147–175.
Heath, J. (2011). *Following the rules – Practical reasoning and deontic constraint*. New York: Oxford University Press.
Hechter, M. and Opp, K.-D. (2005[2001]). What have we learned about the emergence of social norms? In M. Hechter and K.-D. Opp (eds), *Social norms*. New York: Russell Sage Foundation, 394–415.
Hewitt, P. J. (1989). *Dilemmas of the American self*. Philadelphia, PA: Temple University Press.
Hewitt, P. J. and Shulman, D. (2011). *Self and society – A symbolic interactionist social psychology* (11th ed.). Boston, MA: Pearson Education.
Hill, B., Ide, S., Ikuta, S., Kawasaki, A. and Ogino, T. (1986). Universals of linguistic politeness – Quantitative evidence from Japanese and American English. *Journal of Pragmatics*, *10*, 347–371.
Hinds, J. (1980). Japanese conversation, discourse structure, and ellipsis. *Discourse Processes*, *3*, 263–286.
Hinds, J. (1982). *Ellipsis in Japanese*. Carondale and Edmonton, Alberta: Linguistic Research Inc.
Hinds J. (1983). Topic continuity in Japanese. In T. Givón (ed.), *Topic continuity in discourse*. Amsterdam: John Benjamins Publishing Company, 43–93.
Hinds, J. (1984). Topic maintenance in Japanese narratives and Japanese conversational interaction. *Discourse Processes*, *7*, 465–482.
Hofstede, G. (1980). *Culture's Consequences – International Differences in Work-Related Values*. Beverly Hills, CA: Sage.
Hofstede, G. (1991). *Cultures and organizations*. London: McGraw-Hill.
Holmes, J. (2001). *An introduction to sociolinguistics*. Edinburgh: Longman

Holmes, J. and Stubbe, M. (2003). *Power and politeness in the workplace.* London: Longman.

Hyland, K. (2012). *Disciplinary identities.* Cambridge: Cambridge University Press.

Ide, S. (1989). Formal forms and discernment – Two neglected aspects of linguistic politeness. *Multilingua, 8*, 223–248.

Ide, S. (1992). Roots of the *wakimae* aspects of linguistic politeness – Modal expressions and Japanese sense of self. In M. Meeuwis and J.-O. Östman (eds), *Pragmaticizing understanding – Studies for Jef Verschueren.* Amsterdam: John Benjamins Publishing Company, 121–138.

Ide, S. (2006). *Wakimae no goyoo-ron* [*The pragmatics of* wakimae]. Tokyo: Taishukan Shoten

Ide, S., Ogino, T., Kawasaki, A. and Ikuta, S. (1986). *Nihonjin to amerka-jin no keigo koodoo – daigakusei no baai* [*Polite behaviours of the Japanese and Americans – The case of university students*]. Tokyo: Nan-undoo.

Ide, S., Hill, B., Carnes, Y. M., Ogino, T. and Kawasaki, A. (1992). The concept of politeness – An empirical study of American English and Japanese. In R. J. Watts, S. Ide and K. Ehlich (eds), *Politeness in language – Studies in its history, theory and practice* -. Berlin/New York: Mouton de Gruyter, 281–297.

Ikeda, M. (2001). *Hotsumatsutae o yomitoku* [*Reading the mythology of the* Hotsuma *time*]. Tokyo: Tenbosha.

Ikegami, Y. (2000). *Nihongo-ron e no shootai* [*An invitation to* Nihongo-ron]. Tokyo: Kodansha.

Ikuta, S. (1983). Speech level shift and conversational strategy in Japanese discourse. *Language Science, 5*, 37–53.

Inetomi, E. (1963). *Nihonjin to nihon bunka* [*The Japanese and Japanese culture*]. Tokyo: Risosha.

Inoue, F. (1999). *Keigo wa kowakunai* [*Honorifics are not scary*]. Tokyo: Kodansha.

Iritani, T. (1978). Gengo shinri-gaku kara mita keigo no mondai [Issues on politeness from the viewpoint of psycholinguistics]. In Y. Kitahara(ed.), *Keigo – Ronshuu nihongo kenkyuu*, No. 9 [*Honorifics – Selected essays on the study of Japanese language*]. Tokyo: Yuuseido Publishing Co., 187–197.

Irvine, J.T. (1998). Ideologies of honorific language. In B. B. Schieffelin, K. A. Woolard and P. V. Kroskrity (eds), *Language ideologies – Practice and theory.* NY/Oxford: Oxford University Press, 51–67.

Ishizaki, A. (2000). Denwarenraku no kaiwaniokerusupiichireberushifuto [Speech level shifts in message delivery on the phone]. *Gengo Bunka to Nihongo Kyoiku, Ochanomizu Women's College, Japanese and Culture Research Group*, 62–74.

Janney, R. W. and Arndt, H. (1992). Intracultural tact versus intercultural tact. In R. J. Watts, S. Ide and K. Ehlich (eds), *Politeness in language – Studies in its history, theory and practice.* Berlin/New York: Mouton de Gruyter, 21–42.

Jautz, S. (2013). *Thanking formulae in English – Explorations across varieties and genres.* Amsterdam/Philadelphia: John Benjamins Publishing Company.

Johnson, C. G. (2006). The discursive construction of teacher identities in a research interview. In A. de Fina, D. Schiffrina and M. Bamberg (eds), *Discourse and identity.* New York: Cambridge University Press, 213–232.

Jones, K. and Ono, T. (eds) (2008). *Style shifting in Japanese.* Amsterdam: John Benjamins Publishing Company.

Kabaya, H., Kim, T. and Takagi, M. (2009). *Keigo hyoogen handobukku* [*Handbook of honorific expressions*]. Tokyo: Taishukan.

Kádár, Z. D. (2013). *Relational rituals and communication – Ritual interaction in groups.* Basingstoke: Palgrave Macmillan.
Kádár, Z. D. and Haugh, M. (2013). *Understanding politeness.* Cambridge: Cambridge University Press.
Kádár, Z. D. and Mills, S. (2013). Rethinking discernment. *Journal of Politeness Research*, *9*(2), 133–158.
Kádár, Z. D. and Paternoster, A. (2015). Historicity in metapragmatics – A study on 'discernment' in Italian metadiscourse. *Pragmatics*, *25*(3), 369–391.
Kapogianni, E. (2014). Differences in use and function of verbal irony between real and fictional discourse – (mis)interpretation and irony blindness. *Humor*, *27*(4), 597–618.
Kasper, G. (1990). Linguistic politeness. *Journal of Pragmatics*, *14*(2), 193–218.
Kasuga, K. (1977). Keigo no Hensen [Historical changes of honorifics]. In S. Ono and T. Shibata (eds), *Iwanami Kooza Nihongo 4 – Keigo* [*Iwanami series on Japanese language 4: Honorifics*]. Tokyo: Iwanami Shoten, 95–134.
Katriel, T. (1986). *Talking straight – Dugri speech in Israeli Sabra culture.* Cambridge: Cambridge University Press.
Kawai, I. (1982). *Chuukuu koozoo nihon no shinsoo* [*Middle-emptiness structure as Japanese deep-seated consciousness*]. Tokyo: Chuo koronsha.
Kawamoto, A. (1982). *Nihonjin to shudan-shugi – Tochi to chi* [*The Japanese and collectivism: Land and blood*]. Tokyo: Tamagawa University Press.
Kertzer, D. I. (1988). *Ritual, politics and power.* New Haven, CT: Yale University Press.
Kikkawa, E. (1965). *Nihon ongaku no rekishi* [*The history of Japanese music*]. Tokyo: Sogensha.
Kikuchi, Y. (1999[1997]). *Keigo* [*Honorifics*] (5th ed.). Tokyo: Kodansha gakujutsu bunko.
Kikuchi, Y. (2011[2003]). Keigo to sono omona kenkyuu teema no gaikan [Honorifics and a general view of main studies on them]. In Y. Kitahara and Y. Kikuchi (eds), *Asakura Nihongo Kooza, No. 8, Keigo* (4th ed.). Tokyo: Asakura Shoten, 1–30
Kim, M. S. (1994). Cross-cultural comparisons of the perceived importance of interactive constraints. *Human Communication Research*, *21*, 128–151.
Kindaichi, K. (1962[1959]). *Nihon no keigo* [*Japanese honorifics*] (5th ed.). Tokyo: Kadokawa Shinsho.
Kinuhata, T. and Yang, C. (2007). Yakuwari-go toshiteno 'guntai-go' no seiritsu [The development of military terms as role-terms]. In S. Kinsui (ed.), *Yakuwari kenkyuu no chihei* [*The horizon of studies on role-terms*]. Tokyo: Kurosio Shuppan, 179–192.
Kitahara, Y. (1995). *Keigo ishiki to keigo hyoogen* [Consciousness of honorifics and honorific expressions]. *Kokubungaku – Special Issue on Honorifics Today*, 6–9.
Kogi, T. (1967). *Kagaku, gijutsu to nihonjin* [*Science, technology and the Japanese*]. Tokyo: Kodansha.
Koyama, W. (2011). *Kindai gengo ideorogii-ron* [*On linguistic ideologies in modern languages*]. Tokyo: Sangen-sha.
Kumai, H. (2009). Nihongo no politeness to taijin-koodoo ni kansuru ichikoosatsu [=A study on Japanese politeness and acts in personal relationship]. *Bulletin of the Center for International Exchanges, University of Shizuoka*, 1–26.
Kumatoridani, T. (1999). Alternation and co-occurrence in Japanese thanks. *Journal of Pragmatics*, *31*, 623–642.

Kummer, M. (1992). Politeness in Thai. In R. J. Watts, S. Ide and K. Ehlich(eds), *Politeness in language – Studies in its history, theory and practice*. Berlin/New York: Mouton de Gruyter, 325–336.

Lakin, J. L, Jefferis, V. E., Cheng, C. M. and Chartrand, T. (2003). The chameleon effect as social glue: Evidence for the evolutionary significance of nonconscious mimicry. *Journal of Nonverbal Behavior*, *27*, 145–162.

Lakoff, G. and Johnson, M. (2003). *Metaphors we live by*. Chicago, IL: University of Chicago Press.

Lakoff, R. (1973). The logic of politeness – Or, minding your p's and q's. *Papers from the Ninth Regional Meeting of the Chicago Linguistic Society*. Chicago, IL: Chicago Linguistic Society, 292–305.

Lakoff, R. (1975). *Language and woman's place*. New York: Harper & Row.

Lakoff, R. (1977). What you can do with words: Politeness, pragmatics and performatives. In A. Rogers, B. Wall and J. Murphy (eds), *Proceedings of the Texas Conference on Performatives, Presuppositions, and Implicatures*. Arlington, VA: Center of Applied Linguistics, 79–105.

Lave, J. and Wenger, E. (1991). *Situated learning – Legitimate peripheral participation*. Cambridge: Cambridge University Press.

Leech, G. (1980). *Explorations in semantics and pragmatics*. Amsterdam: John Benjamins Publishing Company.

Leech, G. (1983). *Principles of pragmatics*. London: Longman.

Li, D. (2014). *Value theory – A research into subjectivity*. Heidelberg/London: Springer.

Li, W. (2018). *Pragmatic transfer and development – Evidence from EFL learners in China*. Amsterdam/Philadelphia: John Benjamins Publishing Company.

Littleton, C. S. (1979). Outline of a theory of practice by Pierre Bourdieu – Review. *American Anthropologist*, *81*(1), 181–182.

Liu, J., Vohs, K. D. and Smeesters, D. (2011). Money and mimicry – When being mimicked makes people feel threatened. *Psychological Science*, *22*(9), 1150–1151.

Locher, M. A. (2004). *Power and politeness in action*. Berlin/NY: Mouton de Gruyter.

Locher, M. A. (2012). Politeness research from past to future, with a special focus on the discursive approach. In L. F. Amaya, M. O. H. López, R. G. Morón, M. P. Cruz, M. M. Borrero and M. Barranca (eds), *New perspectives on (im)politeness and interpersonal communication*. Cambridge: Cambridge Scholars Publishing, 36–62.

Locher, M. A. and Watts, R. J. (2005). Politeness theory and relational work. *Journal of Politeness Research*, *1*(1), 9–33.

Luce, L. F. and Smith, E. C. (eds) (1987). *Toward internationalism – Reading in cross-cultural communication*. Cambridge, MA: Newbury House.

Makino, S. (1989[1980]). *Kurikaeshi no bunpoo* [*Grammar of repetition*]. Tokyo: Taishukan Shoten.

Makino, S. (1996). *Uchi to soto no gengo bunka-gaku* [*Linguistic-cultural studies of* uchi *and* soto]. Tokyo: Aruku Publishers.

Makino, S. (2002). When does communication turn mentally inward? A case study of Japanese formal-to-informal switching. In N. M. Akatsuka and S. Strauss (eds), *Japanese/Korean linguistics*, Vol. 10. Stanford, CA: CSLI Publications, 121–135.

Mao, L. R. (1994). Beyond politeness theory – 'Face' revisited and renewed. *Journal of Pragmatics*, *21*, 451–486.

Matsumoto, Y. (1988). Reexamination of the universality of face – Politeness phenomena in Japanese. *Journal of Pragmatics*, *12*, 403–426.

Matsumoto, Y. (1989). Politeness and conversational universals – Observation from Japanese. *Multilinguial*, *8*(2/3), 207–221.

Matsumoto, Y. (1993). Linguistic politeness and cultural style: Observation from Japanese. In P. Clancy (ed.), *Japanese /Korean Linguistics*, Vol. 2. Center for the Study of Language and Information, Stanford University, 55–67.

Maynard, S. K. (2001). *Koisurufutari no kanjookotoba – Doramahyoogen no bunseki to nihongoron* [*Emotional language between the couple in love – Analysis of expressions in a drama and discussion on Japanese language*]. Tokyo: KurosioShuppan.

Maynard, S. K. (2004). *Danwa Gengogaku* (Linguistics of Discourse), Tokyo: Kurosio Shuppan.

McCall, G. (2003). Interaction. In L. T. Reynolds and N. J. Herman-Kinney (eds), *Handbook of symbolic interactionism*. Lanham, MD: Rowman & Littlefield, 327–348.

Mead, H. G. (1934). *Mind, self, and society*. Chicago, IL: University of Chicago Press.

Miller, R. (1982). *Japan's modern myth – The language and beyond*. New York: Weatherhill.

Mills, S. (2003). *Gender and politeness*. Cambridge: Cambridge University Press.

Mills, S. (2011). Communities of practice and politeness. In B. L. Davies, M. Haugh and A. J. Merrison (eds), *Situated politeness*. London: Continuum, 73–87.

Mimaki, Y. (1993). Danwa no tenkaihyooshikitoshitenotaiguureberushifuto [Speech level shifts as a marker of development of discourse]. *Osaka Kyoiku University Kiyoo*, *1*(42), 39–51.

Minami, F. (1976[1973]). Koodoo no naka no keigo [Honorifics in behaviour]. In S. Hayashi and F. Minami (eds), *Koodoo no naka no keigo* [*Honorifics in behaviour*]. Tokyo: Meiji Shoin, 7–30.

Minami, F. (1977). Keigo no kinoo to keigo koodoo [The functions of honorifics and honorific behaviours]. In S. Ono and T. Shibata (eds), *Iwanami-kooza, Nihongo, 4, Keigo*. Tokyo: Iwanami shoten, 1–44.

Minami, F. (1987). *Keigo* [*Honorifics*]. Tokyo: Iwanami Shinsho.

Moeran, B. (1998). Japanese language and society – An anthropological approach. *Journal of Pragmatics*, *12*, 427–443.

Moriizumi, S. (2009). Face concern and requests in Japan – Exploring the effects of relational closeness and social status. *Journal of Intercultural Communication Research*, *38*(3), 149–174.

Morisaki, S. and Gudykunst, W. B. (1994). Face in Japan and the United States. In S. Ting-Toomey (ed.), *The challenge of facework*. Albany, NY: State University of New York, 47–93.

Morita, Y. (1995). *Nihongo no shiten* [*The viewpoint of the Japanese language*]. Tokyo: Sotakusha.

Morita, Y. (1998). *Nihonjin no hassoo, nihongo no hyoogen* [*Japanese way of thinking, Japanese expressions*]. Tokyo: Chuo Shinsho.

Moriyama, Y. (1996). Nihongo keigo Hyoogen no shiteki tenkai nitsuiteno kenkyuu [Studies on the historical development of Japanese honorific expressions]. PhD thesis, Nara Women's University.

Moriyama, Y. (2010). Gendai nihongo no keigo no kinoo to poraitonesu (= The functions of Japanese honorifics and politeness). *Nihongo Nihonbungaku, Doshisha Women's College*, *22*, 1–19.

Moriyama, Y. (2011[2003]). Kenjoo-go kara mita keigo-shi, teinei-go kara mita keigo-shi [The history of honorifics in cases of humble styles and addressee honorifics].

In Y. Kitahara and Y. Kikuchi (eds), *Asakura Nihongo kōza, No. 8, Keigo* (4th ed.). Tokyo: Asakura Shoten, 200–224.

Murakami, S. (1977). *Ten-noo no saishi* [*Emperors' religious rites*]. Tokyo: Iwanami Shinsho.

Murakami, Y., Kobun, S. and Sato, S. (1979). *Bunmei toshiteno ie shakai* [*The* ie *society as a civilisation*]. Tokyo: Chuo koronsha.

Nakagawa, H. (2003). Nihongo to ainugo no shiteki kankei [Historical relations between Japanese and Aino languages]. *Perspectives on the origin of the Japanese language*, *31*, 209–220.

Nakane, C. (1970). *Japanese society*. Berkeley/Los Angeles, CA: University of California Press.

Nishida, N. (1995[1987]). *Keigo* [*Honorifics*]. Tokyo: Tokyodo Publishing Co.

Nishida, N. (1998). *Nihon-jin no keigo seikatsu-shi* [*The history of Japanese people's life with honorifics*]. Tokyo: Kanrin Shoboo.

Nishida, N. (2013[2003]). Keigo-shi to gendai keigo [The history of honorifics and modern honorifics]. In Y. Kitahara and Y. Kikuchi (eds), *Asakura nihongo kooza, No. 8 – Keigo* (4th ed.). Tokyo: Asakura Shoten, 225–251.

Obana, Y. (1996). Language diplomacy and Japanese politeness. *New Zealand Journal of East Asian Studies*, *4*(2), 64–75.

Obana, Y. (1999). The speaker's viewpoint and different language constructs – The case of teaching Japanese to English speaking learners. *New Zealand Journal of Asian Studies*, *1*(1), 142–156.

Obana, Y. (2000). *Understanding Japanese – A handbook for learners and teachers.* Tokyo: Kurosio Publishers.

Obana, Y. (2003). Anaphoric choices in Japanese fictional novels – The discourse arrangement of noun phrases, zero and third person pronouns. *TEXT*, *23*(3), 405–443.

Obana, Y. (2009). Politeness strategies in Japanese honorifics – Contrasts between English and Japanese in strategic planning. *Kwansei Gakuin University, Gengo to Bunka*, *12*, 39–53.

Obana, Y. (2012a). Politeness as Role-Identity – Application of Symbolic Interactionism. *Kwansei Gakuin University, Gengo to Bunka*, *15*, 1–16.

Obana, Y. (2012b). Re-examination of yoroshiku onegaishimasu – The routine formula as the linguistic implementation of one's tachiba-role. *Journal of Pragmatics*, *44*, 1535–1548.

Obana, Y. (2015). Kansha hyoogen toshiteno 'arigatoo' to 'sumimasen' no kyookaisen – Shinborikku soogo sayoo-riron o tekiyooshite [The borderline of the thanking formulae between *arigatoo* and *sumimasen*: The application of Symbolic Interactionism]. *Kwansei Gakuin University, Gengo to Bunka*, *18*, 15–28.

Obana, Y. (2016). Speech level shifts in Japanese – A different perspective: The application of Symbolic Interactionist role theory. *Pragmatics*, *26*(2), 247–290.

Obana, Y. (2017). Japanese honorifics re-re-visited. *Journal of Politeness Research*, *13*(2), 4–31.

Obana, Y. (2019). Politeness. In P. Hendrich and Y. Ohara (eds), *Routledge handbook of Japanese sociolinguistics*. London: Routledge, 248–263.

Obana, Y. (2020). Busoosuru keigo – Hi-meidaiteki aironii no koosatsu [Honorifics under arms – The case of non-propositional irony]. *Kwansei Gakuin University, Gengo to Bunka*, *23*, 15–28.

Obana, Y. and Tomoda, T. (1994). Sociological significance of the term politeness in English and Japanese. *Bulletin of Japanese Studies Association of Australia, 14*(2), 37–49.

Oh, S. (2005). *Meirei • irai no hyougen – Nihongo • chuugokugo no taishoo kenkyuu* [*Expressions of command and request – Contrastive studies between Japanese and Chinese*]. Tokyo: Bensei shuppan.

Ohashi, J. (2003). Japanese culture specific face and politeness orientation – A pragmatic investigation of *yoroshiku onegaishimasu. Multilingua, 22*, 257–274.

Ohkubo, K. (2009). Sonkeigo, kenjoogo no kinoonikansurukoosatsu – Kekkonhirooen no shikai no hatsuwa wo rei ni [On the functions of deferential and humble terms – Examples from the wedding MC's utterances]. *Shakai Gengo Kagaku, 12*(1), 162–173.

Oishi, H. (1975). *Keigo* [*Honorifics*]. Tokyo: Chikuma Shobo.

Oishi, H. (1984). *Gendai keigo kenkyuu* [*Studies on modern honorifics*]. Tokyo: Chikuma Shobo.

Okamoto S. (1999). Situated politeness – Manipulating honorific and non-honorific expressions in Japanese conversation. *Pragmatics, 9*, 51–74.

Olshtain, E. (1983). Sociocultural competence and language transfer – The case of apology. In S. Gass and L. Selinker (eds), *Language transfer in language learning*. Rowley, MA: Newbury House, 232–249.

Olshtain, E. and Cohen, A.D. (1989). Speech act behavior across languages. In H. W. Dechert and M. Raupach (eds), *Transfer in language production*. Norwood, NJ: Ablex, 53–67.

Omoniyi, T. and White, G. (2006). Introduction. In T. Omoniyi and G. White (eds), *The sociolinguistics of identity*. London: Continuum, 1–8.

Orikuchi, N. (2009[2003]). *Kodai kenkyuu II – Norito no hassei* [*Studies of ancient times II – The beginning of* norito] (3rd ed.). Tokyo: Chuo-koron Shinsha.

Osugi, K. (1993). *Eigo no keii-hyoogen* [*Expressions of respect in English*] (9th ed.). Tokyo: Taishukan Publishing Co.

Ozora, T. (2002). *Genshi nihongo wa kooshite dekita* [*How the origin of Japanese language was developed*]. Tokyo: Bungei-sha.

Pan, Y. (2000). *Politeness in Chinese – Face-to-face interaction.* Stamford, CT: Ablex Publishing Corporation.

Parsons, T. (1951). *The social system.* New York: Routledge

Peng, G. (2000). Matsushita bunpoo 'taiguu' no honshitsu to sono rironteki kanoosei – 'kachi no imiron' no shikumi [The nature of 'how to treat others' in Matsushita's grammar, and its theoretical feasibility – the framework of semantics of evaluation]. *Sekai no nihongo kyooiku, 10*, 191–206.

Perinbanayagam, R. (2012). *Identity's moments – The self in action and interaction.* Lanham, MD: Lexington Books.

Perrin, L., Deshaies, D. and Paradis, C. (2003). Pragmatic functions of local diaphonic repetitions in conversation. *Journal of Pragmatics, 35*, 1843–1860.

Pizziconi, B. (2003). Re-examining politeness, face and the Japanese language. *Journal of Pragmatics, 35*, 1471–1506.

Pizziconi, B. (2007). The lexical mapping of politeness in British English and Japanese. *Journal of Politeness Research, 3*, 207–241.

Popper, K. (2002 [1934]). *The logic of scientific discovery*. New York: Routledge.

Reischauer, E. O. (1977). *The Japanese.* Cambridge, MA: Belknap Press.

Reischauer, E. O. (1988). *The Japanese today – Change and continuity.* Cambridge, MA: Belknap Press.

Rothenbuhler, W. E. (1998). *Ritual communication*. Thousand Oaks, CA: Sage.
Sagiv, L. and Schwartz, S. H. (1995). Value priorities and readiness for outgroup social contact. *Journal of Personality and Social Psychology*, 69, 437–448.
Saito, J. (2010). Subordinates' use of Japanese plain forms – An examination of superior–subordinate interactions in the workplace. *Journal of Pragmatics, 42*, 3271–3282.
Sakurai, M. (1983). *Keigo ronshuu – Kodai to gendai* [*Essays on honorifics – Past and present*]. Tokyo: Meiji Shoin.
Sandstrom, L. K., Martin, D. D. and Fine, G. A. (2010). *Symbols, selves, and social reality* (3rd ed.). New York/Oxford: Oxford University Press.
Sasagawa, Y. (2016). *Nihongo no poraitonesu saikoo* [*Rethinking of Japanese politeness*]. Tokyo: Shunpu-sha.
Schwartz, S. H. (1990). Individualism–Collectivism – Critique and proposed refinements. *Journal of Cross-Cultural Psychology*, *21*(2), 139–157.
Scollon, R. and Scollon, S. W. (1995). *Intercultural Communication*. Boston, MA: Blackwell.
Scollon, R., Scollon, S. W. and Jones, R. H. (2012). *Intercultural communication – A discourse approach*. Chichester: John Wiley & Sons.
Scott, J. (2014[1994]). *Oxford dictionary of sociology* (4th ed.). Oxford: Oxford University Press.
Searle, J. R. (1975). Indirect speech acts. In P. Cole and J. Morgan (eds), *Syntax and semantics*, Vol. 3: *Speech acts*. New York: Academic Press.
Shibamoto-Smith, J. S. (2011). Honorifics, 'politeness', and power in Japanese political debate. *Journal of Pragmatics*, *43*, 3707–3719.
Shove, E., Pantzar, M. and Watson, M. (2012). *The dynamics of social practice*. Los Angeles, CA: Sage.
Shweder, R. A and Bourne, E. J. (1982). Does the concept of the person vary cross-culturally? In A. J. Marsella and G. M. White (eds), *Cultural conceptions for mental health and therapy*. Dordrecht, The Netherlands: Riedel.
Sifianou, M. (1992). *Politeness phenomena in England and Greece – A cross-cultural perspective*. Oxford: Clarendon Press.
Smith, P. B. and Bond, M. H. (1998). *Social psychology across cultures* (2nd ed.). London: Prentice Hall Europe.
Sofue, T. (1976). *Bunka to paasonaritii* [*Culture and personality*]. Tokyo: Kobundo.
Spencer-Oatey, H. (2005). (Im)politeness, face and perceptions of rapport – Unpackaging their bases and interrelationships. *Journal of Politeness Research*, *1*(1), 95–119.
Spencer-Oatey, H. (2008[2000]). Face, (im)politeness and rapport. In H. Spencer-Oatey (ed.), *Culturally speaking – Culture, communication and politeness theory* (2nd ed.). London: Continuum, 11–47.
Sugimoto, Y. and Mouer, R. (1995). *Nihonjin-ron no hooteishiki* [*The formula of the Japanese-ness*]. Tokyo: Chikuma gakugei bunko.
Takano, Y. (2008). *Shuudan-shugi toyuu sakkaku – Nihonjin-ron no omoi-chigai to sono urai* [*The illusion of collectivism – A misunderstanding of Japaneseness and its origin*]. Tokyo: Shinyosha
Takeda, N. (2011). Dooistu danwa niokeru supiichi reberu shifuto nitsuite no koosatsu [On speech level shifts in the samd discourse]. MA dissertation, Kwansei Gakuin University.
Takekuro, M. (2005). Yoroshiku onegaishimasu – Routine practice of the routine formula in Japanese. In R. T. Lakoff and S. Ide (eds), *Broadening the horizon*

*of linguistic politeness*. Amsterdam/Philadelphia: John Benjamins Publishing Company, 87–97.
Takiura, M. (2005). *Nihon no keigoron* [*On Japanese honorifics*]. Tokyo: Taishukan.
Takiura, M. (2008). *Poraitonesu nyuumon* [*Introducing politeness*]. Tokyo: Kenkyusha.
Tanaka, K. (1999). Keigo wa nihongo wo sekai kara tozasu [Honorifics would make Japanese language close its gate to the world]. *Gekkan Gengo*, *28*(11), 41–47.
Tanaka, S. and Kawade, S. (1982). Politeness strategies and second language acquisition. *Studies in Second Language Acquisition*, *5*, 18–33.
Tannen, D. (1986). *That's not what I meant – How conversational style makes or breaks your relations with others*. New York: W. Morrow and Company, Inc.
Tao, L. (2013). The concept of 'politeness' – A comparative study in Chinese and Japanese verbal communication. *Intercultural Communication Studies*, *XXII*(2), 151–165.
Terkourafi, M. (2005). Beyond the micro-level in politeness research. *Journal of Politeness Research*, *1*(2), 237–262.
Toya, M. (2016). *Joomon no kami* [*Gods in the Jomon times*]. Tokyo: Kawade Shobo.
Triandis, H. C. (1994). Theoretical and methodological approaches to the study of collectivism and individualism. In U. Kim, H. C. Triandis, Ç. Kagitçibasi, S. Choi and G. Yoon (eds), *Individualism and collectivism – Theory, method, and applications*. Thousand Oaks, CA: Sage, 41–51.
Triandis, H. C. (1995). *Individualism and collectivism*. Boulder, CO: Westview Press.
Triandis, H. C. and Brislin, R. W. (eds) (1980). *Handbook of cross-cultural psychology*, Vol. 5. Boston, MA: Allyn & Bacon.
Trompenaars, F. (1993). *Riding the waves of culture – Understanding cultural diversity in business*. London: Nicholas Brealey Publishing Ltd.
Tsujimura, T. (1967). *Gendai no keigo* [*Modern Honorifics*]. Tokyo: Kyobun-sha.
Tsujimura, T. (1977). Nihongo no keigo no koozoo to tokushoku [The structure of Japanese honorifics and their characteristics]. In S. Ono and T. Shibata (eds), *Iwanami Koza Nihongo, 4, Keigo* [*Iwanami Japanese language courses*, No. 4 *Honorifics*]. Tokyo: Iwanami Shoten, 45–94.
Tsujimura, T. (1989). Taiguu hyoogen to nihongo kyooiku [Polite expressions and Japanese teaching]. *Nihongo Kyooiku*, *69*, 1–10.
Turner, J. H. (2002). *Face to face – Toward a sociological theory of interpersonal behavior*. Stanford, CA: Stanford University Press.
Turner, J. H. (2011). Extending the Symbolic Interactionist theory of interaction processes – A conceptual outline. *Symbolic Interaction*, *34*(3), 330–339.
Tsukishima, K. (1976[1973]). Keigo to shakai-shinri [Honorifics and social-psychology]. In S. Hayashi and F. Minami (eds), *Koodoo no naka no keigo* [*Honorifics in behaviour*]. Tokyo: Meiji Shoin, 137–162.
Tyerman, A. and Spencer, C. (1983). A critical test of the Sherifs' robber's cave experiments. *Small Group Behaviour*, *14*, 515–531.
Uryu, N. (2017). *Yoku wakaru norito dokuhon* [*Comprehensive book on* norito]. Tokyo: Kadokawa Sofia-Bunko.
Usami, M. (2001). Dysukoosu poraitonesu to iu kanten kara mita keigo-shiyoo no kinoo (= The functions of honorific use from the viewpoint of discourse politeness). *Gogaku Kenkyuu-sho Ronshuu*, *6*, Tokyo University of Foreign Studies, 1–29.
Van Baaren, R., Holland, R. W., Steenaert, B. and Van Knippenberg, A. (2003). Mimicry for money – Behavioral consequences of imitation. *Journal of Experimental Social Psychology*, *39*, 393–398.

Van Baaren, R., Janssen, L., Chartrand, L. T. and Dijksterhuis, A. (2009). *The Royal Society, Philosophical Transactions B*, 364(1528), 2381–2389.

Van der Bom, I. and Mills, S. (2015). A discursive approach to the analysis of politeness data. *Journal of Politeness Research*, *11*(2), 179–206.

Van Knippenberg, A. and Van Baaren, R. (2008). Baboons, brains, babies and bonding – A multidisciplinary approach to mimicry. In P. A. M. Van Lange (ed.), *Bridging social psychology – Benefits of transdisciplinary approaches*, 173–178.

Vogel, E. (1979). *Japan as number one – Lessons for America.* Cambridge, MA: Harvard University Press.

Vryan, D. K., Adler, A. P. and Adler, P. (2003). Identity. In L. T. Reynolds and N. J. Herman-Kinney (eds), *Handbook of Symbolic Interactionism.* Lanham, MD: Rowman & Littlefield, 367–390.

Warabidani, T. (2017). *Eigyoo de katsu bijinesu keigo* [*How to win in business with honorifics*]. Tokyo: Shinso-sha.

Watanabe, M. (1974). *Kokugo bunpoo-ron* [*On the grammar of Japanese*]. Tokyo: Kazama Shoin.

Watanabe, M. (1994). Gendai nihon niokeru kaikyuu-kakusa to sono koteika, sono ni [Hierarchical differences in modern Japan and their immobilisation, Part II]. *Hitotsubashi University, Yearly Research Report*, *32*, 47–153.

Watts, R. J. (1992). Linguistic politeness and politic verbal behaviour – Reconsidering claims for universality. In R. J. Watts, S. Ide and K. Ehlich (eds), *Politeness in language – Studies in its history, theory and practice.* Berlin/New York: Mouton de Gruyter, 43–69.

Wierzbicka, A. (1991). Japanese key words and core cultural values. *Language in Society*, *20*, 333–385.

Wierzbicka, A. (1994). 'Cultural scripts' – A semantic approach to cultural analysis and cross-cultural communication. *Pragmatics and Language Learning*, *5*, 1–24.

Wierzbicka, A. (1995). Different cultures, different languages, different speech acts. *Journal of Pragmatics*, *9*, 145–161.

Woolard, K.A. (1998). Introduction – Language ideology as a field of inquiry. In B. B. Schieffelin, K. A. Woolard and P. V. Kroskrity (eds), *Language ideologies – Practice and theory.* NY/Oxford: Oxford University Press, 3–47.

Xenitidou, M. and Edmonds, B. (2014). The conundrum of social norms. In M. Xenitidou and B. Edmonds (eds), *The complexity of social norms.* Heidelberg: Springer, 1–8.

Yamada, T. (1924). *Keigo-hoo no kenkyuu* [*The study of how to use honorifics*]. Tokyo: Hobunkan.

Yamashita, H. (1986). *Nihon no kotoba to kokoro* [*The Japanese language and mind*]. Tokyo: Kodansha.

Yoneyama, T. (1976). *Nihonjin no nakama ishiki* [*The comrade-consciousness of the Japanese*]. Tokyo: Kodansha.

Yokomori, D., Yasui, E. and Hajikano, A. (2018). Registering the receipt of information with a modulated stance – A study of *ne*-marked other-repetitions in Japanese talk-in-interaction. *Journal of Pragmatics*, *123*, 167–191.

Yoshida, M. and Sakurai, C. (2005). Japanese honorifics as a marker of sociocultural identity. In R. T. Lakoff and S. Ide (eds), *Broadening the horizon of linguistic politeness.* Amsterdam: John Benjamins Publishing Company, 197–215.

Yoshida, T. (1994). Interpersonal versus non-interpersonal realities – An effective tool individualists can use to better understand collectivists. In R. W. Brislin and

T. Yoshida (eds), *Improving intercultural interactions – Modules for cross-cultural training programs*. Thousand Oaks, CA: Sage, 243–267.
Zimmerman, M. A. (1985). *Dealing with the Japanese*. London: Allen & Unwin.

## Dictionaries and other sources

*Digital Oxford Dictionary of English*. oed.com
*Digital Shin-Kangorin* [*Kanji* dictionary]. Tokyo: Taishu-kan.
世界大百科事典 (*Sekai dai-hyakka jiten* [*The encyclopaedia of the world*]). Tokyo: Heibon-sha.
『脚本の月刊誌　ドラマ』(2014). *Monthly Drama Scenario*, February.
日本経済新聞、(2013). *Nihon-keizai*, newspaper, 16 January).
MedicineNet www.medicinenet.com/script/main/art.asp?articlekey=38857

# Index

*Note*: Page numbers in *italic* refer to figures; those in **bold** refer to tables.

Made in the USA
Las Vegas, NV
24 October 2024

7bb895b2-bef7-4460-9703-cf40bc8815c6R01